Please Note:

This is a hardcopy of an ePublished book. Pagination differs between this and the official digital version.

New Testament Greek Stripped Down
Mastering Greek Essentials in Conjunction with Bible Software

H. Daniel Zacharias

Edited by Tim McLay

Scholar's Publisher Inc.
scholarspub.com

Table of Contents

The Essential Introduction 1

Chapter 1: Signs and Sounds of Greek Stripped Down 9
   1.1: The Greek Alphabet 9
   1.2: Greek Vowels 11
      1.2.1: Vowel Contraction 11
   1.3: Greek Consonants 12
      1.3.1: The Sigma with a Liquid 12
      1.3.2: The Sigma with the Stops 12
   1.4: Jots and Tittles in Greek 13
      1.4.1: Breathing Marks 13
      1.4.2: Accent Marks 14
      1.4.3: Punctuation Marks 15
      1.4.4: Diaeresis, Crasis, Elision 15
      1.4.5: Greek Syllables 16
   1.5: The Least You Need to Know 16
   1.6: Greek@Logos 17
   1.7: Vocabulary 18
   1.8: The Second Time Around 20

Chapter 2: Greek Nouns Stripped Down 21
   2.1: Greek Inflection 21
   2.2: Noun Cases 22
   2.3: Noun Gender 24
   2.4: Noun Number 24
   2.5: Noun Lexical Form 25
   2.6: Noun Declensions 25
   2.7: Noun Case Endings 26
      2.7.1: 1st Declension 26
      2.7.2: 2nd Declension 27
      2.7.3: 3rd Declension 28
   2.8: Noun Parsing 31
   2.9: The Least You Need to Know 31
   2.10: Greek@Logos 32
   2.11: Vocabulary 33
   2.12: The Second Time Around 33

Chapter 3: Case Functions Stripped Down 35
3.1: Nominative 35
3.1.1: Simple Subject 35
3.1.2: Predicate Nominative 36
3.1.3: Apposition 36
3.2: Genitive 36
3.2.1: Possessive 37
3.2.2: Genitive of Relationship 37
3.2.3: Attributive Genitive 37
3.2.4: Apposition 37
3.2.5: Genitive of Comparison 37
3.2.6: Subjective Genitive 38
3.2.7: Objective Genitive 38
3.2.8: Genitive of Time 38
3.2.9: Genitive as Direct Object 38
3.2.10: Descriptive 39
3.3: Dative 39
3.3.1: Indirect Object 39
3.3.2: Dative of Interest 39
3.3.3: Dative of Reference 39
3.3.4: Apposition 39
3.3.5: Dative of Sphere 40
3.3.6: Dative of Time 40
3.3.7: Dative of Association 40
3.3.8: Dative of Means (Instrumental) 40
3.3.9: Dative of Cause 40
3.4: Accusative 41
3.4.1: Direct Object 41
3.4.2: Double Object 41
3.4.3: Apposition 41
3.5: Nouns in the *DBL Greek* Lexicon 41
3.5.1: A Word on Semantic Domains 42
3.5.2: An Analysis of a DBLGreek Noun Entry 44
3.5.2.1: Lexical Form, Stem, Gender, and Part of Speech 44
3.5.2.2: Links to Hebrew Equivalents, Strong's, and TDNT 44
3.5.2.3: Louw & Nida Number 45
3.5.2.4: Gloss 45
3.5.2.5: Brief Explanation, Greek Example, and Scripture Example 45
3.5.3: DBLGreek Noun Example 46

3.5.4: Reading a Louw & Nida Entry 46
3.5.5: Determining The Semantic Domain For A Word Instance 47
3.6: The Least You Need to Know 47
3.7: Greek@Logos 48
3.8: Vocabulary 48
3.9: The Second Time Around 49

Chapter 4: Greek Indicative Verbs Stripped Down 51
4.1: Verb Basics 51
  4.1.1: Types of Verbs 51
  4.1.2: The Efficiency of Greek Verbs 52
  4.1.3: Greek Aspect 53
4.2: Components of a Greek Verb 54
  4.2.1: Tense 55
    4.2.1.1: Present Tense 55
    4.2.1.2: Imperfect Tense 55
    4.2.1.3: Future Tense 55
    4.2.1.4: Aorist Tense 56
    4.2.1.5: Perfect Tense 56
    4.2.1.6: Pluperfect Tense 56
  4.2.2: Voice 57
  4.2.3: Mood 57
  4.2.4: Person 57
  4.2.5: Number 58
4.3: How Greek Indicative Verbs are Formed 58
  4.3.1: The Indicative Slot Machine 58
    4.3.1.1: Slot 1: Augment 60
    4.3.1.2: Slot 2: Reduplication 60
    4.3.1.3: Slot 3: Verb Stems 60
    4.3.1.4: Slot 4: Tense Suffixes 61
    4.3.1.5: Slot 5: Connecting Vowel 62
    4.3.1.6: Slot 6: Primary and Secondary Endings 62
4.4: Strong Verb Example 63
  4.4.1: Verb Translation 64
4.5: Verb Parsing 67
4.6: The Last Word 68
4.7: The Least You Need to Know 68

4.8: Greek@Logos 69
4.9: Vocabulary 69
4.10: The Second Time Around 71

Chapter 5: Alternative Pattern Indicative Verbs and Principal Parts 73
5.1: Greek Principal Parts 73
5.2: Different Types of Verbs 80
   5.2.1: Lexical Middle Verbs 80
   5.2.2: Contract Verbs 81
   5.2.3: Compound Verbs 83
   5.2.4: 2 Aorist Verbs 86
   5.2.5: μι Verbs 87
      5.2.5.1: εἰμί 88
5.3: The Least You Need to Know 89
5.4: Greek@Logos 89
5.5: Vocabulary 90
5.6: The Second Time Around 91

Chapter 6: The Article, Adjectives, Pronouns, and Numbers 93
6.1: Twenty-four Ways to Say "The" 93
   6.1.1: How the Article is Formed 93
   6.1.2: What the Article Can Do 94
      6.1.2.1: Make Something Definite 94
      6.1.2.2: Act Like a Pronoun 94
      6.1.2.3: Rope in a Prepositional Phrase 95
6.2: Adjectives 96
   6.2.1: How Adjectives are Formed 96
      6.2.1.1: Comparatives and Superlatives 97
   6.2.2: What Adjectives Can Do 98
      6.2.2.1: Attribute Value to a Noun 98
      6.2.2.2: Act Like a Noun (act substantivally) 99
      6.2.2.3: Act as a Predicate Nominative 100
6.3: Pronouns 100
   6.3.1: How Pronouns are Formed 101
   6.3.2: Personal Pronouns 101

  6.3.2.1: 1st and 2nd Person Personal Pronoun 102
  6.3.2.2: 3rd Person Personal Pronoun 102
 6.3.3: Pronouns That Act Like Adjectives 103
  6.3.3.1: Special Functions of the 3rd Person Personal Pronoun 103
  6.3.3.2: Demonstrative Pronouns 103
  6.3.3.3: Correlative and Possessive Pronouns 105
 6.3.4: Pronouns That Introduce a Dependent Clause 105
  6.3.4.1: Relative Pronouns 105
  6.3.4.2: Indefinite Relative Pronouns 106
 6.3.5: Pronouns That Ask a Question 106
  6.3.5.1: Interrogative Pronouns 106
  6.3.5.2: Qualitative and Quantitative Interrogative Pronouns............107
 6.3.6: More Pronouns Acting Like Pronouns 107
  6.3.6.1: Indefinite Pronouns 107
  6.3.6.2: Reflexive, Reciprocal, and Negative Pronouns 108

6.4: Numbers 108
 6.4.1: Cardinals 108
 6.4.2: Ordinals 110
6.5: The Least You Need to Know 110
6.6: Greek@Logos 111
6.7: Vocabulary 111
6.8: The Second Time Around 112

Chapter 7: Adverbs, Prepositions, Phrases, and Clauses 117
7.1: Adverbs 117
7.2: Prepositions 117
 7.2.1: Preposition Forms 119
 7.2.2: Preposition Functions 119
7.3: More Little Words 121
 7.3.1: Conjunctions 121
 7.3.2: Interjections 122
 7.3.3: Particles 122
7.4: Word Groups 122
 7.4.1: Phrases 124
 7.4.2: Clauses 124

   7.4.2.1: Independent Clauses 124
   7.4.2.2: Dependent, Participle, and Infinitive Clauses.....................124
   7.4.2.3: Dependent Clause Introducers 125
 7.5: Syntax and Bible Software 126
 7.6: The Least You Need to Know 126
 7.7: Greek@Logos 127
 7.8: Vocabulary 127
 7.9: The Second Time Around 129

Chapter 8: Participles Stripped Down 131
 8.1: Participle Description 131
 8.2: How Participles Are Formed 132
 8.3: What a Participle Can Do, pt.1 136
  8.3.1: Participle Acting Like An Adjective 136
  8.3.2: Participle Acting Like a Verb 137
 8.4: The Least You Need to Know 137
 8.5: Greek@Logos 138
 8.6: Vocabulary 138
 8.7: The Second Time Around 139

Chapter 9: Participle Functions 141
 9.1: What a Participle Can Do..141
  9.1.1: Periphrastic Participle 141
  9.1.2: Genitive Absolute 142
  9.1.3: Adverbial Participle 142
 9.2: Understanding Participle Function and Translation 144
  9.2.1: The Subject of an Adverbial Participle 147
  9.2.2: The Tense Of A Participle 148
 9.3: The Least You Need to Know 148
 9.4: Greek@Logos 149
 9.5: Vocabulary 149
 9.6: The Second Time Around 150

Chapter 10: Non-Indicative Verbs 151
 10.1: Introduction 151
 10.2: Subjunctive Mood 152
  10.2.1: How the Subjunctive is Formed 152
  10.2.2: Understanding Subjunctive Translation and Function 154

10.2.2.1: Subjunctive in Independent Clauses 155
10.2.2.2: Subjunctive in Dependent Clauses 156
  10.2.3: Conditional Sentences 157
10.3: Imperative 158
  10.3.1: How the Imperative is Formed 158
  10.3.2: Understanding Imperative Translation and Function 160
10.4: Optative 161
10.5: The Least You Need to Know 163
10.6: Greek@Logos 163
10.7: Vocabulary 164
10.8: The Second Time Around 165

Chapter 11: Infinitives Stripped Down 167
11.1: Infinitive Description 167
11.2: How Infinitives Are Formed 167
11.3: What An Infinitive Can Do 169
  11.3.1: Infinitive as Subject (nominative) 169
  11.3.2: Infinitive as Object (accusative) 169
  11.3.3: Appositional Infinitive or Epexegetical Infinitive (accusative) ...170
  11.3.4: Infinitive in Indirect Discourse 170
  11.3.5: Complementary Infinitive 171
  11.3.6: Adverbial Infinitive 171
11.4: Understanding Infinitive Function and Translation 173
  11.4.1: The Sort-of-Subject of an Infinitive 175
  11.4.2: The Tense Of An Infinitive 176
11.5: The Least You Need to Know 176
11.6: Greek@Logos 177
11.7: Vocabulary 177
11.8: The Second Time Around 178

Where Do I Go From Here? 179

Appendix A: Additional Vocabulary Lists 181
Appendix B: Principal Parts 197
Appendix C: Nouns in the BDAG Lexicon 201
Appendix D: Glossary 207

List of Tables

Table 1: Greek Alphabet 10
Table 2: Greek Vowels and Diphthongs 11
Table 3: Consonant Categories..12
Table 4: Stop Interactions 13
Table 5: Breathing Marks 14
Table 6: Accent Marks 14
Table 7: Punctuation Marks 15
Table 8: Diaeresis, Crasis, Elision 16
Table 9: Example of Inflected Forms 25
Table 10: 1st Declension Endings (normal) 26
Table 11: 1st Declension Endings (second type) 27
Table 12: 2nd Declension Endings (mostly masculine) 27
Table 13: 2nd Declension Endings (neuter) 28
Table 14: 3rd Declension Endings (masculine or feminine) 29
Table 15: 3rd Declension Endings (neuter) 30
Table 16: Indicative Slot Machine 59
Table 17: Indicative Formation 59
Table 18: Primary and Secondary Endings 62
Table 19: λύω Indicative Paradigm 63
Table 20: Indicative Verb Translation 65
Table 21: Pluperfect Indicative Paradigm 71
Table 22: λύω Indicative Paradigm 74
Table 23: ἀκούω Indicative Paradigm 76
Table 24: λέγω Indicative Paradigm 77
Table 25: Principal Parts 79
Table 26: Lexical Middle Indicative Forms 80
Table 27: φιλέω Indicative Paradigm 82
Table 28: ἀγαπάω Indicative Paradigm 83
Table 29: ἀπαγγέλλω Indicative Paradigm 85
Table 30: 2nd Aorist Indicative Paradigm 86
Table 31: δίδωμι Indicative Paradigm 87

Table 32: εἰμί Indicative table	88
Table 33: The Article	93
Table 34: Lone Article Function	96
Table 35: Adjective following 1st and 2nd declension	97
Table 36: Adjective following 3rd declension (for masculine and neuter)	97
Table 37: 1st Personal Pronoun	102
Table 38: 2nd Personal Pronoun	102
Table 39: 3rd Personal Pronoun	102
Table 40: Demonstrative Pronouns	104
Table 41: Relative Pronouns	106
Table 42: Interrogative Pronouns	107
Table 43: Indefinite Pronouns	108
Table 44: Declined Cardinal Numbers	109
Table 45: Ordinal number "First"	110
Table 46: Correlative Pronouns	113
Table 47: Possessive Pronouns	114
Table 48: Indefinite Relative Pronouns	114
Table 49: Qualitative and Quantitative Pronouns	115
Table 50: Reflexive Pronouns	115
Table 51: Reciprocal Pronouns	116
Table 52: Negative Pronouns	116
Table 53: Preposition Forms	119
Table 54: Greek Word Groups	123
Table 55: Prepositions Spatial Translation Chart	129
Table 56: Participle Formation	132
Table 57: Present Tense λύω Participles	134
Table 58: Aorist Tense λύω Participles	135
Table 59: Perfect Tense λύω Participles	136
Table 60: Participle Flowchart	146
Table 61: Subjunctive Formation	152
Table 62: λύω Subjunctive Paradigm	153
Table 63: εἰμί Subjunctive Paradigm	154
Table 64: Subjunctive Function Table	155

Table 65: Imperative Endings 159
Table 66: Imperative Formation 159
Table 67: λύω Imperative Paradigm 160
Table 68: εἰμί Imperative Paradigm 160
Table 69: Optative Formation 162
Table 70: λύω Optative Paradigm 162
Table 71: Infinitive Formation 168
Table 72: Infinitive Flowchart 174

The Essential Introduction

Many readers typically skip introductions but I really hope you will not. That is why I called this *The Essential Introduction*. The reality is that many students are apprehensive about learning Greek. They may question its usefulness or are even downright hostile towards the idea. Your professor and I were there once and we understand. So this short introduction is to give you some encouragement for the journey as well as to explain why seminaries today are still committed to teaching future ministers how to engage with the biblical text in its original language. I want to give you reasons why Greek is worth the effort.

Encouragement

First, you need to recognize that not only has your teacher been right where you are, but you are probably in a classroom of students in the same boat as you. When we get discouraged we often become very individualistic and think, "no one is suffering with this as much as me!" You are wrong. Second, there are literally thousands and thousands of ministers-in-training across the globe who are engaging in the study of Greek. If you are like I was, Greek was the first language that I learned after English. However, you have many brothers and sisters in Christ throughout the world who are learning Greek as their third or fourth language. Finally, countless thousands have already trod this path. Fathers in church history, spiritual giants in the faith, and even most pastors whose podcasts you listen to faithfully, have trod this path. They did it because they believed it was worth the effort. More specifically, they did it because they believed that diligent study of God's Word meant engaging it in the language in which it was written.

Perhaps it is the changing of the times, the increased skill set required of pastors, the proliferation of modern translations, or some other factor that causes many students today to question the usefulness of Greek. But I assure you, God's Word is still worth the investment of your time and worthy of engagement in its primary languages. We live in a culture of instant gratification, but that is not God's way, and it certainly will not be your experience when learning Greek. It will require hard work, a lot of time, patience with yourself, and a good attitude. If you go through this process with constant resentment for having to work hard and learn something new, then you are in for a bitter few months; but if you keep the end in mind and recognize from the start that you can do this, then you will have an enjoyable few months.

> The main point is, with all and above all, study the Greek and Hebrew Bible, and the love of Christ. — *John Wesley*

> The more a theologian detaches himself from the basic Hebrew and Greek text of Holy Scripture, the more he detaches himself from the source of real theology! And real theology is the foundation of a fruitful and blessed ministry. — *Heinrich Bitzer*

There is another important point of encouragement for you in this process of learning a language. I know you are mature, but learning a language often makes you feel like a kid again. That is okay! You'll forget things, you'll mispronounce things, and you'll ask questions about things you learned only 30 seconds before you asked it. This is normal so don't feel bad or stupid about it, because the rest of your classmates are feeling the same way. Also, the nature of learning a language, especially the grammatical portions, is that you will often not feel like you really "get" it. You will not really feel like you understand chapter 3 until you are finishing chapter 5—particularly those of you in a classroom setting. This is normal, and it is why repetition is so important for learning a language. I often use the (admittedly violent) analogy that it is like treading water in a pool. At the beginning of a new chapter I (and your teacher) will put our foot on top of your head and dunk you down. You will struggle for air and eventually get your nose above the surface of the water for a breath, and the foot will push you down again—chapter after chapter. Perhaps this is an odd way to end a section on encouragement, but part of encouraging is helping you to recognize the way things will be and to give you the confidence that you have the ability to understand it.

Equipping Leaders

With only a few exceptions, most evangelical seminaries today require the study of Greek (and Hebrew) as part of their core curriculum for the training of clergy. If you are a student, please don't think that your professors came to this decision lightly. Many of your professors have been pastors or know enough about ministry to understand that it is not an easy job. In fact, it is one of the most stressful careers and requires a large skill set. The phone does not stop ringing, Sunday morning is always on your mind, someone is always going through a crisis, someone is always dying; and on and on it goes. In the midst of this you must not forget one thing: you are still a minister of God's Word. Professors in seminaries around the world still believe that a pastor needs to be equipped to engage with God's Word in the language in which it was written. Respect that decision. Put your faith in their expertise and life experiences that have brought them to that decision.

One of the essential components of equipping the next generation of pastors to minister effectively and build the kingdom of God is staying grounded in God's Word. Whether you like it or not, you are the main spiritual educator in the life of your congregation. Pop psychology, Christian bestsellers, or the latest sermon series that has trickled down from a mega-church is not going to be the catalyst that drives your congregation towards growth. It will be a large combination of things, one of which is YOU as you model serious study of God's Word, your open example of striving to live a life that conforms to God's will revealed in the scriptures, and your genuine delight in learning more and more about God. You need to continue educating yourself and to be challenged in your study of God's Word so that you can, in turn, challenge those to whom you educate and minister.

> I thank the Lord that from a bitter seed of learning I am now plucking sweet fruits. — *Jerome*

> I have firmly decided to study Greek. Nobody except God can prevent it. It is not a matter of personal ambition, but one of understanding the most Sacred Writings. — *Ulrich Zwingli*

Keeping the End in Mind[1]

God has designed our bodies in a wonderful way: the more we exercise, the stronger we get. The more we do cardio exercise to get our heart pumping, the stronger our heart pumps and the longer it will last. Our brains are the same. They get stronger with more use and exercise. Learning Greek will be difficult, as will your seminary education in general. You may have a crisis of faith (as I did), you may do a complete about-face on a particular theological teaching, and you will study, read, and write so much at times that you will feel numb. This is good! Set high expectations for yourself! The apostle Paul says, "Do your best to present yourself to God as one approved, a worker who has no need to be ashamed, rightly handling the word of truth" (2 Tim 2:15). Yet sometimes

---

[1] For more reasons on the reasons to study Greek beyond what I offer, see Jonathan Pennington's "A Cornucopia of Reasons to Study Greek." http://tiny.cc/pennington

when students come to seminary they complain about the amount of homework, they are irritated at learning about new concepts, and annoyed at having to learn Greek. Do not strive to bypass the approval process. Getting battered and bruised through seminary and through learning Greek is good for you and it shows God that you mean business when it comes to a lifetime of ministry.

As stated previously, whether you like it or not you are the main educator for the majority of your congregation. This means that you are viewed as a theological expert. This does not mean that you need to know the answer to every question. Learning to say "I'm not sure, let me get back to you on that" is a good practice. You also need to know how to delve deeper. You need to be able to read quality resources from top scholars and theologians. In order to engage in higher levels of learning and reading, you need to understand Greek. You do not have to be a master of Greek, but you certainly cannot be ignorant of it. One of the greatest payoffs of learning Greek is that it raises your reading level, which increases your engagement in the conversation surrounding God's Word, so that you can enter into that conversation in order to educate others.

Finally, engaging with God's Word in the original language causes you to *slow down* and see with greater perception than you ever have before. If ever there is a spot to slow down and delay the mentality of instant gratification that prevails in modern society, your time with God and engagement with the Word is that time. I often use the analogy of watching a movie: viewing a 13-inch black and white television is not ideal but you fully understand the story and its characters. Moving to a 27-inch color television is much better as the images are larger and more vibrant. But sitting in a theater with 3-D glasses and watching a movie on the big screen is almost overwhelming as colors and images get right up close to you. Most people in the pews who read just the Bible and occasionally the study notes in their Bible get the story, enjoy it, and have come to know God and his saving grace. Those readers who go to the next level and read some commentaries, some dictionary articles, etc., are reading, perceiving, and enjoying the Scriptures at a different level. But engaging with the text in its primary language is like putting 3-D glasses on. You see things that you have not seen before in stories that you know off by heart already. You are equipped to engage in better research and study of the Bible. And you are forced to slow down. If you are honest with yourself, your Bible reading time probably goes pretty quickly. Christian pastors often become so familiar with God's Word that when they do read the Bible, they skim. Forcing yourself to engage with the Bible in its original language requires you to slow down and observe. You will be so glad you did.

I end this section with a caution—the primary language is not a mystical portal to secret learning. Read the following from Moisés Silva about what competence in Greek means:

> The kind of competence in view here does not necessarily lead to a display of linguistic fireworks. In fact, such knowledge often does not even rise to the surface, but that does not mean it has been unproductive. Language students, to be sure, typically feel cheated if as a result of their hard work they cannot come up with exegetical razzle-dazzle. Teachers, therefore, afraid that their students will lose motivation, try hard to find interpretive "golden nuggets" that prove there is a rich payoff to language study. If used with much care, this approach can be helpful. But there is always the danger of feeding the common mind-set that says, "Something is valuable only if I can see its immediate relevance."
>
> It is not the primary purpose of language study to provide the means for reaching astounding exegetical conclusions, although sound linguistic training can at least prevent students from adopting inadmissible interpretations. The true goal of learning New testament Greek is rather to build a much broader base of knowledge and understanding than the student would otherwise have. Occasionally, this knowledge may indeed supply fairly direct answers to exegetical questions. But what matters most is the newly acquired ability to interpret texts responsibly on the basis of comprehensive rather than fragmented (and therefore distorted) information.
>
> Of course, most people who take up the study of New Testament Greek do not intend to write technical and original works of scholarship. They want skills that will allow them to use commentaries and other reference works effectively. They also hope to do serious exegetical work on their own. But the principles and benefits of language learning remain fundamentally the same. An effective, reliable biblical exposition need not rely on complex discussions of meanings of Greek words or on the supposed subtleties of the aorist tense, but it certainly should arise out of genuine firsthand familiarity with the original text.[2]

---

[2] Moisés Silva, Introduction to *New Testament Greek for Beginners* by J. Gresham Machen and Dan G. McCartney (Prentice Hall, 2003), 10–11. I'm indebted to Rodney Decker for pointing out this quotation on his blog.

Why and How This Grammar is Different

This grammar is different than most. I know every new grammar that comes on the scene justifies its existence by saying this, but this time it really is true. It is different not only in layout, but it is very different in its pedagogical approach and breakdown. Here are the ways in which it is different:

1. This textbook is designed for a twelve-week (or so) class or self learner. That is why there are only 11 chapters in this book. Most (not all) Greek textbooks, and certainly all of the popular ones used in seminaries today, are designed for a full year (i.e. two semester) course and span from 20 to 35 chapters or more.

2. This textbook teaches you to work with Logos Bible software. While most Greek professors want you to avoid Bible Software because it is a crutch (and it certainly can be!), it is increasingly a reality that pastors, if they are working with the original languages *at all*, are doing so with Bible Software. Instead of fighting that trend, I am embracing it and trying to equip you to use Logos Bible Software to its full potential.[3] Indeed, the use of Bible software will *enhance* your knowledge of Greek and enrich your study. If you are about to embark on learning Greek with this grammar, purchase of the Logos 5 *Original Languages* base package is required. If you are a student, Logos is generous with student discounts, so be sure to sign up for their academic discount.

3. Because of the above two realities, this grammar employs a conceptual, or wide-angle approach to teaching you Greek. It is by no means a dumbing down of Greek—there is still plenty of memorization work to be done. But the questions asked are different from a typical grammar. For instance, a typical grammar would ask a student "what is the parsing[4] of λύομαι?" To which your answer would be "present, middle/passive, indicative, first person, singular, from λύω." Instead, this grammar will say, "Your Bible software tells you that λύομαι is present, middle/passive, indicative, first person, singular, from λύω. How does Logos know that? What does it mean to be present? What does it mean to be middle/passive? What does it mean to be indicative? How good of a job did your

---

[3] Logos Bible Software was chosen because it is cross platform (Mac and PC). In the future, I may accommodate users of Accordance Bible Software, as it is another fantastic resource for Mac users. I'm an avid user of both.

[4] I realize you don't even understand this yet, but you will soon enough!

English translation do in translating that word?" This textbook will strive to give you a solid overview of the entire NT Greek system, and challenge you to answer questions relevant to meaning and translation, while helping you understand the basics of how Greek works and how Greek words are formed.

4. I have made the grammar so that it accommodates those who want to go on to study Greek further, and especially those who want to spend another 12 or so weeks to increase their competency in Greek. This is done by going through the book twice. At the end of each chapter, there is a *Second Time Around* section for those who are doing their second pass through the grammar, to suggest some things to focus on and any applicable additional information. The workbook also includes additional sections for those going through the second time.

5. This textbook is designed to be one of the first true multimedia Greek grammars, and is published through an e-publisher. As such, I make extensive use of media and other apps and software. To find the resources for this textbook, please visit NTGreekResources.com where you will find the accompanying workbook, a companion video course, and a Logos tutorial course, and mobile apps recommended within the textbook.

Are you ready? Here we go![5]

---

[5]Recommended prior reading on the history of the Greek language: *Greek Grammar Beyond the Basics* by Daniel Wallace, pp. 12–30.

Chapter 1:
Signs and Sounds of Greek Stripped Down

⇒**What's the Point:** Here is a statistic for you—100% of the New Testament was written using Greek letters. How else can you learn how to read and speak a language than by learning the the alphabet? Learning this chapter thoroughly will equip you for proper reading, recognition, and pronunciation of the Greek New Testament.

1.1: The Greek Alphabet

The first building block to learn a language is the alphabet. While the primary goal for most students of New Testament Greek is to learn to read and interpret the New Testament, being able to read Greek aloud with proper pronunciation is very valuable. After all, how many of you want to go through months of Greek and not even be able to read it aloud! Take the time right from the beginning to *read all the Greek you see aloud*, even if you don't understand it yet.[6]

Scholars are not entirely certain how ancients pronounced Greek, but there are several popular options. Most introductory grammars, including this one, choose what is called the Erasmian method.

The following table of the Greek alphabet shows you the regular and capital letters,[7] as well as the transliteration letter used, and finally a pronunciation example. Transliteration refers to the English letters used to write Greek letters to replicate the sound. While it is not critical that you know how to transliterate, it is good to know because many books, articles, and commentaries employ transliteration when discussing Greek.

---

[6]How to access the audio of the Greek New Testament in Logos will be explained at a later point. Students who own iDevices or Android devices are also encouraged to purchase FlashGreek Pro, a flashcard application keyed to this grammar that also pronounces words. See NTGreekResources.com

[7]Greek capital letters are called majuscules and the small letters are called miniscules. In your Greek New Testament you will encounter mostly miniscules. Capital letters will occur at the beginning of paragraphs (but not sentences), at the beginning of quotations, and as the first letter of proper names.

Table 1: Greek Alphabet

majuscule	minuscule	name	transliteration	pronunciation
Α	α	alpha	a	f**a**ther
Β	β	beta	b	**b**est
Γ	γ	gamma	g, n[8]	**g**ame
Δ	δ	delta	d	**d**irty
Ε	ε	epsilon	e	**e**stablish
Ζ	ζ	zeta	z, dz[9]	**z**oo, a**dds**
Η	η	eta	e	**p**r**ey**
Θ	θ	theta	th	**th**ought
Ι	ι, ᾳ[10]	iota	i, y[11]	**i**diot, **i**gnite (short)
Κ	κ	kappa	k (or c)	**k**ite
Λ	λ	lambda	l	**l**augh
Μ	μ	mu	m	**m**ark
Ν	ν	nu	n	**n**ice
Ξ	ξ	xi	x	bo**x**
Ο	ο	omicron	o	**o**xen
Π	π	pi	p	**p**aint
Ρ	ρ	rho	r	**r**ight
Σ	σ, ς[12]	sigma	s	**s**ound
Τ	τ	tau	t	**t**ight
Υ	υ	upsilon	y, u[13]	s**u**per, **u**sher (short)
Φ	φ	phi	ph	**ph**ilosophy
Χ	χ	chi	ch	**ch**iropractor
Ψ	ψ	psi	ps	li**ps**
Ω	ω	omega	ō	**o**dour

---

[8] A gamma (γ) is pronounced "n" when it comes before γ, κ, ξ, and χ.

[9] A zeta (ζ) is pronounced "dz" when it is in the middle of a word.

[10] The little mark underneath the grey alpha is called an iota subscript. It appears under alphas (ᾳ), etas (ῃ), and omegas (ῳ). When it is a subscript it is still transliterated, it is still there, but it IS NOT pronounced.

[11] An iota (ι) is transliterated with a "y" when followed immediately by another vowel.

[12] This second sigma is called a final sigma, and is used only when the sigma is on the end of a word.

[13] A "u" is used in transliteration when an upsilon (υ) follows another vowel.

1.2: Greek Vowels

Like English, some vowels are always short, some are always long, some can be both, and they can form a tag-team to make a new sound combination called a diphthong. Work especially on identifying diphthongs in words and pronouncing them correctly.

Table 2: Greek Vowels and Diphthongs

Short	Long	Pronunciation
ε, ο		see above
	η, ω	see above
α, ι, υ or	α, ι, υ	see above
	αι[14]	**ai**sle
	αυ	**ou**t
	ει	**ei**ght
	ευ	f**eu**d
	οι	**oi**l
	ου	gr**ou**p
	υι	s**ui**te
	ηυ	**ayoo**
	ωυ	s**ou**l

1.2.1: Vowel Contraction

Another important thing to know is that vowels can lengthen or change. There are a few in particular to be most aware of. When alphas (α) and epsilons (ε) come into contact with another vowel (like another α or ε), they often lengthen to an eta (η). Under similar circumstances, omicrons (ο) lengthen to omegas (ω). Vowels can also contract together to become diphthongs. You do not need to know how or why, just know that it does happen A LOT when vowels come into contact with one another.

☞ Watch this video (http://youtu.be/S8842oS0CtU) to solidify the previous section.

---

[14]Students will most often mispronounce this diphthong because ai in English says "ay" not "eye."

1.3: Greek Consonants

Greek consonants are grouped into categories based on the way they are pronounced with our mouths. Sibilants have an "s" sound, liquid letters keep the air flowing through your mouth, and stop letters stop the air in your mouth at some point. Stop letters are further subdivided into labials (you stop the air with your lips), palatals (you stop the air by touching the roof of your mouth), and dentals (you stop the air by touching your teeth). Read the alphabet in the previous section aloud again and pay attention to what your mouth does.

Table 3: Consonant Categories

Sibilants		σ (ς) ζ ξ ψ		
Liquids		λ μ ν ρ		
Stops[15]		smooth	→→→[16]	rough
	labials	π	β	φ
	palatals	κ	γ	χ
	dentals	τ	δ	θ

1.3.1: The Sigma with a Liquid

Of all of the letters, learn to treat the sigma with the most fear and trepidation because it causes the most problems. The first thing you need to know is that a sigma has an invisibility cloak. When it follows a liquid letter, it often disappears completely (more on this in future chapters). I like to say that it "slips on the liquid." θ also can do this after liquid letters.

1.3.2: The Sigma with the Stops

The second thing about sigma is that it is a bully. When it comes after a labial stop, the two combine to become a ψ. If the sigma comes after a palatal it becomes a ξ. The sigma is most sinister after a dental, I like to say that the dental loses its teeth because the dental will disappear all together. Dentals are also weaklings in that they do not like to end a word. If they do, they disappear.

---

[15] The darkened portion of the table is often referred to as the "square of stops" or "table of stops."
[16] There are times when a smooth stop consonant will change to a rough stop.

Although sigma is the biggest bully, kappa (κ) and theta (θ) also interact with the stop letters in similar ways—they are sigma-wannabees. When a kappa follows a labial, it prefers the rough stop and will cause a pi (π) or a beta (β) to become a phi (φ), but this change makes the kappa disappear. Kappa changes smooth palatals to the rough palatal as well. It acts like a sigma with dentals, making them disappear altogether, while it sticks around. A theta (θ) causes the same changes as a kappa (κ), but it doesn't disappear. The sigma rears its ugly head once more when a theta follows a dental. The dental disappears, and a sigma takes its place!

Table 4: Stop Interactions

	smooth		rough	+ σ[17]			+ κ			+ θ		
labials	π	β	φ	+ σ	=	ψ	+ κ	=	φ	+ θ	=	φθ
palatals	κ	γ	χ	+ σ	=	ξ	+ κ	=	χ	+ θ	=	χθ
dentals	τ[18]	δ	θ	+ σ	=	σ	+ κ	=	κ	+ θ	=	σθ

☞ Watch this video (http://youtu.be/7R4AXepe5p4) to solidify the previous section.

1.4: Jots and Tittles in Greek

There are three sets of marks that are important to know in Greek: breathing marks, accent marks, and punctuation. The first two sets are related to pronunciation. Greek punctuation marks were not part of the original text but were added by later editors.

1.4.1: Breathing Marks

Every Greek word that begins with a vowel (or ρ) has a breathing mark. You may have noticed in the alphabet table that there is no letter that makes an "h" sound. The Greek rough breathing makes the "h" sound while a smooth breathing mark makes no difference in pronunciation. Breathing marks are written: 1) above the first letter of any

---

[17]This section shows what happens when a sigma is added to any of the consonants in that row. With the following sections showing the interactions when a kappa or theta is added.

[18]Sometimes, not always, when a τ is preceded by a nu (ν), the sigma bully may kick them both out.

word beginning with a vowel or ρ, 2) above the second letter if the word begins with a diphthong, or 3) in front of the letter if it is a capital letter.

Table 5: Breathing Marks

Name	Mark	above letter	with capital	with diphthong
smooth breathing (no pronunciation)	᾿	ἐστιν (estin)	Ἰησοῦς (Yesous)	εἰμί (eimi)
rough breathing ("h" sound)	῾	ὑμῶν (humōn)	Ῥαββί (hRabbi)	εἰς (hays)

1.4.2: Accent Marks

Although English does not write accents, most readers have seen accents—on French words for instance. Accents alert the reader where to place emphasis in the word. Do not worry too much about memorizing the accents, but learn to see them and work on emphasizing the syllable that they are on when reading aloud. There are a few times when accents help to identify otherwise identical words, and these will be pointed out when the time comes.

Accents sit over short or long vowels or dpthongs. Finally, you will only ever see an accent over the last three syllables of a word, which are named:

Antepenult	Penult	Ultima
ἄν	θρω	πος
ἐ	αυ	τοῦ
	αὐ	τοῦ
		ὅ

Table 6: Accent Marks

Name	Mark	Quantity	Syllable position	example	w/ breathing mark	
acute	´	short or long	Antepenult / Penult / Ultima	βάλε	ὅτι	ἤδη
circumflex	˜	long	Penult / Ultima	σῶμα	ἦν	ὧδε
grave	`	short or long	Ultima	μὴ	ὸν	ἂν

1.4.3: Punctuation Marks

Punctuation marks are not original to the writing of the scriptures, but nonetheless are important parts of our current Greek text. People that know Greek much better than you (or me!) added punctuation, so in general you can trust them. These punctuation marks will help you recognize sentence divisions, clause divisions, and questions.

Table 7: Punctuation Marks

Name	Mark	Example
period	.	ταῦτα γράφω ὑμῖν ἵνα μὴ ἁμάρτητε.
comma	,	Τεκνία μου,
question	;	τί ἐστιν ἀλήθεια;
semicolon or colon	·	λέγει αὐτῷ ὁ Πιλᾶτος·
quotation mark[19]	capital letter	καὶ λέγει, Οὐκ εἰμί.
	ὅτι	λέγουσιν αὐτῷ· ὅτι οὐδεὶς ἡμᾶς ἐμισθώσατο.

1.4.4: Diaeresis, Crasis, Elision

Diaeresis occurs over the second vowel of what looks like a diphthong. Essentially, diaeresis tells you NOT to treat those two vowels as a diphthong, but to pronounce them separately.

Both crasis and elision are indicators that something odd has happened and they are marked by a *coronis*, which looks like our English apostrophe. Crasis is when two words are smashed together. The result is one word, with a coronis placed over the word to represent the change. Elision happens in English too, with words like "can't" and "don't." The apostrophe in English represents a dropped vowel just like in Greek.

---

[19]Marks of a quotation are not considered punctuation marks, but are important markers to recognize in sentences for divisions.

Table 8: Diaeresis, Crasis, Elision

Name	Mark	example
Diaeresis	¨	Μωϋσῆς
Crasis	᾿	κἀγώ (καὶ + ἐγώ)
Elision	᾿	ἐπ᾿ αὐτήν (ἐπὶ + αὐτήν)

1.4.5: Greek Syllables

Greek syllables function with one main rule just like English syllables: only one vowel (or diphthong) per syllable. There is also another rule that governs syllables, again like English: certain consonants always stick together. Consider in English: sh, ch, st, ck, etc. You would not divide English syllables between these consonants because they form a unit. In Greek many consonants also stick together: βλ, κλ, θλ, πλ, μν, πν, γρ, θρ, κρ, πρ, τρ, χρ, πτ, σκ, σπ, στ, σμ, σχ, _μ, and _ν. Syllabification is not important for meaning, but it does help you learn to pronounce Greek correctly.

1.5: The Least You Need to Know

Each chapter in this textbook will end with a section called *The Least You Need to Know*. It will be a bullet-point list of questions you should understand and be able to answer with a brief explanation (if your teacher is on the ball, they may also appear on tests). There may be times that you are able to answer these questions but don't fully understand the words coming out of your mouth—that's okay! Repetition and exposure will bring understanding. I've also created online flashcards on for these sections to aid in drilling yourself.

Use these online flashcards (http://quizlet.com/_7teo4) to memorize the answers:[20]

- What is a majuscule?
- What is a miniscule?

---

[20]Quizlet© offers a variety of ways to test yourself. Take the time to learn how to use this online flashcard site.

- What is a diphthong?
- What is vowel contraction? When does it occur?
- What is a liquid consonant?
- What is a sibilant consonant?
- What is a labial stop consonant?
- What is a palatal stop consonant?
- What is a dental stop consonant?
- What happens when a sigma follows a liquid?
- What happens when a sigma follows a labial?
- What happens when a sigma follows a palatal?
- What happens when a sigma follows a dental?
- What happens when a kappa follows a labial?
- What happens when a kappa follows a palatal?
- What happens when a kappa follows a dental?
- What happens when a theta follows a labial?
- What happens when a theta follows a palatal?
- What happens when a theta follows a dental?
- What is a rough breathing mark?
- What does an accent do?
- What is the one major governing principle for Greek syllables?

1.6: Greek@Logos

Throughout the textbook chapters you will be learning how to work with Logos Bible Software. If you haven't already, go purchase the Logos 5 *Original Languages* base package. Logos gives great discounts to students, so be sure to sign up for academic pricing before you make your purchase (logos.com/academicdiscount) if this applies to you.

I'm confident that soon Logos Bible Software will soon become one of your best research tools, but it is a big program and takes time to learn. That is why I created a video tutorial course for Logos called ***Mastering Logos Bible Software*** that you can find at NT-GreekResources.com. Through the chapters, I will recommend particular video lessons from this tutorial course. For those of you who do not want to purchase the video course, I've also pointed out some free articles and videos.

For this first chapter, learn the basics of Logos. To do this, you can either go through Section 1 of the Logos tutorial course, or visit logos.com/videos and watch *all* of the videos specific to your platform (Mac or PC). Watch them until you get the basics all down. While you are watching the videos, mimic what you see in your own version of Logos. Through the rest of this book, you learn additional skills in Logos that assume you know the basics taught in these Logos videos.

1.7: Vocabulary

Great news! You already know hundreds of Greek words because of the influence of Greek upon English and your knowledge of the Bible. In the coming chapters, you are asked to memorize the 180 highest frequency words in the New Testament. By the time you are done, you will know all words that occur 100 times or more.

Vocabulary is always presented in a table and includes the following information: 1) the type of word; 2) the frequency of the word in the NT; and 3) (an) applicable English derivative(s) when available to aid in memorization. The following abrreviations identify the type of word:

adj. = adjective

adv. = adverb

conj. = conjunction

inter. = interjection

partic. = particle

pron. = pronoun

pr.noun = proper noun

This first list contains the fourteen most used proper nouns in the Greek New Testament. You should be able to easily remember these, as they sound so similar to their English counterparts. The second list has the fourteen highest frequency words in the NT. For the words that have numerous glosses, try to memorize as many as you can.

Note FlashGreek Pro is an iOS and Android flashcard application that is keyed to each chapter of this grammar. It also includes multimedia components like audio, image mnemonics, and contextual examples. It is recommended that users of this grammar make use of it (full disclosure, I created the app). For those who do not have an iOS or Android device, there are PC and Mac options as well. Visit NTGreekResources.com

Word	Gloss	Type	Freq.	Derivatives
Ἀβραάμ, ὁ[21]	Abraham	pr.noun	73	
Γαλιλαία, -ας, ἡ	Galilee	pr.noun	61	
Δαυίδ, ὁ[22]	David	pr.noun	59	
Ἱεροσόλυμα, τά or ἡ	Jerusalem[23]	pr.noun	62	
Ἱερουσαλήμ, ἡ	Jerusalem	pr.noun	77	
Ἰησοῦς, -οῦ, ὁ	Jesus, Joshua	pr.noun	917	
Ἰωάννης, -ου, ὁ	John	pr.noun	135	
Μωϋσῆς, -έως, ὁ	Moses	pr.noun	80	
Παῦλος, ὁ	Paul	pr.noun	158	
Πέτρος, ὁ	Peter	pr.noun	156	
Πιλᾶτος, ὁ	Pilate	pr.noun	55	
Σίμων, -ωνος, ὁ	Simon	pr.noun	75	
Φαρισαῖος, -ου, ὁ	Pharisee	pr.noun	98	
Χριστός, ὁ	Christ	pr.noun	529	
ὁ, ἡ, τό	the	article	19867	
γάρ	for, so, then	conj.	1041	
δέ	but, and	conj.	2792	
καί	and, even, also	conj.	9161	
ὅτι	because, that, since	conj.	1296	
θεός, -οῦ, ὁ	God, god	noun	1317	*theo*cracy, *theo*logy

---

[21]Right now, do not worry about the grey font in these lists, it will be explained in §3.5.
[22]There is no "v" sound in Greek.
[23]The following 8 names all begin with "J" in English. There is no J sound in Greek (or Hebrew). When you hear a "J" sound in a name in the Bible, it is usually representing an iota, which makes an "ee" sound.

κύριος, -ου, ὁ	lord, Lord	noun	717	
μή	not, no; lest	partic.	1042	
οὐ, οὐκ, οὐχ	not	partic.	1606	
ἐν	(+dat)[24] in, on, by	prep.	2752	*en*demic
εἰς	(+acc) into, in; to, toward; among	prep.	1767	*eis*egesis
ἐκ (ἐξ)[25]	(+gen) from, out of, of, by	prep.	914	*ex*egesis
ἐπί (ἐπ', ἐφ')	(+gen) on, over, when; (+dat) on the basis of, at; (+acc) on, to, against, for	prep.	890	*epi*center
πρός	(+gen) for; (+dat) at; (+acc) to, against	prep.	700	*pros*elyte

1.8: The Second Time Around

The Second Time Around section will be the very last section of each chapter. When necessary, this section provides information for readers who are using the grammar for a second semester and specifies what they should focus. For this chapter, no additional information is necessary.

---

[24]Prepositions can mean different things when paired with different types of nouns. You will learn more about this in Chapter 7. Just memorize what you see for now.

[25]This is an alternative way this word may appear. You will learn more about this in Chapter 7.

Chapter 2:
Greek Nouns Stripped Down

⇒**What's the Point:** 20% of the New Testament is nouns; all of the people, places, and things mentioned in the New Testament are nouns. They are one of the primary parts of any language and, thus, essential to understand.

2.1: Greek Inflection

The English language relies on word order to tell you what nouns are doing in the sentence. Normally, we place the subject in the sentence before the verb, which is often followed by the object. But if you speak or are familiar with another language, you know that not every language works this way. Greek does not care as much about word order,[26] and it identifies what the subject or object is with something called inflection. Inflection is a way of tagging words to indicate their role in the sentence. Take a look at the following sentence:

> The father of Jack threw the ball in the house.

Now, I'm going to color code the same sentence to indicate the functions of the different nouns. The subject is blue, the noun that is indicating possession is green, an indirect object is orange, the object is red, and the verb is black. The small words that work with the nouns (like the word "the" which always goes in front of the noun) is color coded with the noun that they are with.

The father of Jack threw the ball in the house.

If we pretend this sentence is Greek (or if you are Yoda from star wars), we can mix up this sentence however we want.

---

[26] Word order does matter for some things and will be pointed out when appropriate.

Threw in the house the father of Jack the ball.

The ball in the house the father of Jack threw.

In the house the ball threw the father of Jack.

Now, knowing that I have tagged the nouns by color, you can make sense of the sentence by reordering the words to conform to English word order. Instead of using color, Greek inflects (i.e. tags) nouns by changing the end of the word. Here is a Greek example of a made up sentence "the son of man teaches people in the house."

ὁ υἱὸς	ἀνθρώπου	διδάσκει	λαὸν	οἴκῳ.
the son	of man	teaches	people	in the house.

Because of the inflection (i.e. tag) on the end of the nouns, the Greek words can be re-ordered any way the author wants to and we can still understand the sentence because the inflection tells us what the nouns are doing in the sentence:

λαὸν	οἴκῳ	ὁ υἱὸς	ἀνθρώπου	διδάσκει.
people	in the house	the son	of man	teaches.

οἴκῳ	διδάσκει	λαὸν	ὁ υἱὸς	ἀνθρώπου.
in the house	teaches	people	the son	of man.

διδάσκει	ὁ υἱὸς	ἀνθρώπου	οἴκῳ	λαὸν.
teaches	the son	of man	in the house	people.

☞ Watch this video (http://youtu.be/upH6DmOZIgw) to solidify the previous section.

2.2: Noun Cases

Greek inflection tags indicate three things about the noun they are attached to: case, gender, and number. We'll focus on case first. There are four main cases, and one more used only occasionally.

1. NOMINATIVE[27] - A noun is inflected as a nominative mostly to indicate what the *subject* is in the sentence. The blue tag in the above Greek sentence is in the nominative case, which indicates the subject.

2. GENITIVE[28] - A noun is inflected as a genitive to indicate things like *possession, comparison, origin, or an attribute*. When it comes to translating a genitive, it has several "built-in" prepositions that can be used in translation: "of," "from," or "by."[29] So, when you see a genitive noun translated, or when you translate a noun inflected as a genitive, one of these prepositions is often used.[30] We also indicate possession in English with apostrophe+s, so this is also used in translation. The green tag in the above Greek sentence is in the genitive case. Notice how "of" is being used in the translation. Sometimes, the Greek author does not want to use one of the "built-in" prepositions. In this case, Greek gives you a different preposition prior to the genitive noun to use instead. You learn more about prepositions in Chapter 7.

   One more thing about genitive nouns. The genitive noun most often directly follows the noun that it is connected to. Notice in both the English and Greek examples above that the genitive noun followed the nominative because the genitive noun is indicating possession of the nominative. If the genitive was indicating possession of the object, it would have followed the red-tagged word.

3. DATIVE[31] - A noun is inflected as a dative to indicate things like *indirect object, to specify a location, or to specify agency*. Datives have several "built-in" prepositions that can be used in translation: "to," "in," "with," "on," "for" or "by."[32] So, when you see a dative translated or when you translate a dative, use one of these words, unless the sentence gives you a better preposition to use immediately before the dative noun. The orange tag in the above Greek sentence is in the dative case. Notice how "in" is being used in the translation.

---

[27] Abbreviated nom.
[28] Abbreviated gen.
[29] I've listed these roughly in order of use. In other words, "of" is used most often.
[30] Prepositions will be covered in more detail in a later chapter.
[31] Abbreviated dat.
[32] These are listed roughly in order of use.

4. ACCUSATIVE[33] - A noun is inflected as an accusative to indicate the *direct object*[34] in the sentence. The red tag in the above Greek sentence is in the accusative case to indicate the object.

5. VOCATIVE[35] - A noun is inflected as a vocative to indicate *direct address*. It is a formal method of addressing someone, used in direct speech (for example, "*Teacher*, what does this mean?") Most vocatives in the NT are identical to the nominative and would be parsed as such. The only exception is 2nd declension masculine singular nouns (see below). Because this case does not occur that frequently in the NT, it will not be focused on.

2.3: Noun Gender

In Greek, as well as English, nouns have gender. We tend to think of inanimate objects as being "it," not a "him" or "her." But even English speakers sometimes refer to inanimate objects like a boat or car as "her." In Greek, the inflection (those colored parts above) often, but not always, help to indicate the gender of the noun (more on this below).

2.4: Noun Number

English usually marks a noun as plural by adding an "s" after the noun—dog*s*, cat*s*, human*s*. Occasionally, though, English changes how a word is spelled to make it a plural. So, "mouse" is singular, but "mice" is plural; "goose" is singular, but "geese" is plural.

Once again, it is the inflection of a Greek noun (the colored tags) that indicates whether it is singular or plural. A noun's number dictates whether it is translated as a singular or plural.

---

[33] Abbreviated acc.
[34] Some verbs prefer to take a genitive or a dative as their direct object rather than an accusative.
[35] Abbreviated voc.

2.5: Noun Lexical Form

What about the beginning of a Greek noun (i.e. all of the black letters before those colored tags)? Every noun is built upon its stem, which is the most basic part of the word. The lexical form refers to the word as it appears in a lexicon (i.e. a dictionary), which in Greek is always the nominative singular (the blackest box). Consider an English example. If I asked you to look up the word "houses" in a dictionary, you would need to look up "house," and it would tell you "houses" is the plural of "house." The following table takes the Greek word "God" and shows you all the ways it can appear once tagged:

Table 9: Example of Inflected Forms

case	singular		plural	
	Inflected form	*Translation*	*Inflected form*	*Translation*
nominative	θεός	"God"	θεοί	"gods"
genitive	θεοῦ	"of God"	θεῶν	"of gods"
dative	θεῷ	"to/in God"	θεοῖς	"to/in gods"
accusative	θεόν	"God"	θεούς	"gods"

The end of each of these Greek forms of "God" is the inflection, but only θεός occurs as the lexical form in a Greek lexicon. The nominative singular is the form of the word to learn for new vocabulary.

2.6: Noun Declensions

One last item needs to be put into place to understand how Greek nouns are formed. Greek nouns are categorized into three big groups and it is the last letter on the word's stem that determines what category a word belongs to. If the noun stem ends in alpha (α) or eta (η), it is placed in a category called "1st declension." If the noun stem ends in omicron (o), it is placed in a category called "2nd declension." If the noun stem ends in anything else (usually consonants), it is placed in a category called "3rd declension." Why does this matter? Because each declension has its own set of inflection tags to add to the end of the Greek nouns that are in its category.

2.7: Noun Case Endings

The following are the declension endings for the three categories of Greek nouns. Do not be intimidated by the amount of forms. Your goal in the *Stripped Down* approach is to be able to recognize noun forms and understand why they look the way they do. In the next chapter the meaning and function of the Greek noun cases are discussed in greater detail. As you begin to work with bible software, lexicons, etc., work on recognizing the endings from the tables below.

2.7.1: 1st Declension

As previously mentioned, 1st declension nouns have an alpha (α) or an eta (η) as the last letter of the word's stem. In one particular group of 1st declension nouns, the alpha (α) or eta (η) is the second last letter. The majority of 1st declension nouns are feminine in gender. However, the second group that has an alpha (α) or eta (η) as the second last letter in the lexical form are masculine in gender.[36]

Table 10: 1st Declension Endings (normal)

	Singular			Plural		
	end of stem	inflection	final form(s)	end of stem	inflection	final form
nominative	α/η +	--	= α η	α/η +	ι	= αι
genitive	α/η +	ς	= ας ης	α/η +	ων[37]	= ων
dative	α/η +	ι[38]	= ᾳ ῃ	α/η +	ις	= αις
accusative	α/η +	ν	= αν ην	α/η +	ς	= ας

---

[36]There are no neuter nouns in the 1st declension.

[37]The omega will absorb the alpha or eta. This process occurs in the genitive plural of the second type as well.

[38]The iota will subscript. This process occurs in the dative singular of the second type as well.

Table 11: 1ˢᵗ Declension Endings (second type)

	Singular				Plural		
	end of stem	inflection	*final form(s)*		end of stem	inflection	*final form*
nominative	α/η	+	ς	=	ας ης	α/η	+	ι	=	αι
genitive	α/η	+	υ	=	ου ου	α/η	+	ων	=	ων
dative	α/η	+	ι	=	ᾳ ῃ	α/η	+	ις	=	αις
accusative	α/η	+	ν	=	αν ην	α/η	+	ς	=	ας

2.7.2: 2ⁿᵈ Declension

2ⁿᵈ declension nouns are stems that end in an omicron. Nouns that take the first set of endings below are mostly masculine in gender (though sometimes feminine). Nouns that take the second set of endings are neuter in gender. Notice also the similarities with 1ˢᵗ declension.

Table 12: 2ⁿᵈ Declension Endings (mostly masculine)

	singular[39]				plural		
	end of stem	inflection	*final form(s)*		end of stem	inflection	*final form*
nominative	ο	+	ς	=	ος	ο	+	ι	=	οι
genitive	ο	+	υ[40]	=	ου	ο	+	ων[41]	=	ων
dative	ο	+	(#) ι[42]	=	ῳ	ο	+	ις	=	οις
accusative	ο	+	ν	=	ον	ο	+	υς	=	ους

---

[39] The masculine singular vocative is the only vocative form that isn't identical to the nominative, its ending is an ε.

[40] The inflection here and in table 13 is actually an omicron (ο), and ο + ο = ου.

[41] The omega will absorb the omicron.

[42] The iota wants to subscript, but before it happens the omicron will end up being lengthened to an omega, because an iota cannot subscript under on omicron.

Table 13: 2nd Declension Endings (neuter)

	singular			plural		
	end of stem	inflection	**final form(s)**	end of stem	inflection	final form
nominative	ο	+ ν	= ον	ο	+ α	= α
genitive	ο	+ υ	= ου	ο	+ ων	= ων
dative	ο	+ ι	= ῳ	ο	+ ις	= οις
accusative	ο	+ ν	= ον	ο	+ α	= α

2.7.3: 3rd Declension

3rd declension nouns are stems that end in consonants. These nouns are the most difficult to identify because consonants often with one another and change (particularly labials, palatals, and dentals, from sections §1.3.1 and §1.3.2). Whereas 1st declension nouns are mostly feminine and 2nd declension nouns are mostly masculine or neuter, 3rd declension nouns can be any gender.

The stem of 1st and 2nd declension nouns are relatively easy to recognize because of a consistent last letter on the end of the stem, but 3rd declension nouns are not as easy because a stem can end with any consonant. Furthermore, the lexical form of a 1st or a 2nd declension noun clearly shows you the stem: θεός is nominative masculine singular (2nd declension), ἔργον is nominative neuter singular (2nd declension), ἡμέρα is nominative feminine singular (1st declension). In 3rd declension nouns, you cannot trust the nominative singular to reveal the stem of the word because the nominative singular can: 1) change the final letter of the stem, 2) cause the final letter to drop off, 3) cause the final letter to disappear and then change the second-last letter, or 4) cause the final letter to drop off and lengthen the last vowel in the word.[43] *It is the genitive singular form of a 3rd declension noun that will present the stem.*

The complexity of 3rd declension nouns is evident in the table below, but there are even more patterns of 3rd declension nouns. In the Stripped Down approach, you don't need to worry about memorizing all of this. Just understand the inflection and letter interactions.

---

[43]Other things can happen as well, but these are the main changes.

Table 14: 3rd Declension Endings (masculine or feminine)

			singular			plural	
		end of stem	inflection	final form(s)	end of stem	inflection	final form
nominative		[labial] +	ς, --	ψ[44] / --	[labial] +	ες	[π]ες
		[palatal] +		ξ[45] / --	[palatal] +		[κ]ες
		[dental] +		ς[46] / --[47]	[dental] +		[δ]ες
		(ο)ντ +		ων[48]	(ο)ντ +		οντες
		κτ +		ξ[49]	κτ +		κτες
genitive		[labial] +	ος	[π]ος	[labial] +	ων	[π]ων
		[palatal] +		[κ]ος	[palatal] +		[κ]ων
		[dental] +		[δ]ος	[dental] +		[δ]ων
		(ο)ντ +		οντος	(ο)ντ +		οντων
		κτ +		κτος	κτ +		κτων
dative		[labial] +	ι	[π]ι	[labial] +	σι	ψι(ν)[50]
		[palatal] +		[κ]ι	[palatal] +		ξι(ν)
		[dental] +		[δ]ι	[dental] +		σι(ν)
		(ο)ντ +		οντι	(ο)ντ +		ουσι(ν)[51]
		κτ +		κτι	κτ +		ξι(ν)
accusative		[labial] +	α, ν[52]	[π]α	[labial] +	ας	[π]ας
		[palatal] +		[κ]α	[palatal] +		[κ]ας
		[dental] +		[δ]α	[dental] +		[δ]ας
		(ο)ντ +		οντα	(ο)ντ +		οντας
		κτ +		κτα	κτ +		κτας

---

[44] When a sigma follows a labial it transforms to a ψ (§1.3.2). This happens in the dative plural as well.

[45] When a sigma follows a palatal it transforms to a ξ (§1.3.2). This happens in the dative plural as well.

[46] A sigma kicks out a dental (§1.3.2). This happens in the dative plural.

[47] If a Greek noun ends in a τ, and no ending (--) is added, the tau (τ) will drop out.

[48] This type of word adds a sigma, resulting in 2 reactions: 1) dental + ς = ς, 2) the sigma slips on the liquid letter ν. This results in 3) the ο prior to the nu (ν) lengthening to omega (ω).

[49] This type of word adds the sigma (ς), with the two typical reactions of a sigma: 1) Dental+sigma = ς, and then palatal+sigma = ξ.

[50] The nu (ν) here is called a moveable/energic nu. It is often added after a word ending with a vowel.

[51] The sigma of the inflection does damage here, expelling the ντ and causing the ο to lengthen to ου.

Table 15: 3rd Declension Endings (neuter)

	singular			plural		
	end of stem	inflection	final form(s)	end of stem	inflection	final form
nominative	[labial] +		--	[labial] +		[π]α
	[palatal] +		--	[palatal] +		[κ]α
	[dental] +	--	--[53]	[dental] +	α	[δ]α
	(ο)ντ +		ων[54]	(ο)ντ +		οντα
	κτ +		κ[55]	κτ +		κτα
genitive	[labial] +		[π]ος	[labial] +		[π]ων
	[palatal] +		[κ]ος	[palatal] +		[κ]ων
	[dental] +	ος	[δ]ος	[dental] +	ων	[δ]ων
	(ο)ντ +		οντος	(ο)ντ +		οντων
	κτ +		κτος	κτ +		κτων
dative	[labial] +		[π]ι	[labial] +		ψι(ν)[56]
	[palatal] +		[κ]ι	[palatal] +		ξι(ν)
	[dental] +	ι	[δ]ι	[dental] +	σι	σι(ν)
	(ο)ντ +		οντι	(ο)ντ +		ουσι(ν)[57]
	κτ +		κτι	κτ +		ξι(ν)
accusative	[labial] +		--	[labial] +		[π]α
	[palatal] +		--	[palatal] +		[κ]α
	[dental] +	--	--[58]	[dental] +	α	[δ]α
	(ο)ντ +		ων[59]	(ο)ντ +		οντα
	κτ +		κ[60]	κτ +		κτα

[52]This nu (ν) inflection occurs only on a few 3rd declension nouns that end in iota (ι) or upsilon (υ).

[53]If a Greek noun ends in a dental, and no ending (--) is added, the dental will drop out, because dental's do not like to sit on the end of a word.

[54]This type of word adds no ending (--). This results in 2 reactions: 1) The tau (τ) does not like to be on the end and drops out and 2) the omicron (ο) prior to the nu (ν) lengthens to omega (ω).

[55]Remember, dentals will drop off the end of a word.

[56]The nu (ν) here is called a moveable/energic nu. It is often added after a word that ends with a vowel.

[57]The sigma of the inflection does damage here, expelling the ντ and causing the ο to lengthen to ου.

[58]If a Greek noun ends in a dental, and no ending (--) is added, the dental will drop out, because dental's do not like to sit on the end of a word.

☞ Watch this video (http://youtu.be/RMqZd-NsUJo) to solidify the previous section.

2.8: Noun Parsing

When we come to any noun in the New Testament, we need to identify four essential elements of the noun: *case, gender, number, and lexical form*. The first three elements come from the inflection, and the lexical form is the nominative singular form of the word. All of these are essential in the translation of the word:

- Case indicates the function of the noun in the sentence.
- Gender is not always crucial in the translation, but will be important when we come to discuss items we will learn in Chapter 6.
- Number tells you whether or not to translate something as singular or plural.
- The lexical form carries the meaning of the word.

2.9: The Least You Need to Know

You should be able to clearly and accurately answer these questions. Use these online flashcards (http://quizlet.com/_7tft3) to memorize the answers:

- What is inflection?
- What does the nominative case signify?
- What does the genitive case signify?
- What does the dative case signify?
- What does the accusative case signify?
- What does the vocative case signify?
- What does noun gender signify?
- What does noun number signify?
- What are noun declensions and what is the parameter for deciding which declension a noun falls into?

---

[59] This type of word adds no ending (--). This results in 2 reactions: 1) The tau (τ) does not like to be on the end and drops out and 2) the omicron (o) prior to the nu (ν) lengthens to omega (ω).

[60] Remember, dentals will drop off the end of a word.

- What genders are *most* 1st declension nouns?
- What genders are *most* 2nd declension nouns?
- Why is the 3rd declension so troublesome?
- What are the four essential elements of noun parsing?
- How do you identify the stem of a noun?

2.10: Greek@Logos

In the remainder of the chapters you are encouraged to learn how to use Logos Bible Software. There are numerous aids by Logos and its community to help you. In the top right corner of your Logos window is a [?] icon that provides a link to the internal help files, which are indexed and searchable. In addition, links are provided to the Logos forums and the Logos user-edited wiki. In each of the Greek@Logos sections a list of Logos features will be listed that users should learn how to use. All aspects of Logos Bible Software are taught in the ***Mastering Logos Bible Software*** course, but if you do not want to purchase the course, I have provided alternative links when available.

Users should take the time this chapter to learn:

- How to put your Greek Bible and English Bible side by side so they scroll together using link sets.
    - See Lecture 9 of ***Mastering Logos Bible Software***
    - Alternative: "The Resource Panel—Advanced" article at logos.com/videos
- How to access Logos' reverse interlinear Bibles
    - See Lecture 11 of ***Mastering Logos Bible Software***
    - Alternative: http://youtu.be/e7Ualk4oB5s
- How to turn on Logos' sympathetic highlighting
    - See Lecture 12 of ***Mastering Logos Bible Software***
    - Alternative: http://youtu.be/4xt7utfZvZo
- How to search for Greek nouns with specific tags (i.e. inflection) searching for nouns
    - See Lecture 34 of ***Mastering Logos Bible Software***
    - Alternative: http://youtu.be/yn0-GUJiPEk

- Alternative: http://youtu.be/2yT2hP4h_Tg
* Get the Greek read to you using the Audio Greek New Testament resource
  - See Lecture 8 of *Mastering Logos Bible Software*

2.11: Vocabulary

Word	Meaning	Type	Freq.	Derivatives
ἀλλά (ἀλλ')	but, yet, except	conj.	638	
ἵνα	in order that, that	conj.	663	
οὖν	therefore, then, accordingly	conj.	499	
ὡς	as, while	conj.	504	
ἀδελφός, -οῦ, ὁ	brother	noun	343	Phil*adelph*ia
ἄνθρωπος, -ου, ὁ	man, person	noun	550	*anthropo*logy
ἡμέρα, -ας, ἡ	day	noun	389	
λόγος, -ου, ὁ	word, matter	noun	330	dia*log*ue
οὐρανός, -οῦ, ὁ	heaven, sky	noun	273	*Uran*us
πατήρ, -τρός, ὁ	father	noun	413	*patr*iarch
πνεῦμα, -ματος, τό	wind, spirit	noun	379	*pneum*atics
υἱός, -οῦ, ὁ	son, descendant; child	noun	377	
εἰ	if	partic.	502	
ἀπό (ἀπ', ἀφ')	[+gen] (away) from	prep.	646	*apo*stle
διά (δι')	(+gen) through (+acc) because of	prep.	667	*dia*meter

2.12: The Second Time Around

It is recommended that students who are passing through this chapter the second time around concentrate on the memorization of the case endings of each declension. Use The Singing Grammarian to assist you with this. This chapter should also be paired with the next chapter, and the bulk of your energy should be devoted to the memorization of the case endings and parsing nouns.

Chapter 3:
Case Functions Stripped Down

⇒**What's the Point**: In the previous chapter you learned about the base definitions of the four Greek cases. The truth is that the Greek cases can do much more than what their base definition implies. This is no different than English, and as you look at Greek cases always evaluate them alongside your preferred English translation. In the following examples, the noun case in question is in bold, and any verbs are underlined.

Before you begin—please remind yourself of a few things:
1. You do NOT need to memorize all of this!
2. When understanding the functions of nouns in the examples below and the NT in the future, ALWAYS evaluate alongside the English translation of your choice.
3. These types of questions are not solely unique to Greek—these types of functions are present in our own language as well. We just rarely take the time to put English under the microscope.

Finally, the truth of the matter is that even the many examples I give you below are still only a sampling. For a full view of all of the functions of Greek cases, see an advanced grammar like Daniel Wallace, *Greek Grammar Beyond the Basics*.[61]

3.1: Nominative

The nominative is the most straightforward of the cases, almost always indicating the subject of the sentence.

3.1.1: Simple Subject

The simple subject is the most basic and frequent function of a nominative noun.
- ἠγάπησεν ὁ **θεός** τὸν κόσμον (John 3:16)
- **God** loved the world....

---

[61] The substance of this chapter is largely indebted to Daniel Wallace's fine work.

3.1.2: Predicate Nominative

The word "predicate" means *a verb and all of its modifiers*. You will learn later about equative verbs, which are types of verbs do not describe an action. Rather, they tell you more about the subject. For example, "Jerry is the teacher." Notice how the subject Jerry is not doing anything, and the verb "is" tells us more about Jerry—the predicate nominative is renaming or telling more about the subject. Because the subject is being renamed, Greek uses another nominative that is called the *predicate nominative*. In the following verse, we have two nominative nouns: one is the subject and the other is the predicate nominative.

- **κύριός** ἐστιν ὁ **υἱὸς** τοῦ ἀνθρώπου καὶ (even) τοῦ σαββάτου (Mk 2:28)
- The **son** of man is **lord** even of the sabbath.

3.1.3: Apposition

Apposition is a common grammatical function of nouns in both Greek and English. A noun in apposition is a noun in parallel with another noun, giving you more information about the noun in parallel.

- παραγίνεται Ἰωάννης ὁ **βαπτιστὴς** κηρύσσων (Matt 3:1)
- John the **baptizer** came preaching...

3.2: Genitive

The genitive is the most versatile of all of the cases. If you recall from the last chapter, the "built-in" word to use for genitive is "of." Consider these sentences:

- The husband *of* Maria.
- Please take care *of* my cat.
- That is the dog *of* my next door neighbor.

All three of these sentences use the word "of" and yet none of the nouns that follow it are doing the same type of things. The first is expressing a relationship, the second is expressing the object, the third is indicating possession. Greek genitive nouns are also versatile. Do not be intimidated by this! In the *Stripped Down* approach, you are looking at Greek right alongside English.

3.2.1: Possessive

Many genitives indicate possession. The noun in the genitive case possesses the noun it is connected to. The word "of," or apostrophe+s is what is most often used to translate the function into English.

- τὸν δοῦλον τοῦ **ἀρχιερέως** (Matt 26:51)
- The slave of the **high priest**

3.2.2: Genitive of Relationship

The genitive is used in Greek to indicate relationship, particularly family relationshipσ. Sometimes translation even warrants adding a word to indicate the relationship.

- Σίμων **Ἰωάννου** (John 21:15)
- Simon, [son] of **John**

3.2.3: Attributive Genitive

An attributive genitive is much like an adjective in that it is describing an attribute of the noun it is connected to. Using "of," or translating the genitive immediately prior to the other noun, is how these types of genitives are often translated.

- ὁ κριτὴς τῆς **ἀδικίας** (Lk 18:6)
- Judge of **unrighteousness** [or unrighteous judge]

3.2.4: Apposition

Apposition is a category introduced under the nominative. The apposition function occurs in all of the cases. Remember that apposition is restating the noun it is connected to, often shedding a little more light.

- σωτῆρος ἡμῶν **Ἰησοῦ Χριστοῦ** (Tit 2:13)
- Our Savior, **Jesus Christ**

3.2.5: Genitive of Comparison

A genitive will often be coupled with a comparative adjective (see §6.2.1.1). The word "than" is the word that often needs to be added to best translate the function.

- ὁ ἄλλος μαθητὴς προέδραμεν τάχιον τοῦ **Πέτρου** (Jn 20:4)
- The other disciple ran more quickly than **Peter**

3.2.6: Subjective Genitive

Sometimes a noun has a verbal idea baked right in, like love. In these cases a genitive that follows one of these nouns-with-a-verbal-idea-baked-in is the subject of that noun's baked-in action. The word "of," or apostrophe+s is what is most often used to translate the function into English.

- τίς ἡμᾶς χωρίσει ἀπὸ τῆς ἀγάπης τοῦ **Χριστοῦ**; (Rom 8:35)
- Who shall separate us from the love **of Christ** (or Who shall separate us from Christ's love for us?)

3.2.7: Objective Genitive

Like the subjective genitive, a noun-with-a-verbal-idea-baked-in may indicate the object of the baked-in verbal idea with a genitive. The word "of," or apostrophe+s is what is most often used to translate the function into English.

- ἡ δὲ **τοῦ πνεύματος** βλασφημία οὐκ ἀφεθήσεται
- But the blasphemy **of the Spirit** shall not be forgiven (or "blasphemy against the Spirit")

3.2.8: Genitive of Time

A genitive noun can be used when talking about time. In these instances a word like "during," "act," or "a" are used to translate the function into English.

- ἦλθεν πρὸς αὐτὸν **νυκτός** (Jn 3:2)
- He came to him during the **night**

3.2.9: Genitive as Direct Object

Certain verbs, in both English and Greek, require a genitive as their object. In particular, they need the word "of."

- ἐπιμελήθητι **αὐτοῦ** (Lk 10:35)
- Take care of **him**

3.2.10: Descriptive

A descriptive genitive gives some general description of the noun it is connected to. This category is a bit of a general category for when a noun doesn't fall into any of the other categories.

- Ἰωάννης . . . κηρύσσων βάπτισμα **μετανοίας** (Mark 1:4)
- John . . . [was] preaching a baptism of **repentance**

3.3: Dative

3.3.1: Indirect Object

A dative noun indicating an indirect object is a common function of the dative case.

- καὶ ἔδωκεν ἄν **σοι** ὕδωρ ζῶν (Jn 4:10)
- And he would have given **to you** living water

3.3.2: Dative of Interest

A dative of interest specifies the noun that is interested in the action of the sentence. The words "to" or "for" are often used when translating this type of dative noun.

- ἥτις ἐστὶν **αὐτοῖς** ἔνδειξις ἀπωλείας (Phil 1:28)
- which is a sign of destruction **to them**

3.3.3: Dative of Reference

A dative of reference noun is providing a frame of reference for the sentence. Often the words "with reference to" could be added before this type of noun. Typically, the words "to," "concerning," or "about" are used when translating this type of function into English.

- λογίζεσθε ἑαυτοὺς εἶναι νεκροὺς μὲν τῇ **ἁμαρτίᾳ** (Rom 6:11)
- Consider yourselves to be dead [with reference] **to sin**

3.3.4: Apposition

Like the other noun cases, the dative can also function in apposition.

- παρέδωκαν Πιλάτῳ τῷ **ἡγεμόνι** (Matt 27:2)
- they handed [him] over to Pilate, the **governor**

3.3.5: Dative of Sphere

The dative of sphere describes location in which the word or action takes place or exists. Typically the word "in" is used to translate this function into English.

- ἐκκλησίαι ἐστερεοῦντο τῇ **πίστει** (Acts 16:5)
- the churches grew **in faith**

3.3.6: Dative of Time

The dative of time indicates the time when the action of the verb in the sentence happens. Typically the words "in" or "on" are used to translate this function into English.

- **τῇ τρίτῃ ἡμέρᾳ** ἐγερθήσεται (Matt 17:23)
- **on the third day** he will be raised

3.3.7: Dative of Association

The dative of association indicates an association between one noun and another. Typically the words "with" is used to translate this function into English.

- οἱ δὲ ἄνδρες οἱ συνοδεύοντες **αὐτῷ** (Acts 9:7)
- the men who were traveling **with him**

3.3.8: Dative of Means (Instrumental)

The dative of means indicates the instrument with which the action in the sentence happens. Typically the words "with," "by," or "by means of" are used to translate this function into English.

- ἐξέβαλεν τὰ πνεύματα **λόγῳ** (Matt 8:16)
- he cast out the spirits **by [means of] a word**

3.3.9: Dative of Cause

The dative of cause indicates the cause or reason for the action in the sentence. Typically the words "because of" are used to translate this function into English.

- ἵνα τῷ **σταυρῷ** τοῦ Χριστοῦ μὴ διώκωνται (Gal 6:12)
- only that they might not be persecuted **because of the cross** of Christ

3.4: Accusative

3.4.1: Direct Object

The most common use of an accusative is to indicate the direct object.
- ἠγάπησεν ὁ θεὸς τὸν **κόσμον** (Jn 3:16)
- God loved the **world**

3.4.2: Double Object

Sometimes a verb requires two objects in order to make sense. often, not always, the word "of" is needed to translate the function into English.
- ἐξέδυσαν αὐτὸν τὴν **χλαμύδα** (Matt 27:31)
- They stripped him of [his] **robe**

3.4.3: Apposition

Like the other cases, the accusative can function in apposition.
- πίστευσον ἐπὶ τὸν κύριον **Ἰησοῦν** (Acts 16:31)
- believe in the Lord **Jesus**

By now you might be feeling information overload, I don't blame you! Remember, once again, that you do not need to memorize all of this but you do need to understand when you see these things in the Greek New Testament. Take the time before going on to the next section to go back up and look at each example. Look at the nouns that are in bold and ask yourself "what is that noun doing?" In many instances without looking at the description you would be able to say on your own already "this noun is the subject," or "this noun is indicating location," or "this noun is indicating relationship." The exercises for this chapter will further challenge you in identifying noun function.

3.5: Nouns in the *DBL Greek* Lexicon

The goal of the *Stripped Down* approach is to help you access the language using the best tools. One of the most important items in your toolkit when working with Greek is a good lexicon. *The Dictionary of Biblical Languages With Semantic Domains* is a lexicon included in the Logos Original Languages package. The *DBLGreek* lexicon is a centralized resource that relies on the *Greek-English Lexicon of the New Testament: Based on Semantic Domains* by Louw & Nida.

You will come to see that all translation is interpretation.[62] Simply take a look at the entry of a few different words in your lexicon and you will see that there can sometimes be numerous translation options for a single word.[63] This is why it is important to not only learn the main gloss while learning vocabulary, but also to be able to access a lexicon when looking closer at New Testament passages. Words have a range of meaning, so the proper translation of a word is only yielded when the meaning of the word in **that specific** context in understood.

3.5.1: A Word on Semantic Domains

Since the *DBLGreek* lexicon relies on the Louw & Nida semantic domains lexicon, it is important to have some understanding of semantic domains. In brief, semantic domains refer to the relationships that exist between words and how they are used. Therefore, the meaning of words in general as well as their meaning in a specific context is derived from their connections to other words. It is the selection and combination of different words due to their relationships to one another that reflects the lexical structure of a language and semantic domains provide a map of these relations. For example, the words strong and powerful may be used to describe a person. "He is strong" or "She is powerful." In contrast, though we may refer to our morning coffee as being too "strong," we would never describe it as too "powerful."

The usage of "strong" and "powerful" illustrates that the selection and combination of words (or the relationship between words) is affected at two levels: the horizontal relationship between words, i.e. *how words are combined in a running sequence*; and the vertical relations between words, i.e. *how words are chosen in a particular context in contrast to other words*. Thus, in many instances "strong" and "powerful" can be interchanged because their range of meaning overlaps, but not in all. The importance of the relationship between words for determining meaning is illustrated when we sit down to

---

[62] That's why not every English translation is the same and why it is important for you to be able to work with the primary language of the New Testament.

[63] These options for translating a word are often called glosses.

write. How often do we stop (or pause, reflect, reconsider?) and insert a more appropriate (or concise, specific, meaningful?) word in a particular context?

So the choice of what word we use at any particular time is influnced by a number of factors. In the first place it is influenced by the overall discussion or piece that we are writing. What is the topic of discussion? We use different terms when discussing the study of Greek than we do about sports or politics. Then there is the specific topic at a specific time. For example, how many times have you been instructed by a teacher not to use the same word too many times or to find another way to say the same thing? Sometimes we choose words *simply for the sake of variety (or because we want to explain it in a different way)*. In other cases we choose words because it sounds better to say it this way or because we would not say it a certain way. Think of the times that you hear someone who is not a native speaker of English (or whatever your native language is) who uses a word or an expression in an odd way. We know what they mean but we would never say it that way! Our choices are also infuenced by our culture, education, and vocabulary. All of these factors and more have come together and exerted an influence on the exact choice of words you are reading right now. I could have explained the same concept using different words, grammar, and sentences!

Understanding semantic domains helps us appreciate the complex relationships that exist between words and the relevance of the use of a word in a particular context in contrast to other words. Louw & Nida use 93 semantic domains in total to classify the whole range of vocabulary in the New Testament! Thus, each domain is a broad category with a number of sub-categories that ultimately may include hundreds of words that are employed within that domain. A word may have only one range of meaning and so only be in a single domain, but many words have multiple usages, and so fit into several semantic domains.

Let's take κύριος as an example. Several words can be used to translate κύριος because it fits into several semantic domains. Two of the common translation options are 1) "Lord" and 2) "owner." κύριος is translated as "Lord" when referring to God and in some cases Jesus, so it is in Louw & Nida's semantic domain 12, "Supernatural Beings and Powers" (there are 49 other Greek words that also fall into that domain). But when κύριος is best translated as "owner," κύριος falls into semantic domain 57, "Possess, Transfer, Exchange" (there are 248 other words that also fall into that domain). It is important to reiterate one more time that it is the context of a passage that determines the best way to translate a word. Semantic domains help us to understand why one word may have been chosen rather than another. In some cases they help us to understand that there is nothing important at all!

3.5.2: An Analysis of a DBLGreek Noun Entry

The following sections will detail the sections of a word entry. All *DBLGreek* entries include a transliteration in italics and parentheses.

3.5.2.1: Lexical Form, Stem, Gender, and Part of Speech

Beyond giving you the various glosses for a word, some of the first information a lexicon relates to a reader is the stem of a word and its gender. Remember, a noun's stem determines what declension endings a word uses. The biggest reason readers need a lexicon to help them with identifying a stem is because of 3rd declension nouns (those pesky consonant interactions!) because the lexical form (nominative singular) of a 3rd declension noun does not show the stem the way 1st and 2nd declension nominative singular nouns do. A lexicon identifies the stem by showing you the genitive singular ending directly after the word is introduced (see examples below).

In Chapter 6 you will learn more about the Greek article (the word "the"), which was in chapter one's vocabulary. The masculine singular form of "the" is ὁ; the feminine singular form is ἡ; and the neuter singular form is τό. In a lexicon, after a noun and its genitive ending, an article will occur to indicate the gender of the noun. DBLGreek does this but it also provides an explicit identification. The entry below is identified as a n(oun).masc(uline).

3.5.2.2: Links to Hebrew Equivalents, Strong's, and TDNT

When available, *DBLGreek* will link to Hebrew equivalents in the *DBLHebrew* or *DBLAramaic* lexicon. Following this is the Strong's number for the word.[64] The very beginning of every entry is also a number, the Goodrick-Kohlenberger number. These two numbering systems were created for the vocabulary of the Greek New Testament, particularly for the days of research using printed books.

A link to the *Theological Dictionary of the New Testament* entry is also provided. Think of a theological dictionary as a commentary on the lexicon. It looks at the theologi-

---

[64] Although the Strong's number is linked, it will also take you to *TDNT* unless you own the Strong's lexicon in your Logos library.

cal significance and usage of the word prior to and within the NT. *TDNT* is an important resource with invaluable information, but it must be used with caution. At the time it was written many of the contributors were not as sensitive to the importance of the relationships between words (semantic domains) and put too much emphasis on the usage of words in other contexts to explain the meaning in another context.

3.5.2.3: Louw & Nida Number

The entry in *DBLGreek* will list with numbers all of the relevant meanings of a word (the example below contains 9). Each of the numbered sections begins with the Louw & Nida (LN) number and link. This is the most valuable aspect of the *DBLGreek* lexicon—not only does it provide a tidy one paragraph overview of a word, it also provides direct links to the Louw & Nida lexicon. If you are not using *DBLGreek* to immediately access Louw & Nida, you are not using the lexicon correctly. The actual lexicon entries and discussion is in Louw & Nida, not *DBLGreek*.

3.5.2.4: Gloss

A gloss is the most often used English word to translate a Greek word in that particular semantic domain. A gloss will usually be in bold, unless the gloss is an idiom.

3.5.2.5: Brief Explanation, Greek Example, and Scripture Example

If any brief explanation on the gloss or notes is warranted, it will follow the gloss. This may be followed by a brief Greek example (with transliteration), and every numbered section will include at least one verse as an example. If the scripture example has a + sign, this indicates that the scripture example is the only verse in which the word is used in that manner.

3.5.3: DBLGreek Noun Example

Lexical form (nom. sing.), genitive ending, gender	Links to Hebrew equivalents, Strong's, and TDNT[65]	Louw & Nida number and link	Gloss	Brief explanation if necessary	Greek example	Scripture example (+ indicates only occurrence)

476 ἄνθρωπος (*anthrōpos*), ου (*ou*), ὁ (*ho*): n.masc.; ≡ DBLHebr 132, 408, 632; Str 444; TDNT 1.364—**1.** LN 9.1 **human being** (Jn 10:33); **2.** LN 9.24 **man**, *a male human* (Mt 10:35); **3.** LN 10.53 **husband** (Mt 19:3, 10); **4.** LN 9.3 υἱὸς τοῦ ἀνθρώπου (*huios tou anthrōpou*), **Son of Man** (Mt 8:20); **5.** LN 9.2 υἱοὶ τῶν ἀνθρώπων (*huioi tōn anthrōpōn*), **people**, *those of the class of humanity* (Eph 3:5+); **6.** LN 41.43 παλαιὸς ἄνθρωπος (*palaios anthrōpos*), **former behavior** (Ro 6:6; Eph 4:22; Col 3:9+), *note: others would see more than behavior in this idiom, but also ontological implications, see next entries*; **7.** LN 8.3 ὁ ἔξω ἄνθρωπος (*ho exō anthrōpos*), **body, physical form** (2Co 4:16+); **8.** LN 26.1 ὁ ἔσω ἄνθρωπος (*ho esō anthrōpos*), **inner being** (Ro 7:22; Eph 3:16+); **9.** LN 26.1 ὁ ἐν τῷ κρυπτῷ ἄνθρωπος (*ho en tō kryptō anthrōpos*), **inner being** (1Pe 3:4+)

This noun example is typical of most *DBLGreek* entries. When necessary, future chapters will indicate any items of note for understanding different types of words in the lexicon.

3.5.4: Reading a Louw & Nida Entry

As mentioned previously, it is absolutely necessary to move to Louw & Nida in order to gain a better understanding of the different semantic meanings of a word. *Louw & Nida is where the actual definition of the word occurs*. In the example of ἄνθρωπος above, clicking on entry 1 (LN 9.1) will open Louw & Nida to the word in that particular

---

[65]*Theological Dictionary of the New Testament* (edited by Gerhard Kittel, Geoffrey W. Bromiley, and Gerhard Friedrich; Grand Rapids, MI: Eerdmans, 1964).

semantic domain. The menu bar tells you that you are in semantic domain 9, "People," and from there you can explore related terms in that domain.

3.5.5: Determining The Semantic Domain For A Word Instance

The word entries in *DBLGreek* and Louw & Nida provide the definitions of a word based on its semantic domains. However, neither of these lexicons provides an exhaustive list for every time a word occurs, nor does it tell you which semantic domain is preferable. Luckily, Logos has done the hard work for you by providing direct links to the semantic domain for a word instance. For example, open your Greek NT to Matt 8:9, which has the word ἄνθρωπος. If you right-click the word in Logos, a Louw & Nida number is provided. This number is also provided in the reverse interlinear bibles.

Keep in mind that lexicographers are not infallible, so you may disagree with the choice made for the se- mantic domain. However, in general we can trust the work of scholars who have made these determinations for users.

3.6: The Least You Need to Know

You should be able to clearly and accurately answer these questions. Use these online flashcards (http://quizlet.com/_7tfw1) to memorize the answers:

- What does "predicate" mean?
- What is a predicate nominative?
- What is apposition? Which cases can indicate apposition?
- What is a genitive of relationship?
- What is an attributive genitive? Make up an English sentence example.
- What is a genitive of comparison? Make up an English sentence example.
- What is a subjective genitive? Make up an English sentence example.
- What is an objective genitive? Make up an English sentence example.
- What is a dative of interest? Make up an English sentence example.
- What is a dative of reference? Make up an English sentence example.
- What is a dative of association? Make up an English sentence example.
- What is a dative of means? Make up an English sentence example.
- What is a dative of cause? Make up an English sentence example.

- How does a lexicon show you the root of the noun?
- What indicates the gender of a noun in a lexicon?

3.7: Greek@Logos

Utilizing the ***Mastering Logos Bible Software*** course or the Logos help files, Logos forums, Logos wiki, and videos provided, users should take the time to learn:

- How to build a filter to highlight nouns in the Greek New Testament
    - See Lecture 39 of ***Mastering Logos Bible Software***
    - Alternative: http://youtu.be/7COLQXP7S8E
- How to access various ways you can learn more about a single word, particularly in using the right-click menu.
    - See Lecture 12 & 14 of ***Mastering Logos Bible Software***
    - Alternative: See the "Using the Context Menu" article at logos.com/videos
- How to do a Bible Word Study on a Greek noun.
    - See Lecture 17 of ***Mastering Logos Bible Software***
    - Alternative: http://youtu.be/B40vPTRVJXY

3.8: Vocabulary

In the above section on nouns in a lexicon (§3.5), you learned about how a lexicon shows you the stem of words, as well as their gender. These additional details are provided in your vocabulary lists from now on (these were grey font portions from chapter 1 & 2 vocabulary as well).

Word	Gloss	Type	Freq.	Derivatives
οὕτως	thus, so, in this manner	adv.	208	
ἐάν	if (ever), when (ever), although (+subj.)	conj.	351	
τέ	and (so), so [consec: both...and]	conj.	215	

ἀνήρ, ἀνδρός, ὁ	man, husband	noun	216	*andr*oid
γῆ, -ῆς, ἡ	land, earth	noun	250	*geo*graphy
γυνή, -αικός, ἡ	woman, wife	noun	215	*gyne*cology
μαθητής, -οῦ, ὁ	disciple, student	noun	261	*math*
νόμος, -ου, ὁ	law	noun	194	Deutero*nom*y
ὄνομα, -ματος, τό	name, reputation	noun	231	pseud*onym*
πίστις -εως, ἡ	faith, belief, trust	noun	243	
ἤ	or, than; (ἤ... ἤ either...or)	partic.	343	
κατά (κατ', καθ')	(+gen) down from, against (+acc) according to, throughout, during	prep.	473	*cata*clysm
μετά (μετ', μεθ')	(+gen) with (+acc) after	prep.	469	*meta*phor
περί	(+gen) about, concerning (+acc) around	prep.	333	*peri*meter

3.9: The Second Time Around

Please read the *Second Time Around* from the previous chapter, as these two chapters should be read and worked through together the second time around.

Chapter 4:
Greek Indicative Verbs Stripped Down

⇒**What's the Point**: 20% of the words in the New Testament are verbs (28,110 in total), and half of these are in what is called the Indicative mood (you'll understand what this means soon enough!). Greek verbs are also very nuanced, robust, and flexible; they are inflected like nouns. Having a thorough knowledge of Greek verbs is essential to understanding the Greek New Testament, because they are literally where all of the action is!

4.1: Verb Basics

4.1.1: Types of Verbs

Greek (and English) has three main types of verbs. It is not especially important that you always recognize what type every verb is, but one of them is more difficult to understand when working in a Greek sentence.

1. *Transitive*: A transitive verb is the standard way we think of verbs, transferring action from subject to object. "The dog *bites* the boy" is a transitive verb because action is being transferred from subject to object. Notice also that we can make the verb passive: "The boy *was bitten by* the dog."

2. *Intransitive:* An intransitive verb is not indicating transfer of action, it is only indicating the action of the subject. "The boy *went* to bed" is an intransitive verb because action is not being transferred to an object but is telling you about an action the subject is performing—the object is where the subject is going. Notice that we cannot neatly make the verb passive: "The bed *was being gone to by* the boy" is bad English! Intransitive verbs also do not need an object. Compare "the dog bites" and "I left." The first statement expects an object—it is hard to discuss a dog biting without talking about what it is biting! With the second example, the statement does not need anything else.

3. *Equative*:[66] An equative verb does not indicate action at all. "Danny *is* the author" is not transferring action nor is it describing an action the subject is performing. At the same time, we could also say, 'The author is Danny," so in these types of sentences, both "Danny" and "the author" are in the *nominative case*.[67] In the sentence, "Danny *is* the author", "the author" is referred to as the *predicate nominative* (§3.1.2). Equative verbs can be very tricky, so it important to understand the different ways they can be used. For example, it is very different to say, "God *is* love" than it is to say, "Love *is* God." There are four different ways that equative verbs can be used: Indentification, "She is the teacher;" Membership in a class, "She is a teacher; State-"He is old;" and Existential, "There is a teacher."

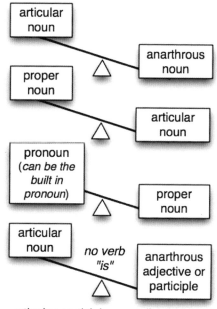

articular participle= usually object
anarthrous participle= object

Finally, because an equative verb has a nominative as subject AND a nominative as object, there are rules for determining which one gets to be the subject and which one gets to be the object. Again, it is not essential that you memorize this, just that you recognize that there are rules which govern the decisions made by translators (some items in the image you will not understand until later in the book).

4.1.2: **The Efficiency of Greek Verbs**

Greek verbs pack quite a punch in that they contain a lot of information in a single word. Not only does a Greek verb tell you about the actual action (*bite, run, know*, etc.),

---

[66] An Equative verb is also often called a "copulative verb."

[67] There are numerous equative verbs used in the New Testament. These will be pointed out in your vocabulary lists and do need to be recognized in Greek, because the sentence will NOT have an accusative noun as the object. There will, rather, be two nominative nouns in the sentence. One is the subject and the other is the object. This special object of an equative verb is called a *predicate nominative*.

but a Greek verb can also have the subject built in, as well as the type of action and sometimes even when it happened. Consider the following English sentences:

- I will follow.
    - "I" is the subject.
    - "will" puts the action into the future.
    - This sentence would translate a single Greek verb, ἀκολουθήσω. The verb means "follow" and is inflected to be future (the "will" part) and first person (the "I" part).
- I have been found.
    - "I" is the subject.
    - "have" places the action into the past.
    - "been" makes the subject passive, meaning the action is happening to the subject, rather than the subject doing the action.
    - This sentence would translate a single Greek verb, εὑρέθην. The verb means "find" and is inflected to be in the past (the "have" part), first person (the "I" part), and passive (the "been" part).

4.1.3: Greek Aspect[68]

Greek tenses[69] are improperly named because the main point of Greek's six[70] tenses is NOT primarily to tell you about when the action occurs (past, present, or future). Just remember, when you hear the word tense when in reference to Greek, time is not the major issue. The aspect, or viewpoint, of the verb is the more important issue. Aspect relays how the author viewed the action of the verb.

- INTERNAL ASPECT: Internal aspect[71] views the action up close. It is more descriptive of the action of the verb. Think of it as a camera zooming in on the action showing you *unfolding action that is in process.* Using a popular parade

---

[68]Scholars of New Testament Greek are divided on their understanding of Greek verbs. The issue basically boils down to whether verbs indicate time (past, present, future) or not. I have chosen to stay in sync with Daniel Wallace's *Greek Grammar Beyond the Basics*.

[69]Some grammarians prefer to use the term "tense-form" in attempts to avoid the issue of time that is so closely related to the word tense.

[70]The New Testament actually has a seventh tense, but this final tense occurs a whopping one time in Heb 8:11.

[71]Other grammarians call this *Imperfective aspect.*

analogy, internal aspect is like standing on the side of the street while a parade goes by. Your focus is not on the whole parade, but rather on one particular part of the parade unfolding before you. If someone were to ask you what you are looking at, you probably would not say you are looking at the parade, but that you are looking at the jugglers passing in front of you at that point.

- EXTERNAL ASPECT: External aspect[72] views the action like a snapshot, as *a whole and completed event* without regard for the details. Think of it as a camera zooming out on the action to show the whole thing. Using the parade analogy, you are lucky enough to be living on the 30th floor of an apartment that the parade is going by. As you sit on your balcony, you see the parade in its entirety from beginning to end, but you are so high up that the details are a little fuzzy.
- STATIVE ASPECT: Stative aspect views the action as *done and in a completed state*. This aspect combines both internal and external aspects in that the action is viewed as complete, but its result is viewed internally as having a continuing effect. Using the parade analogy, you are one of the unlucky crew members cleaning up after the parade (which had horses and elephants). You know the parade is complete but it had plenty of consequences affecting you now!

4.2: Components of a Greek Verb

Greek (and English) verbs have six main components, one of which is the lexical form. A verb's stem will take affixes[73] and endings (tags) to indicate tense, voice, person, and number.

In Chapter 2 the components that made up noun parsing were introduced (case, gender, number, lexical form). For Greek verbs, the components are: tense, voice, mood, person, number, lexical form.[74] Each of these will be talked about in order.

---

[72]Other grammarians call this *Perfective aspect*.
[73]Affixes are parts added to the beginning or end of a word—prefixes and suffixes.
[74]**T**V **M**akes **P**eople **N**auseous is a way I learned to remember the order of Greek parsing.

4.2.1: Tense

4.2.1.1: Present Tense
- *Aspect*: The present tense describes internal aspect.
- *Time*: Remember that time is not the primary part of Greek tenses, and some grammarians would argue that time is not a factor in a Greek tense at all. The present tense will tend to be in the present time, but is not confined to it.
- *Translation*: The translation of Greek tenses is tricky business because Greek tenses can convey so many different things and are not confined to past, present, or future. When the present tense is translated, translators will often use an "ing" on the verb to indicate the internal aspect (i.e. he is kick*ing*). However, this is not always an exact science and the translation depends the most on the context in which it occurs.[75]

4.2.1.2: Imperfect Tense
- *Aspect*: Like the present tense, the imperfect tense describes internal aspect.
- *Time*: The imperfect tense is most often used in a past time context, especially in narrative sequences to "zoom" in on a particular detail.
- *Translation*: The imperfect tense most often occurs in a narrative context, which is often past time, and also conveys the internal aspect, so a basic translation will often use the past form of the copulative (i.e. was, were) and an "ing" on the verb (i.e. he *was* kick*ing*). Again, translation depends the most on the context in which the word occurs.

4.2.1.3: Future Tense
- *Aspect*: The future tense describes external aspect.
- *Time*: As the name implies, the future tense describes a future action. The future tense in Greek is the truest tense by name in terms of time.

---

[75] As you begin to work with Greek verbs and English translations, you will see how hard translation can be. It is often very difficult to convey Greek verbs into English without making a very unreadable translation. This is why learning the primary languages is so important.

- *Translation*: The future tense in Greek is translated the same as the future tense in English would, using the word "will" (i.e. he *will* kick).

4.2.1.4: Aorist Tense
- *Aspect*: The aorist tense describes external aspect.
- *Time*: Although time is not the main issue in Greek verbs, the aorist tends to be used mostly in past time, especially in narrative contexts.
- *Translation*: The aorist is the most used tense in the indicative mood and is the default verb tense in narrative. Although aorist is most often used in a past time context, past time is not the main thing that is conveyed in the aorist tense form. In translation the aorist tense is usually translated with a past time English form using "–ed," or sometimes by using the simple form of the verb (i.e. he kick*ed* or I kick).

4.2.1.5: Perfect Tense
- *Aspect*: The perfect tense portrays stative aspect.
- *Time*: Like the other tenses, the perfect tense is not very concerned about time but in general stays in the present tense.
- *Translation*: When used in a time-specific context, the perfect tense describes a completed action with ongoing results (i.e. he *has* kicked). When used to describe a state of affairs (stative) the perfect can be translated in different ways depending on context: I am (in a state of) hopefulness, I am hoping, I hope.

4.2.1.6: Pluperfect Tense
- *Aspect*: Like the perfect tense, the pluperfect tense portrays stative aspect.
- *Time*: The pluperfect tense works in much the same way as the perfect, but tends to be confined to narrative and most often in past time.
- *Translation*: When in a time-specific context the pluperfect refers to a completed action that has ongoing results in the past, but those results have also ceased (i.e. he *had* kicked). When used to describe a state of affairs (stative) the pluperfect can be translated much like the perfect.

4.2.2: Voice

In English, voice describes whether the subject is doing the action or having the action done to them. If the subject is doing the action, it is active voice. If the subject is having the action done to them, it is passive voice. Greek adds one more voice called middle. The middle voice is right in between active and passive—the subject does the action with self-interest. Middle voice is often hard to communicate and English translations of the middle voice often end up sounding active.

1. ACTIVE: The subject performs the action.
   - "The dog *bit* the child."
2. MIDDLE: The subject performs the action upon themselves or out of self-interest.
   - "The dog *bit* the child." (the self interest of the Greek voice is usually left untranslated)
3. PASSIVE: The subject is having the action being done to them.
   - "The child *was bitten by* the dog."

Every Greek tense can be combined with the active, middle, or passive voice. Of the six tenses, four of them (present, imperfect, perfect, pluperfect) have identical middle and passive forms. In these four tenses, context will decide whether to translate it as middle or passive.

4.2.3: Mood

The mood of a verb describes the action's relation to reality, or presentation of certainty. The action may be real or the action may just possibly happen depending on circumstances. English shares the first three moods with Greek, with one additional mood in Greek as well. Only the first mood, the indicative, will be covered in this chapter, with the final three moods being covered in Chapter 10. The indicative mood is the presentation of certainty. Verbs in the indicative mood are being asserted as having happened, in the process of happening, or will happen.

4.2.4: Person

The person of a verb tells us about the subject.

1. FIRST PERSON: "I" or "we" is a first person subject. "I" is singular, "we" is plural.
2. SECOND PERSON: "you" or "y'all"[76] is a second person subject. "You" is singular, "y'all" is plural.
3. THIRD PERSON: "he, she, it" or "they" are third person subjects. "He, she, it" are singular, "they" is plural. Notice that "they" can be used for the plural of "he" to mean a bunch of men, or the plural of "she" to indicate a bunch of women, etc.

4.2.5: Number

The number of a verb is similar to a noun in that it makes it singular or plural. The difference is that a plural verb is telling you that the subject (the actor) is plural. "I kick" is singular, "we kick" is plural. "You kick" is singular, "y'all kick" is plural. "He/she/it kicks" is singular, "they kick" is plural.

4.3: How Greek Indicative Verbs are Formed

4.3.1: The Indicative Slot Machine

An easy(-ish) way to learn about the indicative mood is with the indicative slot machine. There are six slots that can be filled in the construction of a Greek verb (not every slot will always be filled). Certain combinations in the slot machine will result in different tense & verb combination. This slot-type patterning is most recognizable with *strong verbs*. Strong verbs, in Greek and English, are verbs whose spelling stays consistent and/or follows recognizable patterns. For instance, "kick" is a strong verb because k-i-c-k always stays in the verb ("kick," "kicking," "was kicked," "will kick"). The verb "go" is a *weak verb*—its past tense is "went," which bears no resemblance to "go" whatsoever. English speakers have simply learned that "went" is the past tense of "go."

---

[76]Only certain parts of the world use "y'all" as the second person plural form of you. Most use "you" as singular and plural. I find it better to use "y'all" for learning Greek.

Table 16: Indicative Slot Machine

1	2	3	4	5	6
augment	reduplication	stem	suffix	connecting vowel	inflection

These attributes form the stem of each principal part[77]

Each slot of the slot machine will be discussed in turn. Before discussing these, though, examine closely the following table while reading about the different slots. You can see from the table that combinations of different slots create the different tense & voice combinations. Slot 6 (inflection tags) determines the person and number of a verb.

Table 17: Indicative Formation

Principal part	tense & voice		augment	redupl.	stem	suffix	connecting vowel	inflection
1st	present	active			λυ		ο/ε	primary active
		m/p			λυ		ο/ε	primary mid/pas
	imperfect	active	ε		λυ		ο/ε	secondary active
		m/p	ε		λυ		ο/ε	secondary mid/pas
2nd	future	active			λυ	σ	ο/ε	primary active
		middle			λυ	σ	ο/ε	primary mid/pas
3rd	aorist	active	ε		λυ	σα		secondary active
		middle	ε		λυ	σα		secondary mid/pas
4th	perfect	active		λε	λυ	κα		secondary active
	pluperf.	active	ε	λε	λυ	κει		secondary active
5th	perfect	m/p		λε	λυ			primary mid/pas
	pluperf.	m/p	ε	λε	λυ			secondary mid/pas
6th	aorist	passive	ε		λυ	θη		secondary active
	future	passive			λυ	θησ	ο/ε	primary mid/pas

Composes the principal part

---

[77]There is not always an augment and the vowel in the suffix slot is not always part of the principal part. Principal parts will be discussed in §5.1.

4.3.1.1: Slot 1: Augment

An augment is an epsilon added to the beginning of a verb. If the verb stem begins with a vowel, then the augment and the first vowel will contract together and result in a long vowel or diphthong. Aorist, Imperfect, and Pluperfect are the tenses that have an augment. Focus on the orange affixes below:

- Word with no augment: λύω[78]
- Word with augment: ἔλυον
- Word beginning with vowel (ἀκούω) with an augment: ἤκουον[79]

4.3.1.2: Slot 2: Reduplication

Reduplication take the first consonant of a word and reduplicates it with an epsilon. If the verb stem begins with: 1) a vowel, 2) a sibilant, or 3) two or three consonants in a row; it will use an augment instead of reduplicating, and the augment may or may not cause lengthening. If the word begins with a rho (ρ) it will still reduplicate it, but slightly differently. If the word begins with a stop consonant (see §1.3) the consonant will reduplicate with the smooth stop consonant. Perfect and Pluperfect are the tenses that have reduplication. Focus on the purple affixes below:

- Word with no reduplication: λύω
- Word with reduplication: λέλυκας, πεφιλήκατε, ἐρρυήκατε
- Word beginning with a vowel, sibilant, or consonant group:[80] ἠγαπήκαμεν, ἐξήρανται, ἐσταύρωται

4.3.1.3: Slot 3: Verb Stems

The stem of the verb is the basic part of a verb. The stem does not change with strong verbs, or only changes in a very minor way. The strong verb that Greek students continually work with is λύω, "I loose." λύω is a strong verb because no matter what affixes are added to the word, the -λυ- part never changes. In reality, there are also so-called "weak pattern" verbs. There are in fact 6 potential ways a verb stem may be spelled, called principal parts, which will be discussed in Chapter 5.

---

[78] In this example, the connecting vowel has been absorbed into the inflected ending.
[79] Remember from §1.2.1 that vowels contract when next to one another.
[80] Although these look like the augment, it is reduplication.

4.3.1.4: Slot 4: Tense Suffixes

A tense suffix follows the verb stem for some tenses. The following are the different tense suffixes, along with some changes that may occur:

1. σ future active and future middle verbs take a sigma (σ) suffix.
   - If you recall from Chapter 1, the sigma is sinister;
   - If the stem ends with a liquid verb, the sigma slips away entirely. These are called *liquid verbs*. (recall §1.3.1)
   - If the stem ends with a stop consonant a change will occur (recall §1.3.2).

2. σα aorist active and aorist middle verbs take a sigma-alpha (σα) suffix.
   - Like the σ future suffix, the same changes (sigma disappearing and sigma+stop interactions) will occur with the sigma in the σα suffix.
   - In the 3rd person singular form, the σα suffix is σε.

3. κα perfect active verbs take a kappa-alpha (κα) suffix.
   - The kappa at the beginning of the suffix may cause changes to the final letter of the stem (Table 4: Stop Interactions). This includes dentals on the end of the stem becoming a sigma.
   - Some verbs like a buffer vowel between the stem and the κα-suffix and will first add an η or ω, particularly liquid consonants.
   - In the 3rd person singular form, the κα suffix is κε.
   - Some verb stems just don't like that kappa at all and will take just an alpha as the suffix.

4. κει pluperfect active verbs take kappa-epsilon-iota (κει) suffix.
   - The same changes that occur because of the kappa (κ) in the above suffix also occur here.

5. θη aorist passive verbs take a theta-eta (θη) suffix.
   - Like sigma (σ) and kappa (κ), theta causes changes when it follows a stop. (Table 4: Stop Interactions)
   - Like the kappa in the above two suffixes, it may take a buffer vowel.

6. θησ future passive verbs take a theta-eta-sigma (θησ) suffix.
   - All of the same θ interactions detailed in the previous suffix occur here.

4.3.1.5: Slot 5: Connecting Vowel

The connecting vowel (often called a thematic vowel) is simply an omicron (o) or epsilon (ε) that occurs in all present, imperfect, and future tense & voice combinations. These are the tense & voice combinations that are built off of the first and second principal parts. The only real difficulty the connecting vowel can cause is in the present and imperfect tense. Remember that when vowels are next to one another, they often contract into a long vowel or diphthong (§1.2.1). Contract verbs (see below) have stems that ends with a vowel, so the connecting vowel will contract with the end of the stem.

4.3.1.6: Slot 6: Primary and Secondary Endings

Different tense and voice combinations have either primary or secondary endings. There are both active voice endings and middle/passive voice endings. Therefore, the inflected endings in combination with a tense suffix will make it active or middle/passive. The inflected endings indicate the subject of the verb.

Table 18: Primary and Secondary Endings

	Primary				Secondary	
	Active			Middle/Passive	Active	Middle/Passive
	connecting vowel+inflection=		*ending*[81]	*μι verbs*[82]		
1 sg	o	+	--[83] = ω	μι	μαι	ν, (--)	μην
2 sg	ε	+	ες[84] = εις	ς	σαι (η)	ς	ου, σο
3 sg	ε	+	ε[85] = ει	σι	ται	-- (εν)[86]	το
1 pl	o	+	μεν = ομεν	μεν	μεθα	μεν	μεθα
2 pl	ε	+	τε = ετε	τε	σθε	τε	σθε
3 pl	o	+	οσι(ν)[87] = ουσι(ν)	ασι	νται	ν, σαν, σι(ν)	ντο

---

[81] Because the connecting vowel and the primary active endings end up merging, it is broken down.
[82] You will learn about verbs that use these endings in §5.2.5.
[83] No ending is added, so the connecting vowel is lengthened to an omega (ω).
[84] Vowel contraction occurs here to create the ει diphthong in the final form.
[85] Vowel contraction occurs here to create the ει diphthong in the final form.
[86] No ending is added here, so a nu (ν) is often added to the end (moveable nu).
[87] Vowel contraction occurs here to create the ου diphthong in the final form.

☞ Watch this video (http://youtu.be/6YSCYML0Z0k) to solidify the previous section:

4.4: Strong Verb Example

All of the information in §4.3 above is best understood by looking now at an example. The following table displays the entire indicative paradigm of the strong verb λύω. *Stop and dwell on the following table for a long time.* Compare it to the information given to you above. Take the time to understand how every single form was built. In this *Stripped Down* approach, you don't need to memorize and replicate this, just understand the formation of the verbs.

Table 19: λύω Indicative Paradigm

Parts	1st λύω				2nd λύσω	
tense & voice	*present active*	*present m/p*	*imperfect active*	*imperfect m/p*	*future active*	*future middle*
1 sg	λύω	λύομαι	ἔλυον	ἐλυόμην	λύσω	λύσομαι
2 sg	λύεις	λύῃ	ἔλυες	ἐλύου	λύσεις	λύσῃ
3 sg	λύει	λύεται	ἔλυε(ν)	ἐλύετο	λύσει	λύσεται
1 pl	λύομεν	λυόμεθα	ἐλύομεν	ἐλυόμεθα	λύσομεν	λυσόμεθα
2 pl	λύετε	λύεσθε	ἐλύετε	ἐλύεσθε	λύσετε	λύσεσθε
3 pl	λύουσι(ν)	λύονται	ἔλυον	ἐλύοντο	λύσουσι(ν)	λύσονται

Parts	3rd ἔλυσα		4th λέλυκα	5th λέλυμαι	6th ἐλύθην	
tense & voice	aorist active	aorist middle	perfect active	perfect m/p	aorist passive	future passive
1 sg	ἔλυσα	ἐλυσάμην	λέλυκα	λέλυμαι	ἐλύθην	λυθήσομαι
2 sg	ἔλυσας	ἐλύσω	λέλυκας	λέλυσαι	ἐλύθης	λυθήσῃ
3 sg	ἔλυσε(ν)	ἐλύσατο	λέλυκε(ν)	λέλυται	ἐλύθη	λυθήσεται
1 pl	ἐλύσαμεν	ἐλυσάμεθα	λελύκαμεν	λελύμεθα	ἐλύθημεν	λυθησόμεθα
2 pl	ἐλύσατε	ἐλύσασθε	λελύκατε	λέλυσθε	ἐλύθητε	λυθήσεσθε
3 pl	ἔλυσαν	ἐλύσαντο	λελύκασι(ν)	λέλυνται	ἐλύθησαν	λυθήσονται

4.4.1: Verb Translation

As you work with your bible software of choice take time to see how each verb is translated in your English translation. Use the following table as a guideline in your understanding of the translation of verbs.

Table 20: Indicative Verb Translation

	Present Tense					
	active		middle		passive	
1 sg	λύω	I am loosing / I loose	λύομαι	I loose (for myself)	λύομαι	I am (being) loosed
2 sg	λύεις	you are loosing / you loose	λύῃ	you loose (for yourself)	λύῃ	you are (being) loosed
3 sg	λύει	(s)he/it is loosing / (s)he/it looses	λύεται	(s)he/it looses (for himself)	λύεται	(s)he/it is (being) loosed
1 pl	λύομεν	we are loosing / we loose	λυόμεθα	we loose (for ourselves)	λυόμεθα	we are (being) loosed
2 pl	λύετε	y'all are loosing / y'all loose	λύεσθε	y'all loose (for yourselves)	λύεσθε	y'all are (being) loosed
3 pl	λύουσι(ν)	they are loosing / they loose	λύονται	they loose (for themselves)	λύονται	they are (being) loosed

	Imperfect Tense					
	active		middle		passive	
1 sg	ἔλυον	I was loosing / I loose	ἐλυόμην	I was loosing (for myself)	ἐλυόμην	I was (being) loosed
2 sg	ἔλυες	you were loosing / you loose	ἐλύου	you were loosing (for yourself)	ἐλύου	you were (being) loosed
3 sg	ἔλυε(ν)	(s)he/it was loosing / (s)he/it looses	ἐλύετο	(s)he/it was loosing (for himself)	ἐλύετο	(s)he/it was (being) loosed
1 pl	ἐλύομεν	we were loosing / we loose	ἐλυόμεθα	we were loosing (for ourselves)	ἐλυόμεθα	we were (being) loosed
2 pl	ἐλύετε	y'all were loosing / y'all loose	ἐλύεσθε	y'all were loosing (for yourselves)	ἐλύεσθε	y'all were (being) loosed
3 pl	ἔλυον	they were loosing / they loose	ἐλύοντο	they were loosing (for themselves)	ἐλύοντο	they were (being) loosed

Future Tense

	active		middle		passive	
1 sg	λύσω	I will loose	λύσομαι	I will loose (for myself)	λυθήσομαι	I will be loosed
2 sg	λύσεις	you will loose	λύσῃ	you will loose (for yourself)	λυθήσῃ	you will be loosed
3 sg	λύσει	(s)he/it will loose	λύσεται	(s)he/it will loose (for himself)	λυθήσεται	(s)he/it will be loosed
1 pl	λύσομεν	we will loose	λυσόμεθα	we will loose (for ourselves)	λυθησόμεθα	we will be loosed
2 pl	λύσετε	y'all will loose	λύσεσθε	y'all will loose (for yourselves)	λυθήσεσθε	y'all will be loosed
3 pl	λύσουσι(ν)	they will loose	λύσονται	they will loose (for themselves)	λυθήσονται	they will be loosed

Aorist Tense

	active		middle		passive	
1 sg	ἔλυσα	I loose(d)	ἐλυσάμην	I loosed (for myself)	ἐλύθην	I was loosed
2 sg	ἔλυσας	you loose(d)	ἐλύσω	you loosed (for yourself)	ἐλύθης	you were loosed
3 sg	ἔλυσε(ν)	(s)he/it loose(d)	ἐλύσατο	(s)he/it loosed (for himself)	ἐλύθη	(s)he/it was loosed
1 pl	ἐλύσαμεν	we loose(d)	ἐλυσάμεθα	we loosed (for ourselves)	ἐλύθημεν	we were loosed
2 pl	ἐλύσατε	y'all loose(d)	ἐλύσασθε	y'all loosed (for yourselves)	ἐλύθητε	y'all were loosed
3 pl	ἔλυσαν	they loose(d)	ἐλύσαντο	they loosed (for themselves)	ἐλύθησαν	they were loosed

	active		middle		passive	
	Perfect Tense *note: for pluperfect translation "have/has" would be replaced with "had"*					
1 sg	λέλυκα	I have loosed	λέλυμαι	I have loosed (for myself)	λέλυμαι	I have (been) loosed
2 sg	λέλυκας	you have loosed	λέλυσαι	you have loosed (for yourself)	λέλυσαι	you have (been) loosed
3 sg	λέλυκε(v)	(s)he/it has loosed	λέλυται	(s)he/it has loosed (for himself)	λέλυται	(s)he/it has (been) loosed
1 pl	λελύκαμεν	we have loosed	λελύμεθα	we have loosed (for ourselves)	λελύμεθα	we have (been) loosed
2 pl	λελύκατε	y'all have loosed	λέλυσθε	y'all have loosed (for yourselves)	λέλυσθε	y'all have (been) loosed
3 pl	λελύκασι(v)	they have loosed	λέλυνται	they have loosed (for themselves)	λέλυνται	they have (been) loosed

4.5: Verb Parsing

The main difference in the *Stripped Down* approach as compared to other grammars is that they take many chapters to teach you how to parse a verb from memory. In this approach, the assumption is that you are not (at least initially) aiming on parsing on your own. Bible software is there to do the parsing for you. What you need to know, rather, is what the information provided to you by bible software means. Verb parsing will be provided to you in the following way (as per §4.2):

tense	voice	mood	person	number	lexical form
present	active	indicative	3	singular	λύω

T.V. Makes **P**eople **N**auseous is a simple way to remember the order in which the information is usually given to you. Most importantly, though, you need to understand what these things mean. What does the present tense convey? What does it mean to be active voice? What is the indicative mood? etc. These are the types of questions you need to ask and be able to answer from memory.

4.6: The Last Word

You are likely dazed and confused right now. I don't blame you. This is a whirlwind of information. As you work through the exercises things will become clearer. Remember, this approach aims to help you understand how Greek verbs are formed and what verb parsing means. Familiarity with all of the items is important, but not memorization.

4.7: The Least You Need to Know

You should be able to clearly and accurately answer these questions. Use these online flashcards (http://quizlet.com/_7tfwd) to memorize the answers:

- What are the 3 types of verbs?
- What is internal aspect?
- What is external aspect?
- What is stative aspect?
- What does the Greek present tense convey? In what time is it most often used?
- What does the Greek imperfect present tense convey? In what time is it most often used?
- What does the Greek future tense convey? In what time is it most often used?
- What does the Greek aorist tense convey? In what time is it most often used?
- What does the Greek perfect tense convey? In what time is it most often used?
- What does the Greek pluperfect tense convey? In what time is it most often used?
- What 3 voices occur in Greek? What does each one convey?
- What is the indicative mood?
- What are the 6 slots of the indicative slot machine?
- What tenses receive the augment?
- What tenses receive reduplication?
- Which tenses take which suffixes (slot 4)?
- Which tense&voice combinations take primary endings?
- Which tense&voice combinations take secondary endings?

4.8: Greek@Logos

Utilizing the ***Mastering Logos Bible Software*** course or the Logos help files, Logos forums, Logos wiki, and videos provided, users should take the time to learn:

- Add to a filter to highlight indicative verbs
    - See Lecture 39 of ***Mastering Logos Bible Software***
    - Alternative: http://youtu.be/7COLQXP7S8E
- How to search for a lexical form of a verb and how to search for an inflected form of a verb
    - See Lecture 34 of ***Mastering Logos Bible Software***
    - Alternative: http://youtu.be/2yT2hP4h_Tg and http://youtu.be/TrPW8h4TdMo)
- How to access the parsing of any Greek verb using the information window and its translation
    - See Lecture 12 of ***Mastering Logos Bible Software***
    - http://youtu.be/GF8qHbRUoyM

4.9: Vocabulary

One of the things this chapter has in the verb stem section (§4.3.1.4) is that verbs are built upon 6 principal parts. In other words, there are 6 possible variations on how a verb can look (yikes!). Lexicons (and the vocabulary tables in this textbook) list the lexical form as the one to learn. The reality, though, is that the other principal parts are just as, and sometimes more, important to recognize as well. In the vocabulary below, and in the remaining chapters, principal parts will be listed with verbs as they occur. The lexical form (the one you memorize) is the 1st principal part. When a dash appears in the principal parts, it is because that form of the word does not occur in the NT.

You don't fully understand principal parts yet, but don't worry about it. You will learn about them in the next chapter, and the grey words added below the verbs here will start to make more sense to you over time.

Word	Gloss	Type	Freq.	Derivatives
ἄγγελος, -ου, ὁ	messenger, angel	noun	175	angel
κόσμος, -ου, ὁ	world, universe	noun	186	cosmos
χείρ, χειρός, ἡ	hand; arm; finger	noun	177	*chiro*practor
παρά (παρ')	(+gen) from (+dat) beside, in the presence of, with (+acc) alongside of, other than	prep.	194	*para*llel
ἀκούω	I hear	verb	428	*acou*stics
ἀκούω, ἀκούσω, ἤκουσα, ἀκήκοα, ἤκουσμαι, ἠκούσθην				
ἀποκρίνομαι	I answer	verb	231	
ἀποκρίνομαι, ——, ἀπεκρινάμην, ——, ——, ἀπεκρίθην				
γράφω	I write	verb	191	*graph*ics
γράφω, γράψω, ἔγραψα, γέγραφα, γέγραμμαι, ἐγράφην				
δύναμαι	I am able, I am powerful, I can	verb	210	*dynam*ic
δύναμαι, δυνήσομαι, ——, ——, ——, ἠδυνήθην				
ἔχω	I have	verb	708	
ἔχω (imperfect εἶχον), ἕξω, ἔσχον, ἔσχηκα, ἔσχημαι, ——				
θέλω	I want, wish, will, desire	verb	208	
θέλω (imperf. ἤθελον), θελήσω, ἠθέλησα, ἠθέληκα, ——, ἠθελήθην				
καλέω	I call, name, invite	verb	148	
καλέω, καλέσω, ἐκάλεσα, κέκληκα, κέκλημαι, ἐκλήθην				
λαλέω	to sound, talk, speak	verb	296	glossa*lal*ia
λαλῶ, λαλήσω, ἐλάλησα, λελάληκα, λελάλημαι, ἐλαλήθην				
λύω	I loosen, release	verb	42	
λύω, λύσω, ἔλυσα, λέλυκα, λέλυμαι, ἐλύθην				
πιστεύω	I believe (in), have faith, trust	verb	241	
πιστεύω, πιστεύσω, ἐπίστευσα, πεπίστευκα, πεπίστευμαι, ἐπιστεύθην				
ποιέω	I do, make	verb	568	
ποιέω, ποιήσω, ἐποίησα, πεποίηκα, πεποίημαι, ἐποιήθην				

πορεύομαι	I go, proceed, live	verb	153
πορεύομαι, πορεύσομαι, ἐπορευσάμην, πεπόρευκα, πεπόρευμαι, ἐπορεύθην			

4.10: The Second Time Around

The second time around in this chapter is all about memorization and paradigms. You should not only thoroughly memorize the endings and indicative slot machine, but be able to create the paradigms from memory (use the practice tables from the workbook). You should also pay attention to the ways that verbs may be translated.

The following is the pluperfect paradigm of λύω, which wasn't presented during the chapter.

Table 21: Pluperfect Indicative Paradigm

Parts	4th λέλυκα	5th λέλυμαι
tense & voice	pluperfect active	pluperfect middle/passive
1 sg	ἐλελύκειν	ἐλελύμην
2 sg	ἐλελύκεις	ἐλέλυσο
3 sg	ἐλελύκει	ἐλέλυτο
1 pl	ἐλελύκειμεν	ἐλελύμεθα
2 pl	ἐλελύκειτε	ἐλέλυσθε
3 pl	ἐλελύκεισαν	ἐλέλυντο

Chapter 5:
Alternative Pattern Indicative Verbs and Principal Parts

⇒**What's the Point**: While you may feel like you barely understand the Greek Indicative verb system from the last chapter, the truth is that Greek verbs get even more complicated (don't blame me!). The last chapter focused on the strong verb, using the example of λύω, as well as vowel contractions and consonant interactions that can happen. With λύω, the -λυ- part was consistent. Since it was consistent, we could clearly see the affixes attached to make the different tense & voice combinations. The reality, though, is that most verbs aren't neat and tidy like this. Furthermore, there is another group of verbs, called μι verbs, that are very different. This chapter will begin by discussing principal parts of verbs and then introduce you to alternative verbal patterns. The chapter will conclude with discussing how to read about verbs in a Greek lexicon.

5.1: Greek Principal Parts

In the previous chapter you learned about the indicative slot machine and how the slot patterns is best seen with a strong verb like λύω. It is important to understand that the slot machine *is a recognition of patterns in a verb*. The slot patterns are easily recognizable with strong verbs. For some verbs, the pattern can change a little bit:

- If a verb stem begins with a vowel there is contraction when slot 1 (the augment) is attached. The vowel that begins the stem also cannot be reduplicated (slot 2) and so lengthens instead.
- If a verb stem ends with a vowel, and a connecting vowel (slot 5) is added, there is vowel contraction.
- If a verb stem ends in a liquid letter, the sigma that is part of the future and aorist suffix disappears (they slip on the liquid).
- If a verb stem ends with any of the stop consonants, there is consonant interaction with all of the suffixes, because the suffixes begin with sigma, kappa, or theta (see §1.3.2).

All of these changes are manageable because the slot machine pattern is there, though altered slightly. BUT, this is not the only problem we can run into. Another problem is *the stem itself*. Unlike nouns, a Greek verb stem is not always consistent in its spelling. In contrast to the strong verb λύω, there are many verbs whose stem (slot 3) changes depending on the tense & voice combination. For English speakers, there are three primary ways verbs are spelled, i.e. they have three *principal parts*. For example, there are times a verb is somewhat consistent and only changes a little bit so the stem will still be recognizable (e.g. fight, fight*s*, f*ou*ght). Other verbs are very different depending on the tense; this a weak verb. The past tense of "go" is "went." Children will often say "goed" because they have not yet learned that for this particular verb you don't simply stick "-ed" on the end of the verb to make it past tense. As native speakers, we learn these as related words even when they are spelled very differently.

The same thing occurs in Greek except it has six principal parts for each verb or six possible spelling varia- tions. In this Stripped Down approach you do not need to worry about learning all the various ways a verb may look; just know that it is not always consistent and there are more weak verbs than strong verbs.

Look at the following λύω table again, but this time note how the stem of the principal part in the top row (the bold and underlined portion) flows down to all of the forms that are built off of it (also underlined):

Table 22: λύω Indicative Paradigm

Parts	1st λύω				2nd λύσω	
tense & voice	present active	present m/p[88]	imperfect active	imperfect m/p	future active	future middle
1 sg	λύω	λύομαι	ἔλυον	ἐλυόμην	λύσω	λύσομαι
2 sg	λύεις	λύῃ	ἔλυες	ἐλύου	λύσεις	λύσῃ
3 sg	λύει	λύεται	ἔλυε(ν)	ἐλύετο	λύσει	λύσεται
1 pl	λύομεν	λυόμεθα	ἐλύομεν	ἐλυόμεθα	λύσομεν	λυσόμεθα
2 pl	λύετε	λύεσθε	ἐλύετε	ἐλύεσθε	λύσετε	λύσεσθε
3 pl	λύουσι(ν)	λύονται	ἔλυον	ἐλύοντο	λύσουσι(ν)	λύσονται

---

[88]See §4.2.2.

Alternative Pattern Indicative Verbs and Principal Parts

Parts	3rd ἔλυσα		4th λέλυκα	5th λέλυμαι	6th ἐλύθην	
tense & voice	aorist active	aorist middle	perfect active[89]	perfect m/p	aorist passive	future passive
1 sg	ἔλυσα	ἐλυσάμην	λέλυκα	λέλυμαι	ἐλύθην	λυθήσομαι
2 sg	ἔλυσας	ἐλύσω	λέλυκας	λέλυσαι	ἐλύθης	λυθήσῃ
3 sg	ἔλυσε(ν)	ἐλύσατο	λέλυκε(ν)	λέλυται	ἐλύθη	λυθήσεται
1 pl	ἐλύσαμεν	ἐλυσάμεθα	λελύκαμεν	λελύμεθα	ἐλύθημεν	λυθησόμεθα
2 pl	ἐλύσατε	ἐλύσασθε	λελύκατε	λέλυσθε	ἐλύθητε	λυθήσεσθε
3 pl	ἔλυσαν	ἐλύσαντο	λελύκασι(ν)	λέλυνται	ἐλύθησαν	λυθήσονται

Notice how, for the most part, the inflected endings (the red font along with the connecting vowel), are the main change that occur as one goes down the columns (with a few exceptions). Since λύω is a strong verb, the patterns work out nicely. The following table takes ἀκούω, which is not as "strong" as λύω. It begins with a vowel, so there is some vowel contraction. Observe in the 4th-6th principal parts that it starts to look quite different and the slot machine pattern (§4.3.1) is not as easy to recognize. Notice, however, that the stem for each principal part flows down through the forms that are built off of it, and the endings (the red font) are the main change.

---

[89] Pluperfect active and middle is also built off of this part. It is rare so is not added here.

Table 23: ἀκούω Indicative Paradigm

Parts	1st **ἀκούω**				2nd **ἀκούσω**	
tense & voice	present active	present m/p[90]	imperfect active	imperfect m/p	future active	future middle
1 sg	ἀκούω	ἀκούομαι	ἤκουον	ἠκουόμην	ἀκούσω	ἀκούσομαι
2 sg	ἀκούεις	ἀκούῃ	ἤκουες	ἠκούου	ἀκούσεις	ἀκούσῃ
3 sg	ἀκούει	ἀκούεται	ἤκουε(ν)	ἠκούετο	ἀκούσει	ἀκούσεται
1 pl	ἀκούομεν	ἀκουόμεθα	ἠκούομεν	ἠκουόμεθα	ἀκούσομεν	ἀκουσόμεθα
2 pl	ἀκούετε	ἀκούεσθε	ἠκούετε	ἠκούεσθε	ἀκούσετε	ἀκούσεσθε
3 pl	ἀκούουσι(ν)	ἀκούονται	ἤκουον	ἠκούοντο	ἀκούσουσι(ν)	ἀκούσονται

Parts	3rd **ἤκουσα**		4th **ἀκήκοα**	5th **ἤκουσμαι**	6th **ἠκούσθην**	
tense & voice	aorist active	aorist middle	perfect active[91]	perfect m/p	aorist passive	future passive
1 sg	ἤκουσα	ἠκουσάμην	ἀκήκοα	ἤκουσμαι	ἠκούσθην	ἠκουσθήσομαι
2 sg	ἤκουσας	ἠκούσου	ἀκήκοας	ἤκουσαι	ἠκούσθης	ἀκουσθήσῃ
3 sg	ἤκουσε(ν)	ἠκούσετο	ἀκήκοε(ν)	ἤκουσται	ἠκούσθη	ἀκουσθήσεται
1 pl	ἠκούσαμεν	ἠκουσάμεθα	ἀκηκόαμεν	ἠκούσμεθα	ἠκούσθημεν	ἠκουσθησόμεθα
2 pl	ἠκούσατε	ἠκούσεσθε	ἀκηκόατε	ἤκουσθε	ἠκούσθητε	ἠκούσθησεσθε
3 pl	ἤκουσαν	ἠκούσοντο	ἀκηκόασιν	ἤκουσνται	ἠκούσθησαν	ἠκουσθήσονται

So to recap, Greek verbs have 6 potential ways they can be spelled whereupon the inflection tags (the primary or secondary endings) are attached and these endings change. The 6 principal parts of each verb are the representation of the variances in spelling for

---

[90] See §4.2.2.
[91] Pluperfect active and middle is also built off of this part. It is rare so is not added here.

the verb. For some verbs, like λύω, the slot machine pattern is easy to recognize because the -λυ- part stays the same. For ἀκούω, the pattern is less consistent in that much of the pattern is recognizable. But some verbs are VERY different. This final example is λέγω, which is one of the highest frequency verbs in the New Testament. Notice how different the principal parts are, BUT you should also notice how the stem of the principal part flows down to all of forms that are built off of it.

Table 24: λέγω Indicative Paradigm

Parts	1st λέγω				2nd ἐρῶ	
tense & voice	present active	present m/p[92]	imperfect active	imperfect m/p	future active	future middle
1 sg	λέγω	λέγομαι	ἔλεγον	ἐλεγόμην	ἐρῶ	---[93]
2 sg	λέγεις	λέγῃ	ἔλεγες	ἐλέγου	ἐρεῖς	---
3 sg	λέγει	λέγεται	ἔλεγε(ν)	ἐλέγετο	ἐρεῖ	---
1 pl	λέγομεν	λεγόμεθα	ἐλέγομεν	ἐλεγόμεθα	ἐροῦμεν	---
2 pl	λέγετε	λέγεσθε	ἐλέγετε	ἐλέγεσθε	ἐρεῖτε	---
3 pl	λέγουσι(ν)	λέγονται	ἔλεγον	ἐλέγοντο	ἐροῦσιν	---

---

[92] See §4.2.2.
[93] No NT forms.

Parts	3rd __εἶπον__		4th __εἴρηκα__	5th __εἴρημαι__	6th __ἐρρέθην__	
tense & voice	*aorist active*	*aorist middle*	*perfect active*[94]	*perfect m/p*	*aorist passive*	*future passive*
1 sg	εἶπον	εἰπόμην	εἴρηκα	εἴρημαι	ἐρρέθην	---
2 sg	εἶπες	εἶπου	εἴρηκας	εἴρησαι	ἐρρέθης	---
3 sg	εἶπε(ν)	εἶπετο	εἴρηκε(ν)	εἴρηται	ἐρρέθη	---
1 pl	εἴπομεν	εἰπόμεθα	εἰρήκαμεν	εἰρήμεθα	ἐρρέθημεν	---
2 pl	εἴπετε	εἴπεσθε	εἰρήκατε	εἴρησθε	ἐρρέθητε	---
3 pl	εἶπον	εἶποντο	εἰρήκασι(ν)	εἴρηνται	ἐρρέθησαν	---

A final word about principal parts that I hope you recognize by now. If you had a photographic memory and memorized all Greek principal parts and the primary and secondary endings, you would be able to recognize any verb form! Now, of course you do not need to do that in the *Stripped Down* approach, but you do need to understand the formation of indicative verbs. The table below is a sampling of Greek verb principal parts. Some are strong, some are manageable, some are annoying, and some are downright ugly. I have color-coded these principal parts as best as can be done, but with some verbs the slot machine pattern is not easily recognizable. Appendix B is a fuller list of Greek principal parts.

As you go through the remainder of this chapter, keep your head in "principal part mode." As tables of different types of verbs are introduced, observe how the stem of the principal part flows down to all of the forms that are built off of it.

---

[94] Pluperfect active and middle is also built off of this part. It is rare so is not added here.

Table 25: Principal Parts

First	Second	Third	Fourth	Fifth	Sixth
λύω [95]	λύσω	ἔλυσα	λέλυκα	λέλυμαι	ἐλύθην
ἀκούω	ἀκούσω	ἤκουσα	ἀκήκοα	ἤκουσμαι	ἠκούσθην
γινώσκω [96]	γνώσομαι	ἔγνων	ἔγνωκα	ἔγνωσμαι	ἐγνώσθην
γίνομαι [97]	γενήσομαι	ἐγενόμην	γέγονα	γεγένημαι	ἐγενήθην
λαλῶ [98]	λαλήσω	ἐλάλησα	λελάληκα	λελάλημαι	ἐλαλήθην
πληρῶ	πληρώσω	ἐπλήρωσα	πεπλήρωκα	πεπλήρωμαι	ἐπληρώθην
γεννῶ	γεννήσω	ἐγέννησα	γεγέννηκα	γεγέννημαι	ἐγεννήθην
ἀποστέλλω [99]	ἀποστελῶ	ἀπέστειλα	ἀπέσταλκα	ἀπέσταλμαι	ἀπεστάλην
λέγω	ἐρῶ	εἶπον	εἴρηκα	εἴρημαι	ἐρρέθην
ὁράω	ὄψομαι	εἶδον	ἑώρακα	ἑώραμαι	ὤφθην
δίδωμι [100]	δώσω	ἔδωκα	δέδωκα	δέδομαι	ἐδόθην
tense & voice combinations that build off of these principal parts					
present (all), imperfect (all)	*future active & middle*	*aorist active & middle*	*(plu)perfect active*	*(plu)perfect middle/passive*	*aorist & future passive*

In the nouns chapter you learned that the nominative singular form of every noun is the lexical form. With verbs, the first principal part is the lexical form of every verb (usually the present, active, indicative, 1st, singular). This is why it is important to understand that the Greek verb system is built upon principal parts—sometimes the form of a verb is VERY different from its lexical form.

---

[95] In both the first and second principal part, certain inflected endings will absorb the connecting vowel.
[96] This is a "future middle" verb, which is discussed below.
[97] This is a lexical middle verb, which is discussed below.
[98] The following three verbs are called contract verbs, which are discussed below.
[99] This is a compound verb, which is discussed below.
[100] This is a μι verb, which is discussed below.

5.2: Different Types of Verbs

5.2.1: Lexical Middle Verbs

Certain Greek verbs do not have active voice forms. Instead, they look like a middle/passive verb because they only take the middle/passive endings, which also makes them fairly easy to recognize. So for example, the word γίνομαι has -μαι as the ending (the middle/passive ending). In the table below, all of the verbs are middle or passive, with the exception of the perfect, which has an active form.[101] Remember that middle voice indicates that the action is being done with self-interest, and is often translated into English sounding like an active.

Table 26: Lexical Middle Indicative Forms

Parts	1st γίνομαι				2nd γενήσομαι	
tense & voice	*present active*	*present m/p*	*imperfect active*	*imperfect m/p*	*future active*	*future middle*
1 sg	---	γίνομαι	---	ἐγινόμην	---	γενήσομαι
2 sg	---	γίνῃ	---	ἐγίνου	---	γενήσῃ
3 sg	---	γίνεται	---	ἐγίνετο	---	γενήσεται
1 pl	---	γινόμεθα	---	ἐγινόμεθα	---	γενησόμεθα
2 pl	---	γίνεσθε	---	ἐγίνεσθε	---	γενήσεσθε
3 pl	---	γίνονται	---	ἐγίνοντο	---	γενήσονται

---

[101] Many past and current grammars have called these forms "deponent verbs." A deponent verb is a Latin concept, where verbs look like middle, but are translated as active. Research in the past few decades, however, have shown that deponency is foreign to Greek. These lexical middle forms do indeed get translated as active in English, but the idea of self-interest is still core to its meaning in Greek.

Parts	3rd ἐγενόμην		4th γέγονα	5th γεγένημαι	6th ἐγενήθην	
tense & voice	aorist active	aorist middle	perfect active	perfect m/p	aorist passive	future passive
1 sg	---	ἐγενόμην	γέγονα	γεγένημαι	ἐγενήθην	γενηθήσομαι
2 sg	---	ἐγένου	γέγονας	γεγένησαι	ἐγενήθης	γενηθήσῃ
3 sg	---	ἐγένετο	γέγονε(ν)	γεγένηται	ἐγενήθη	γενηθήσεται
1 pl	---	ἐγενόμεθα	γεγόναμεν	γεγενήμεθα	ἐγενήθημεν	γενηθησόμεθα
2 pl	---	ἐγένεσθε	γεγόνατε	γεγένησθε	ἐγενήθητε	γενηθήσεσθε
3 pl	---	ἐγένοντο	γεγόνασι(ν)	γεγένηνται	ἐγενήθησαν	γενηθήσονται

5.2.2: Contract Verbs

You have already learned from Chapter 1 that vowels frequently contract when placed side by side. Verb stems that end in an alpha (α), epsilon (ε), or omicron (ο) are called contract verbs because the vowel at the end of the stem contracts with the connecting vowel *for all present and imperfect forms* (i.e. the 1st principal part). When a contract verb occurs in the rest of the tenses the vowel at the end of the stem will automatically lengthen: α/ε = η and ο = ω. In the following paradigms I've underlined the vowel contraction or lengthening.

Table 27: φιλέω Indicative Paradigm

Parts	1st φιλέω				2nd ---	
tense & voice	present active	present m/p	imperfect active	imperfect m/p	future active	future middle
1 sg	φιλῶ	φιλοῦμαι	ἐφίλουν	ἐφιλούμην	---[102]	---
2 sg	φιλεῖς	φιλῇ	ἐφίλεις	ἐφιλοῦ	---	---
3 sg	φιλεῖ	φιλεῖται	ἐφίλει	ἐφιλεῖτο	---	---
1 pl	φιλοῦμεν	φιλούμεθα	ἐφιλοῦμεν	ἐφιλούμεθα	---	---
2 pl	φιλεῖτε	φιλεῖσθε	ἐφιλεῖτε	ἐφιλεῖσθε	---	---
3 pl	φιλοῦσι(ν)	φιλοῦνται	ἐφίλουν	ἐφιλοῦντο	---	---

Parts	3rd ἐφίλησα		4th πεφίληκα	5th ---	6th ---	
tense & voice	aorist active	aorist middle	perfect active	perfect m/p	aorist passive	future passive
1 sg	ἐφίλησα	ἐφιλησάμην	πεφίληκα	---	---	---
2 sg	ἐφίλησας	ἐφιλήσω	πεφίληκας	---	---	---
3 sg	ἐφίλησε(ν)	ἐφιλήσατο	πεφίληκε(ν)	---	---	---
1 pl	ἐφιλήσαμεν	ἐφιλησάμεθα	πεφιλήκαμεν	---	---	---
2 pl	ἐφιλήσατε	ἐφιλήσασθε	πεφιλήκατε	---	---	---
3 pl	ἐφίλησαν	ἐφιλήσαντο	πεφιλήκασι(ν)	---	---	---

---

[102]The sections that are left blank indicate that the verb in question does not occur in this form in the NT, so it is not taught. This is different than the Lexical Middle verbs above that are greyed out, as those forms don't exist at all.

Table 28: ἀγαπάω Indicative Paradigm

Parts	1st ἀγαπάω				2nd ἀγαπήσω	
tense & voice	present active	present m/p	imperfect active	imperfect m/p	future active	future middle
1 sg	ἀγαπῶ	ἀγαπῶμαι	ἠγάπων	ἠγαπώμην	ἀγαπήσω	ἀγαπήσομαι
2 sg	ἀγαπᾷς	ἀγαπᾷ	ἠγάπας	ἠγαπῶ	ἀγαπήσεις	ἀγαπήσῃ
3 sg	ἀγαπᾷ	ἀγαπᾶται	ἠγάπα	ἠγαπᾶτο	ἀγαπήσει	ἀγαπήσεται
1 pl	ἀγαπῶμεν	ἀγαπώμεθα	ἠγαπῶμεν	ἠγαπώμεθα	ἀγαπήσομεν	ἀγαπησόμεθα
2 pl	ἀγαπᾶτε	ἀγαπᾶσθε	ἠγαπᾶτε	ἠγαπᾶσθε	ἀγαπήσετε	ἀγαπήσεσθε
3 pl	ἀγαπῶσι	ἀγαπῶνται	ἠγάπων	ἠγαπῶντο	ἀγαπήσουσιν	ἀγαπήσονται

Parts	3rd ἠγάπησα		4th ἠγάπηκα	5th ἠγάπημαι	6th ἠγαπήθην	
tense & voice	aorist active	aorist middle	perfect active	perfect m/p	aorist passive	future passive
1 sg	ἠγάπησα	ἠγαπησάμην	ἠγάπηκα	ἠγάπημαι	ἠγαπήθην	ἀγαπηθήσομαι
2 sg	ἠγάπησας	ἠγαπήσω	ἠγάπηκας	ἠγάπησαι	ἠγαπήθης	ἀγαπηθήσῃ
3 sg	ἠγάπησε(ν)	ἠγαπήσατο	ἠγάπηκεν	ἠγάπηται	ἠγαπήθη	ἀγαπηθήσεται
1 pl	ἠγαπήσαμεν	ἠγαπήσαμεθα	ἠγαπήκαμεν	ἠγάπημεθα	ἠγαπήθημεν	ἀγαπηθησόμεθα
2 pl	ἠγαπήσατε	ἠγαπήσασθε	ἠγαπήκατε	ἠγάπησθε	ἠγαπήθητε	ἀγαπηθήσεσθε
3 pl	ἠγάπησαν	ἠγαπήσαντο	ἠγαπήκασι(ν)	ἠγάπησαν	ἠγαπήθησαν	ἀγαπηθήσονται

5.2.3: Compound Verbs

Compound verbs are made up of a normal verb with the addition of a preposition to the front of it.[103] The compound form is an entirely new verb that may be used (though not always!) within the same semantic domain (see §3.5.1) as the original form. For instance:

- γινώσκω = I know
- ἀναγινώσκω = I read (the preposition ἀνα, which means up, has been added to the front of the verb to make a new word), which is not in the same semantic domain, but a pneumonic device to remember the primary gloss for the compound verb is the knowledge of the written word floats "up" so you can "know" it.

The most important thing to know about compound verbs is that the epsilon augment (slot 1) appears *after the preposition* that has been added to make the new word. So ανα + [ε] + γινώσκω. In the table below the example used is ἀπαγγέλλω, απ'[104] + [ε] + αγγέλλω.

The underlined letters represent the contraction that has occurred because of the augment, which shows up in the imperfect, aorist, and perfect.

---

[103] You've already learned numerous prepositions in vocabulary and you will learn more about them in §7.2.

[104] This is the shortened form for ἀπό.

Alternative Pattern Indicative Verbs and Principal Parts

Table 29: ἀπαγγέλλω Indicative Paradigm

Parts	1st ἀπαγγέλλω				2nd ἀπαγγελῶ	
tense & voice	present active	present m/p[105]	imperfect active	imperfect m/p	future active	future middle
1 sg	ἀπαγγέλλω	ἀπαγγέλλομαι	ἀπήγγελλον	ἀπηγγελλόμην	ἀπαγγελῶ	ἀπαγγελοῦμαι
2 sg	ἀπαγγέλλεις	ἀπαγγέλλῃ	ἀπήγγελλες	ἀπηγγέλλου	ἀπαγγελεῖς	ἀπαγγελῇ
3 sg	ἀπαγγέλλει	ἀπαγγέλλεται	ἀπήγγελλεν	ἀπηγγέλλετο	ἀπαγγελεῖ	ἀπαγγελεῖται
1 pl	ἀπαγγέλλομεν	ἀπαγγελλόμεθα	ἀπηγγέλλομεν	ἀπηγγελλόμεθα	ἀπαγγελοῦμεν	ἀπαγγελούμεθα
2 pl	ἀπαγγέλλετε	ἀπαγγέλλεσθε	ἀπηγγέλλετε	ἀπηγγέλλεσθε	ἀπαγγελεῖτε	ἀπαγγελεῖσθε
3 pl	ἀπαγγέλλουσι	ἀπαγγέλλονται	ἀπήγγελλον	ἀπηγγέλλοντο	ἀπαγγελοῦσι	ἀπαγγελοῦνται

Parts	3rd ἀπήγγειλα		4th ---	5th ἀπήγγελμαι	6th ἀπηγγέλην	
tense & voice	aorist active	aorist middle	perfect active	perfect m/p	aorist passive	future passive
1 sg	ἀπήγγειλα	ἀπηγγειλάμην	---	ἀπήγγελμαι	ἀπηγγέλην	ἀπαγγελήσομαι
2 sg	ἀπήγγειλας	ἀπηγγείλω	---	ἀπήγγελσαι	ἀπηγγέλης	ἀπαγγελήσῃ
3 sg	ἀπήγγειλε	ἀπηγγείλατο	---	ἀπήγγελται	ἀπηγγέλη	ἀπαγγελήσεται
1 pl	ἀπηγγείλαμεν	ἀπηγγειλάμεθα	---	ἀπηγγέλμεθα	ἀπηγγέλημεν	ἀπαγγελησόμεθα
2 pl	ἀπηγγείλατε	ἀπηγγείλασθε	---	ἀπήγγελσθε	ἀπηγγέλητε	ἀπαγγελήσετε
3 pl	ἀπήγγειλαν	ἀπηγγείλαντο	---	ἀπήγγελνται	ἀπηγγέλησαν	ἀπαγγελήσονται

---

[105]See §4.2.2.

5.2.4: 2 Aorist Verbs

Some aorist stems are so different in their principal part that their is no trace of the σα suffix. These aorists are often called 2nd Aorist. 2nd Aorist forms end up looking just like an imperfect tense in that they only take an augment (slot 1) and secondary endings. The key, again, is that the principal part is different.

Table 30: 2nd Aorist Indicative Paradigm

Parts	1st ἄγω				2nd ἄξω	
tense & voice	present active	present m/p[106]	imperfect active	imperfect m/p	future active	future middle
1 sg	ἄγω	ἄγομαι	ἦγον	ἠγόμην	ἄξω	ἄξομαι
2 sg	ἄγεις	ἄγῃ	ἦγες	ἤγου	ἄξεις	ἄξῃ
3 sg	ἄγει	ἄγεται	ἦγε(ν)	ἤγετο	ἄξει	ἄξεται
1 pl	ἄγομεν	ἀγόμεθα	ἤγομεν	ἠγόμεθα	ἄξομεν	ἀξόμεθα
2 pl	ἄγετε	ἄγεσθε	ἤγετε	ἤγεσθε	ἄξετε	ἄξεσθε
3 pl	ἄγουσι(ν)	ἄγονται	ἦγον	ἤγοντο	ἄξουσι(ν)	ἄξονται

Parts	3rd ἤγαγον		4th ἀγείοχα	5th ἦγμαι	6th ἤχθην	
tense & voice	aorist active	aorist middle	perfect active[107]	perfect m/p	aorist passive	future passive
1 sg	ἤγαγον	ἠγαγόμην	ἀγείοχα	ἦγμαι	ἤχθην	ἀχθήσομαι
2 sg	ἤγαγες	ἠγάγου	ἀγείοχας	ἦγσαι	ἤχθης	ἀχθήσῃ
3 sg	ἤγαγε(ν)	ἠγάγετο	ἀγείοχεν	ἦγται	ἤχθη	ἀχθήσεται
1 pl	ἠγάγομεν	ἠγαγόμεθα	ἀγειόχαμεν	ἦγμεθα	ἤχθημεν	ἀχθησόμεθα
2 pl	ἠγάγετε	ἠγάγεσθε	ἀγειόχατε	ἦγσθε	ἤχθητε	ἀχθήσεσθε
3 pl	ἤγαγον	ἠγάγοντο	ἀγειόχασι(ν)	ἦγνται	ἤχθησαν	ἀχθήσονται

---

[106]See §4.2.2.
[107]Pluperfect active and middle is also built off of this part. It is rare so is not added here.

5.2.5: μι *Verbs*

μι verbs are a special class of Greek verbs that occur pretty regularly in the New Testament. Their stems are often short and end in a vowel, which causes them to act much like contract verbs in that the vowel may lengthen to a long vowel or diphthong. The other oddity of a μι verb occurs mainly in the present and imperfect tenses (those built off of the 1st principal part). In the 1st principal part, μι verbs have a special type of iota reduplication. It is like Perfect reduplication, but using an iota instead. The present active forms of μι verbs also have their own set of endings (see Table 18: Primary and Secondary Endings). Finally, aorist active μι verbs have a -κα suffix instead of -σα. In the middle forms, it has no suffix. The following table shows the full indicative paradigm of δίδωμι, with the unique iota reduplication in the 1st principal part underlined.

Table 31: δίδωμι Indicative Paradigm

Parts	1st δίδωμι				2nd δώσω	
tense & voice	present active	present m/p	imperfect active	imperfect m/p	future active	future middle
1 sg	δίδωμι	δίδομαι	ἐδίδουν	ἐδιδόμην	δώσω	δώσομαι
2 sg	δίδως	δίδοσαι	ἐδίδους	ἐδίδοσο	δώσεις	δώσῃ
3 sg	δίδωσι(ν)	δίδοται	ἐδίδου	ἐδίδοτο	δώσει	δώσεται
1 pl	δίδομεν	διδόμεθα	ἐδίδομεν	ἐδιδόμεθα	δώσομεν	δωσόμεθα
2 pl	δίδοτε	δίδοσθε	ἐδίδοτε	ἐδίδοσθε	δώσετε	δώσεσθε
3 pl	διδόασι(ν)	δίδονται	ἐδίδοσαν	ἐδίδοντο	δώσουσι(ν)	δώσονται

Parts	3rd ἔδωκα		4th δέδωκα	5th δέδομαι	6th ἐδόθην	
tense & voice	aorist active	aorist middle	perfect active[108]	perfect middle	aorist passive	future passive
1 sg	ἔδωκα	ἐδόμην	δέδωκα	δέδομαι	ἐδόθην	δοθήσομαι
2 sg	ἔδωκας	ἔδου	δέδωκας	δέδοσαι	ἐδόθης	δοθήσῃ
3 sg	ἔδωκε(ν)	ἔδοτο	δέδωκε(ν)	δέδοται	ἐδόθη	δοθήσεται
1 pl	ἐδώκαμεν	ἐδόμεθα	δεδώκαμεν	δεδόμεθα	ἐδόθημεν	δοθησόμεθα
2 pl	ἐδώκατε	ἔδοσθε	δεδώκατε	δέδοσθε	ἐδόθητε	δοθήσεσθε
3 pl	ἔδωκαν	ἔδοντο	δέδωκαν	δέδονται	ἐδόθησαν	δοθήσονται

☞ Watch this video (http://youtu.be/Ij1Nq53zpEU) to solidify the previous section.

5.2.5.1: εἰμί

εἰμί is an equative verb (see §4.1). It is also a μι verb, but is treated separately because it is so frequent in the New Testament. εἰμί only occurs in present, imperfect, and

---

[108] Pluperfect active and middle is also built off of this part. It is rare so is not added here.

future in the Indicative mood. It is also unique from other verbs in that it does not have voice. So a form of εἰμί would be parsed as tense, mood, person, number, lexical form (eg. present, indicative, 2, singular, εἰμί).

Table 32: εἰμί Indicative table

	Present		Imperfect		Future	
1 sg	εἰμί	I am	ἤμην	I was	ἔσομαι	I will be
2 sg	εἶ	you are	ἦς (ἦσθα)	you were	ἔσῃ	you will be
3 sg	ἐστί(ν)	(s)he/it is	ἦν	(s)he/it was	ἔσται	(s)he/it will be
1 pl	ἐσμέν	we are	ἦμεν (ἤμεθα)	we were	ἐσόμεθα	we will be
2 pl	ἐστέ	y'all are	ἦτε	y'all were	ἔσεσθε	y'all will be
3 pl	εἰσί(ν)	they are	ἦσαν	they were	ἔσονται	they will be

5.3: The Least You Need to Know

You should be able to clearly and accurately answer these questions. Use these online flashcards (http://quizlet.com/_7tfwx) to memorize the answers:

- What are principal parts?
- Which tense&voice combinations build off of the 1st principal part?
- Which tense&voice combinations build off of the 2nd principal part?
- Which tense&voice combinations build off of the 3rd principal part?
- Which tense&voice combinations build off of the 4th principal part?
- Which tense&voice combinations build off of the 5th principal part?
- Which tense&voice combinations build off of the 6th principal part?
- What are deponent verbs?
- What are future deponent verbs?
- What are contract verbs? Describe their behavior.
- What are compound verbs? Describe their behavior, particularly with the augment.
- What are 2Aorists?
- What are μι verbs? What makes μι verbs different from other verb forms?

- What is the first bit of information a lexicon gives about verbs?

5.4: Greek@Logos

Utilizing the *Mastering Logos Bible Software* course or the Logos help files, Logos forums, Logos wiki, and videos provided, users should take the time to learn:

- Get started on managing your Logos library to empower your searching
  - See Lecture 24, 26–28 of *Mastering Logos Bible Software*
  - Alternative: http://youtu.be/DXsyzbYiiic
- How to prioritize resources
  - See Lecture 25 of *Mastering Logos Bible Software*
  - Alternative: http://youtu.be/RHF8a1UsYJU

5.5: Vocabulary

Word	Meaning	Type	Freq.	Derivatives
μέν	on the one hand, indeed [or left untranslated]	partic.	179	
γίνομαι	I become, am, exist, happen, take place, am born, am created	verb	669	
γίνομαι, γενήσομαι, ἐγενόμην, γέγονα, γεγένημαι, ἐγενήθην				
γινώσκω	I know, come to know, realize, learn	verb	222	dia*gnos*tic
γινώσκω, γνώσομαι, ἔγνων, ἔγνωκα, ἔγνωσμαι, ἐγνώσθην				
δίδωμι	I give (out), entrust, give back, put, grant, allow	verb	415	
δίδωμι, δώσω, ἔδωκα, δέδωκα, δέδομαι, ἐδόθην				
εἰμί	I am	verb	2462	
εἰμί, ἔσομαι, ἤμην, ——, ——,				
εἰσέρχομαι	I enter, come in(to), go in(to)	verb	194	
εἰσέρχομαι, εἰσελεύσομαι, εἰσῆλθον, εἰσελήλυθα, ——,				

ἐξέρχομαι	I go out	verb	218	
ἐξέρχομαι, ἐξελεύσομαι, ἐξῆλθον, ἐξελήλυθα, ——, ——				
ἔρχομαι	I come, go	verb	634	
ἔρχομαι, ἐλεύσομαι, ἦλθον, ἐλήλυθα, ——, ——				
ἐσθίω	I eat	verb	158	
ἐσθίω, φάγομαι, ἔφαγον, ἐδήδοκα, ἐδήδεσμαι, ——				
εὑρίσκω	I find	verb	176	*heuris*tic
εὑρίσκω, εὑρήσω, εὗρησα (εὗρον), εὕρηκα, ——, εὑρέθην				
ἵστημι	I stand set, place; I cause to stand	verb	155	
ἵστημι, στήσω, ἔστησα (ἔστην), ἕστηκα, ——, ἐστάθην				
λαμβάνω	I take, receive	verb	258	
λαμβάνω, λήμψομαι, ἔλαβον, εἴληφα, ——, ἐλήμφθην				
λέγω	I say, speak	verb	2354	*leg*end
λέγω, ἐρῶ, εἶπον, εἴρηκα, εἴρημαι, ἐρρέθην				
οἶδα	I know, understand	verb	318	
οἶδα, εἰδήσω, ᾔδειν, ——, ——, ——				
ὁράω	I see, notice, experience	verb	454	pan*ora*ma
ὁράω, ὄψομαι, εἶδον, ἑώρακα (ἐόρακα), ἑώραμαι, ὤφθην				

5.6: The Second Time Around

This chapter very much builds off of the foundation laid in the previous chapter. Learning the differences in these alternative patterns, in addition to the paradigms and endings learned in the previous chapter, will help you to recognize them when parsing. Take the time also to memorize the εἰμί indicative paradigm, as it is the most frequent verb in the NT.

Chapter 6:
The Article, Adjectives, Pronouns, and Numbers

⇒**What's the Point:** 32% of the New Testament is composed of words that fill in detail and give life to the text. Pronouns stand in place of nouns, the word "the" in Greek does a lot more than "the" in English, and adjectives have a robust life in the Greek language. Learning and appreciating these types of words will bring out the life and color of the Greek New Testament as you read and study it.

6.1: Twenty-four Ways to Say "The"

Greek has no word like "a" or "an," but the definite article "the" comes in abundance. In English, "the" always come right before the word it is paired with.[109] In Greek, the article can be paired with any noun no matter how it is inflected. When words are paired together in Greek, they have to be inflected in the exact same way (same case, gender, and number). So, unlike Greek nouns which have only one gender (masculine, feminine, or neuter), the article can be any gender.

6.1.1: How the Article is Formed

The article must be inflected the same way as the noun it is paired with, so it has 24 forms.

Table 33: The Article

	masculine		feminine		neuter	
	singular	*plural*	*singular*	*plural*	*singular*	*plural*
nominative	ὁ(ς)	οἱ	ἡ	αἱ	τό(ν)	τά
genitive	τοῦ	τῶν	τῆς	τῶν	τοῦ	τῶν
dative	τῷ	τοῖς	τῇ	ταῖς	τῷ	τοῖς
accusative	τόν	τούς	τήν	τάς	τό(ν)	τά

---

[109]Recall in §2.1 that the article was color-coded along with the noun it is paired with.

Notice that apart from the masculine and feminine nominative forms, all of the articles start with a tau (τ). Those four that do not have a τ have rough breathing instead. Finally, take note that the masculine and neuter articles use 2nd declension endings, and feminine articles use 1st declension endings. I have added in grey font the letters that complete the declension endings. It is only the grey font portions that are not used in article formation.

6.1.2: What the Article Can Do

6.1.2.1: Make Something Definite

The article will simply say "the" to make something definite when it is directly before a noun that it is paired with. Remember, when the article is paired with a noun they are inflected in exactly the same case, gender, and number. The case of the article and noun pair will be translated accordingly: e.g.: ὁ λογός = "the word," τοῖς λόγοις = "to the words." This exact pairing is why grammarians often tell students that the article is one of your best friends. It never lies to the reader. Whereas some nouns are more difficult to figure out (especially those pesky 3rd declension nouns) the article is always crystal clear.

Even though the article makes something definite, it is not always translated into English. For example, proper names like God and Jesus often appear with an article but translations usually do not have "the God" or "the Jesus."

6.1.2.2: Act Like a Pronoun

The article can stand all by itself in Greek. When this happens it is functioning in a unique way that is unparalleled in English. The first thing the article can do when it is by itself is act like a pronoun. Consider this example:

- ὁ δὲ εἶπεν αὐτοῖς (Matt 12:3)
    - ὁ (article="the") δὲ ("but" or untranslated) εἶπεν (verb="said") αὐτοῖς (pronoun="to them")
    - Translation: He said to them (Matt 12:3, NRSV)

Notice how the translation is NOT "the said to them." Notice also that the article is *all by itself*. Whenever the article is all by itself, it is not making something definite or saying "the." In this example, the article is working like a pronoun, and just like a pronoun it has an antecedent. Since the article is nominative, masculine, singular we know that it is translated as "he" (and the "he" in the context is Jesus). The English pronoun used to translate the article will correspond to the inflection of the article/noun:

- ἡ δὲ εἶπεν αὐτοῖς
  She said to them
- τό δὲ εἶπεν αὐτοῖς
  It said to them
- οἱ δὲ εἶπαν αὐτοῖς
  they said to them

6.1.2.3: Rope in a Prepositional Phrase

The second thing a Greek article can do when it is *sitting all by itself* is rope in a prepositional phrase. Consider the following Greek sentence (and its breakdown):

word	ὁ	ναὸς	τοῦ	θεοῦ	ὁ	ἐν	τῷ	οὐρανῷ
meaning	the	temple	the	God	the	in	the	heaven
type	*article*	*noun*	*article*	*noun*	*article*	*preposition*	*article*	*noun*
parsing	nom, masc, sg	gen, masc, sg			nom, masc, sg	--	date, masc, sg	
Translation:	"the temple of God which is in heaven (Rev 11:19) *or* "the temple of God that is in heaven (Rev 11:19)							

Looking at the English translation ask yourself, what is "in heaven," the temple or God? In English it is unclear, but in Greek it is crystal clear. In the example, there are four articles. The article all by itself is not paired with anything and comes right before the prepositional phrase ἐν τῷ οὐρανῷ. You will learn more about prepositions and phrases in chapter 7. For now, what you need to know is that a preposition works with a few other words to further describe something in the sentence.

Take note that the lone article has the identical case as the very first article. The agreement in gender, number, and case makes it clear that the prepositional phrase is telling you *more about the matching word.*

Table 34: Lone Article Function

matching, therefore…

ὁ ναὸς τοῦ θεοῦ ὁ ἐν τῷ οὐρανῷ

this phrase is describing this noun

The lone article matches "the temple" (ὁ ναὸς) the thing "in heaven" is the temple. This type of article is often translated with "which" or "that." f we were to change the lone article to match God, then it would be saying that God is in heaven:

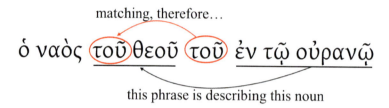

this phrase is describing this noun

Now the English translation would read, "the temple of God, who is in heaven."

6.2: Adjectives

Adjectives in Greek function in much the same way they do in English. They can attribute value to a noun (*good* person, *bad* dog, *ugly* house) or they can sit all by themselves and act like a noun (the *good*, the *bad*, and the *ugly*). This last function is called acting as a substantive (i.e. it has substance all on its own and can stand alone). Therefore, as you work with Greek and come across an adjective, the main questions to ask are: Is it attributing value to a noun? If so, what noun is it paired with?

6.2.1: How Adjectives are Formed

The great thing about adjectives (and the article) is that they use the declension endings just like nouns do, so there are no new endings to memorize (yeah!). Just like nouns, the last letter on the stem determines which declension endings are chosen. Like the article, adjectives are also multi-gendered and the inflection corresponds to the gender, number, and case of any article, noun or pronoun that it is used with. In the following examples the case inflection is colored red. Finally, remember that the case endings affect the translation of adjectives just like they affect nouns: nominative adjectives are the subject, genitive adjectives indicate possession, etc.

Table 35: Adjective following 1st and 2nd declension

	Masculine		Feminine		Neuter	
	sg.	*pl.*	*sg.*	*pl.*	*sg.*	*pl.*
nominative	ἀγαθός	ἀγαθοί	ἀγαθή	ἀγαθαί	ἀγαθόν	ἀγαθά
genitive	ἀγαθοῦ	ἀγαθῶν	ἀγαθῆς	ἀγαθῶν	ἀγαθοῦ	ἀγαθῶν
dative	ἀγαθῷ	ἀγαθοῖς	ἀγαθῇ	ἀγαθαῖς	ἀγαθῷ	ἀγαθοῖς
accusative	ἀγαθόν	ἀγαθούς	ἀγαθήν	ἀγαθάς	ἀγαθόν	ἀγαθά

Table 36: Adjective following 3rd declension (for masculine and neuter)

stem is παντ for masc/neut	Masculine		Feminine		Neuter	
	sg.	*pl.*	*sg.*	*pl.*	*sg.*	*pl.*
nominative	πᾶς	πάντες	πᾶσα	πᾶσαι	πᾶν	πάντα
genitive	παντός	πάντων	πάσης	πασῶν	παντός	πάντων
dative	παντί	πᾶσι(ν)	πάσῃ	πασαις	παντί	πᾶσι(ν)
accusative	παντα	πάντας	πᾶσαν	πάσας	πᾶν	πάντα

6.2.1.1: Comparatives and Superlatives

Just like in English, Greek has comparatives and superlatives.
- "Good" is an adjective.
- "Better" is the comparative of good.
- "Best" is the superlative of good.

Greek comparatives and superlatives are built off of Greek adjectives. Like English, some comparatives and superlatives are just like their adjectives (small, small*er*, small*est*). Greek adjectives that are more regular add -τερ- to their stem for the comparative and -τατ- for the superlative, and these are followed by the declension endings. Other adjectives, though, will be totally different (e.g. good, better, best). Higher frequency comparatives and superlatives will appear in vocabulary as their own words. All comparatives and superlatives will take declension endings just like any other adjective.

	normal	**comparative**	**superlative**
regular	νεός	νεώτερος	νεώτατος
irregular	ἀγαθός	κρείσσων	ἄριστός

6.2.2: What Adjectives Can Do

Adjectives in Greek do the same things English adjectives do, but the grammar of Greek is different from English.

6.2.2.1: Attribute Value to a Noun

Take a look at these three English examples and the three different ways Greek can say the same thing. Each noun used is a different gender and all are nominative singular:

- the good man (*masculine noun*)
    - ἀγαθὸς ἄνθρωπος
    - ὁ ἀγαθὸς ἄνθρωπος
    - ὁ ἀγαθὸς ὁ ἄνθρωπος
    - ὁ ἄνθρωπος ὁ ἀγαθὸς
- the good woman (*feminine noun*)
    - ἀγαθὴ γυνή
    - ἡ ἀγαθὴ γυνή
    - ἡ ἀγαθὴ ἡ γυνή
    - ἡ γυνὴ ἡ ἀγαθή
- the good tree (*neuter noun*)
    - ἀγαθὸν δένδρον
    - τόν ἀγαθὸν δένδρον
    - τόν ἀγαθὸν τόν δένδρον
    - τόν δένδρον τόν ἀγαθὸν

Take the time to look carefully at each set above to recognize the similarities in every group. The first thing to notice is that the adjective and the noun it is paired with are *identical in case, gender, and number* (the articles are identical too). The second thing to notice is that in examples 2–4 *the adjective always has an article*. Think of this as the **AAA rule** = an **A**djective preceded by an **A**rticle is **A***ttributive*. Even when the noun does not have the article, the adjective still does. This demonstrates a simple rule about Greek adjectives: *the article is key to understanding adjective function*. Here are the rules governing an attributive adjective:

1. The adjective MUST be in concord (i.e. same case, gender, number) as the noun it is paired with.
2. If the noun has an article, the adjective MUST have it too for it to be an attributive.

6.2.2.2: Act Like a Noun (act substantivally)

Like English, an adjective can act alone. In this case, the gender of the adjective may become part of the translation. When an adjective stands alone, words are sometimes added to make it more substantive. Examples:

- ὁ ἀγαθὸς
    - This is nominative, masculine, singular.
    - It can be translated as "the good," "the good *one*," or "the good *man*."
    - This same adjective without an article, and with no nearby noun in concord, would also be translated substantivally, i.e. "a good (man)"
- ἡ ἀγαθή
    - This is nominative, feminine, singular.
    - It can be translated as "the good," "the good *one*," or "the good *woman*."
    - This same adjective without an article, and with no nearby noun in concord, would also be translated substantivally, i.e. "a good (woman)"
- τόν ἀγαθὸν
    - This is nominative, neuter, singular.
    - It can be translated as "the good," "the good *one*," or "the good *thing*."

- This same adjective without an article, and with no nearby noun in concord, would also be translated substantivally, i.e. "a good (thing)"

In all of the above cases, the adjective has the article but **it is not in concord with a nearby noun** (remember the rules from above). Think of it as the **A(A) noN rule** = an Adjective (that can also have an Article) but **no** Noun in concord is *substantival*.

6.2.2.3: Act as a Predicate Nominative

This is a bit of a hybrid function of the previous two. Here is an example:
- ἀγαθὸς ὁ ἄνθρωπος
    - Both the noun and the adjective are nominative, masculine, singular.
    - Notice that the noun has the article but the adjective **does not.**
    - It is translated as "the man *is* good."

You may be wondering where "is" came from? It is a good question because it is foreign to English. In English, we always need a verb for a proper sentence, but not so in Greek. In Greek (and other languages) a sentence can be verbless. This does not mean that you can insert any verb you want there, but only one verb in particular. When a Greek sentence has no verb, the verb assumed to be invisibly present is a form of εἰμί. In these types of Greek sentences, "is," "was," "am," "were," or "are" is added in translation. In these types of verbless sentences, the adjective *with no article is the predicate nominative* of the invisible equative verb (remind yourself about the equative verb in §4.1). We can call this the **noA noV rule** = an adjective with **no** Article and in a clause with **no** Verb is a *predicate nominative*.

6.3: Pronouns

Greek has a somewhat complicated set of pronouns that have different functions beyond a traditional English pronoun. The baseic use of a pronoun from Greek to English remains the same: it is a smaller word that stands in the place of noun. For example, "John ate pizza. *He* liked it," uses the pronoun "he." Readers know from context that the "he" is John, which is called the antecedent. In the same way, most Greek pronouns have an antecedent. It is not necessary to cover every pronoun in detail, as some are infrequent and others essentially act like adjectives. The pronouns will be discussed in order of importance and frequency, and some pronouns that do not occur regularly will only be discussed in the *Second Time Around* section. In the future, if you come across pronouns you are unfamiliar with, you can also take the time to read about them in Daniel Wallace's *Greek Grammar Beyond the Basics*.

6.3.1: How Pronouns are Formed

The great thing about pronouns (*and* the article *and* adjectives) is that they use the declension endings just like nouns do, so there are no new endings to become familiar with. Just like nouns and adjectives, the last letter on the stem determines the declension endings that are chosen. Like adjectives and the article, pronouns are also multi-gendered. In the following examples the case inflection is colored red, which changes on the pronoun depending on its case and number. Finally, remember that the case ending affects the translation of pronouns just like it does nouns: nominative pronouns are the subject, genitive pronouns indicate possession, etc.

6.3.2: Personal Pronouns

Personal pronouns occur the most frequently. The previous chapter on verbs taught how verbs have the subject built into them, i.e. person and number indicate the subject. When a verb is translated on its own, a personal pronoun is used in the translation (e.g., *I* loose, *you* loose, *they* loose). These pronouns are built into Greek verbs, but they also have a life of their own. As you come across personal pronouns in the Greek New Testament, notice that they are not always necessary. This is one case where the Greek seems inefficient. A personal pronoun may occur with a verb that already has the subject built in. Example:

- ἐγὼ βαπτίζω ἐν ὕδατι = I baptize in water   (verb is pres, act, ind, 1, sg)
- βαπτίζω ἐν ὕδατι = I baptize in water   (verb is pres, act, ind, 1, sg)

In the above examples the sentence is translated the same, as the verb has the subject built in, so the presence of the pronoun "I" (ἐγὼ) does not seem necessary.[110]

---

[110] At times the Greek authors may be emphasizing the subject when they use the pronoun.

6.3.2.1: 1ˢᵗ and 2ⁿᵈ Person Personal Pronoun

There is no gender in the 1ˢᵗ and 2ⁿᵈ person personal pronoun. In the singular forms of the 1ˢᵗ person, the epsilon is in parentheses as it does not always occur. Although these personal pronouns are inflected for case and number, they do not take a very recognizable pattern of inflection. The genitive and dative forms are similar to the noun declensions, but not the nominative and accusative.

Table 37: 1ˢᵗ Personal Pronoun

	singular		*plural*	
nominative	ἐγώ	*I*	ἡμεῖς	*we*
genitive	(ἐ)μοῦ	*my* or *of/from me*	ἡμῶν	*our* or *of/from us*
dative	(ἐ)μοί	*to/in me*	ἡμῖν	*to/in us*
accusative	(ἐ)μέ	*me*	ἡμᾶς	*us*

Table 38: 2ⁿᵈ Personal Pronoun

	singular		*plural*	
nominative	σύ	*you*	ὑμεῖς	*y'all*
genitive	σοῦ	*your* or *of/from you*	ὑμῶν	*your* or *of/from y'all*
dative	σοί	*to you*	ὑμῖν	*to y'all*
accusative	σέ	*you*	ὑμᾶς	*y'all*

6.3.2.2: 3ʳᵈ Person Personal Pronoun

The 3ʳᵈ person personal pronoun is fully inflected and multi-gendered like adjectives.

Table 39: 3ʳᵈ Personal Pronoun

	Masculine				**Feminine**				**Neuter**			
	sg.		*pl.*		*sg.*		*pl.*		*sg.*		*pl.*	
nom	αὐτός	he	αὐτοί	they	αὐτή	she	αὐταί	they	αὐτό	it	αὐτά	they
gen	αὐτοῦ	his	αὐτῶν	their	αὐτῆς	her	αὐτῶν	their	αὐτοῦ	its	αὐτῶν	their
dat	αὐτῷ	to him	αὐτοῖς	to them	αὐτῇ	to her	αὐταῖς	to them	αὐτῷ	to it	αὐτοῖς	to them
acc	αὐτόν	him	αὐτούς	them	αὐτήν	her	αὐτάς	them	αὐτό	it	αὐτά	them

6.3.3: Pronouns That Act Like Adjectives

6.3.3.1: Special Functions of the 3rd Person Personal Pronoun

The 3rd person personal pronoun can function like a regular pronoun (as per the translations given in Table 39 above) but can also function in an adjectival way. The word will look exactly the same as above, but an article may be involved in the construction. There are two different ways it can work:

- ADJECTIVAL INTENSIFICATION
    - τὸν αὐτὸν λόγον = the same word (Mark 14:39) or
      αὐτῇ τῇ ὥρᾳ = the same hour (Luke 10:21)
    - The pronoun is in full concord with the noun it is paired with.
    - The noun and pronoun may or may not have an article
- REFLEXIVE INTENSIFICATION
    - αὐτὴ ἡ κτίσις = the creation itself (Rom 8:21)
    - The pronoun is in full concord with the noun it is paired with but never has the article.
    - The pronoun is translated like a reflexive pronoun (himself, herself, itself, etc.)

6.3.3.2: Demonstrative Pronouns

Demonstrative pronouns function just like adjectives (refer to §6.2.2) and so are in full concord with the noun they are paired with. The one exception is that demonstrative pronouns never take an article. Like adjectives, the demonstrative will pair with a nearby noun in full concord. Far more frequent, however, is the demonstrative by itself acting substantivally (see §6.2.2.2). "This/these" are often referred to as the close or proximate demonstrative. "That/those" are often referred to as the far or remote demonstrative. Demonstrative pronouns use 2nd declension endings for masculine and neuter, and 1st declension for feminine. The following are some examples:

1. DEMONSTRATIVE PAIRED WITH A NOUN
    - Ἔχομεν δὲ τὸν θησαυρὸν τοῦτον ἐν ὀστρακίνοις σκεύεσιν
      But we have *this treasure* in clay jars (2 Cor 4:7)

- Ἐν δὲ ταῖς ἡμέραις ἐκείναις παραγίνεται Ἰωάννης ὁ βαπτιστὴς
  But in *those days* John the baptizer appeared (Matt 3:1)

2. DEMONSTRATIVE BY ITSELF

- οὗτός ἐστιν ὁ υἱός μου
  this is my son (Matt 3:17)

- ταῦτα δὲ αὐτοῦ ἐνθυμηθέντος
  But just when he had resolved to do *these things* (Matt 1:20)

Table 40: Demonstrative Pronouns

NEAR	Masculine		Feminine		Neuter	
	sg.	*pl.*	*sg.*	*pl.*	*sg.*	*pl.*
nominative "this/these"	οὗτος	οὗτοι	αὕτη	αὗται	τοῦτο	ταῦτα
genitive "of this/these"	τούτου	τούτων	ταύτης	τούτων	τούτου	τούτων
dative "to this/these"	τούτῳ	τούτοις	ταύτῃ	ταύταις	τούτῳ	τούτοις
accusative "this/these"	τοῦτον	τούτους	ταύτην	ταύτας	τοῦτο	ταῦτα

FAR	Masculine		Feminine		Neuter	
	sg.	*pl.*	*sg.*	*pl.*	*sg.*	*pl.*
nominative "that/those"	ἐκεῖνος	ἐκεῖνοι	ἐκείνη	ἐκεῖναι	ἐκεῖνο	ἐκεῖνα
genitive "of that/those"	ἐκείνου	ἐκείνων	ἐκείνης	ἐκείνων	ἐκείνου	ἐκείνων
dative "to that/those"	ἐκείνῳ	ἐκείνοις	ἐκείνῃ	ἐκείναις	ἐκείνῳ	ἐκείνοις
accusative "that/those"	ἐκεῖνον	ἐκείνους	ἐκείνην	ἐκείνας	ἐκεῖνο	ἐκεῖνα

Notice that the near demonstrative is like the article, with the masculine and feminine nominative singular having rough breathing and no tau, but the rest do.

6.3.3.3: Correlative and Possessive Pronouns

Correlative pronouns and possessive pronouns also act just like adjectives, but occur infrequently. As you come across them, you can take time to read about them in the *Second Time Around* section. You can also read Wallace's *Greek Grammar Beyond the Basics*.

6.3.4: *Pronouns That Introduce a Dependent Clause*

Clauses will be introduced in the next chapter but for now the important thing to know is that clauses are units of words centered around a verb. In English we separate clauses by periods, commas, semicolons, colons, etc. If you take a minute to look at your Greek New Testament in bible software or paperback, you will notice that there is punctuation. This punctuation is not original to the text, but modern editors know where to put the punctuation because of the way Greek grammar works. One such example are the following two types of pronouns; they introduce clauses and thus the editors knew to place punctuation immediately prior to these pronouns. These pronouns are unique, then, in that they are both a pronoun AND they work like a conjunction between clauses.

6.3.4.1: Relative Pronouns

A relative pronoun will be translated as "who," "whom," "which," or "that" depending on context. It is a pronoun that agrees with its antecedent in gender and number and it introduces a dependent clause. The relative pronoun is the subject or the object of the new clause it introduces. Relative pronouns are fairly easy to recognize because they look just like the declension endings with rough breathings. Relative pronouns use 2nd declension for masculine and neuter, and 1st declension for feminine. The following are some examples:

1. αὕτη ἐστὶν ἡ ἀγγελία ἣν ἠκούσατε ἀπ' ἀρχῆς (1Jn 3:11)
   this is the message which you heard from the beginning.
2. ἐπίστευσαν τῇ γραφῇ καὶ τῷ λόγῳ ὃν εἶπεν ὁ Ἰησοῦς (John 2:22)
   they believed in the scripture and in the word that Jesus spoke.

Table 41: Relative Pronouns

who, whom, which, that	Masculine		Feminine		Neuter	
	sg.	pl.	sg.	pl.	sg.	pl.
nominative	ὅς	οἵ	ἥ	αἵ	ὅ	ἅ
genitive	οὗ	ὧν	ἧς	ὧν	οὗ	ὧν
dative	ᾧ	οἷς	ᾗ	αἷς	ᾧ	οἷς
accusative	ὅν	οὕς	ἥν	ἅς	ὅ	ἅ

Another frequent use of a relative pronoun is with ἄν following it. ἄν is often an untranslated word, but when it follows a relative pronoun it adds "-ever" to the pronoun. So ὅς ἄν would be translated as "whoever" or "whatever."

6.3.4.2: Indefinite Relative Pronouns

Indefinite relative pronouns occur infrequently. They are translated like the relative pronoun followed by ἄν and function in the same way that relative pronouns do. As you come across them, you can take time to read about them in the **Second Time Around** section. You can also read Wallace's *Greek Grammar Beyond the Basics*.

6.3.5: Pronouns That Ask a Question

Like the relative pronouns above, three types of pronouns sit at the front of a clause that is asking a question.

6.3.5.1: Interrogative Pronouns

Interrogative pronouns ask "who?" "which?" "what?" or "why?" The context determines the best English translation. An accusative interrogative often ends up being translated like the subject. These pronouns use 3rd declension endings, and are interesting because they are identical to the indefinite pronoun (§6.3.6.1) except that the indefinite does NOT have an accent. The stem of the interrogative pronoun is τιν-, which classifies it as 3rd declension (remind yourself of the changes to the final consonant of 3rd declension word §2.7.3).

1. Τίς [δέ] ἐστιν ὁ νικῶν τὸν κόσμον εἰ μὴ ὁ πιστεύων ὅτι Ἰησοῦς ἐστιν ὁ υἱὸς τοῦ θεοῦ; (1Jn 5:5)

Who is it that conquers the world but the one who believes that Jesus is the Son of God?

- Notice how the sentence ends with a Greek question mark.

Table 42: Interrogative Pronouns

"who? which? what? why?"	Masculine		Feminine		Neuter	
	sg.	pl.	sg.	pl.	sg.	pl.
nominative	τίς	τίνες	τίς	τίνες	τί	τίνα
genitive	τίνος	τίνων	τίνος	τίνων	τίνος	τίνων
dative	τίνι	τίσι(ν)	τίνι	τίσι(ν)	τίνι	τίσι(ν)
accusative	τίνα	τίνας	τίνα	τίνας	τί	τίνα

6.3.5.2: Qualitative and Quantitative Interrogative Pronouns

The qualitative (which? what?) and quantitative (how much? how many?) interrogative pronouns also ask questions, but occur infrequently. As you come across them, you can take time to read about them in the **Second Time Around** section. You can also read Wallace's *Greek Grammar Beyond the Basics*.

6.3.6: More Pronouns Acting Like Pronouns

The remaining pronoun types stand on their own (i.e. not paired with a noun) and are translated in the same way as personal pronouns.

6.3.6.1: Indefinite Pronouns

Indefinite pronouns make inexact reference and do not have an antecedent. They are usually translated as "any(one)," "some(one)," "a certain one," etc. The stem of the interrogative pronoun is τιν-, which classifies it as 3rd declension (remind yourself of the changes to the final consonant of 3rd declension word §2.7.3). Indefinite pronouns are identical to interrogative pronouns with the exception of the accent position.

1. ἐάν τις εἴπῃ ὅτι ἀγαπῶ τὸν θεὸν... (1Jn 4:20)
   If anyone says "I love God"...

Table 43: Indefinite Pronouns

someone, something, a certain one/person	Masculine		Feminine		Neuter	
	sg.	*pl.*	*sg.*	*pl.*	*sg.*	*pl.*
nominative	τις	τινές	τις	τινές	τι	τινά
genitive	τινός	τινῶν	τινός	τινῶν	τινός	τινῶν
dative	τινί	τισί(ν)	τινί	τισί(ν)	τινί	τισί(ν)
accusative	τινά	τινάς	τινά	τινάς	τι	τινά

6.3.6.2: Reflexive, Reciprocal, and Negative Pronouns

Reflexive pronouns ("myself," "yourself," "himself," etc.), reciprocal pronouns ("one another"), and negative pronouns ("no one" or "nothing") occur infrequently. As you come across them, you can take time to read about them in the **Second Time Around** section. You can also read Wallace's *Greek Grammar Beyond the Basics*.

6.4: Numbers

As in English, Greek numbers do not occur with great frequency in prose, but happen often enough that a reader needs to be familiar with some high frequency numbers.

6.4.1: Cardinals

Cardinal numbers are normal counting numbers (1, 2, 3 or one, two, three). Only the numbers 1, 2, 3, 7, 12 occur in high frequency. Only numbers 1-4 are declined, and occur in all genders just like adjectives. All remaining cardinals are not declined. The number 1 is always and only singular, while 2-4 are always and only plural. All of them follow 3rd declension, except for 3 which follows 1st declension for feminine, though like other 3rd declension words, they do not always follow a neat and tidy pattern.

Table 44: Declined Cardinal Numbers

	Masculine				Feminine				Neuter			
	sing	*plural*			*sing*	*plural*			*sing*	*plural*		
	"1"	"2"	"3"	"4"	"1"	"2"	"3"	"4"	"1"	"2"	"3"	"4"
nom	εἷς	δύο	τρεῖς	τέσσαρες	μία	δύο	τρεῖς	τέσσαρες	ἕν	δύο	τρία	τέσσαρα
gen	ἑνός	δύο	τριῶν	τεσσάρων	μιᾶς	δύο	τριῶν	τεσσάρων	ἑνός	δύο	τριῶν	τεσσάρων
dat	ἑνί	δυσί	τρισί	τέσσαρσι	μιᾷ	δυσί	τρισί	τέσσαρσι	ἑνί	δυσί	τρισί	τέσσαρσι
acc	ἕνα	δύο	τρεῖς	τέσσαρας	μίαν	δύο	τρεῖς	τέσσαρας	ἕν	δύο	τρία	τέσσαρα

The higher cardinal numbers do not occur in high frequency, but it is good to understand how Greek formulates numbers.

- 10 is its own word, δέκα. To make a teen number, the number ten is added to the numbers 1–9. So for example δεκατέσσαρες is 14 (δέκα=10 and τέσσαρες=4).
- 20 is its own word (εἴκοσι).
    - A suffix which means "x 10" is -κοντα. So for example τεσσεράκοντα is 40 (τέσσαρες=4 and -κοντα= x10).
- 100 is its own word (ἑκατόν).
    - A suffix which means "x 100" is -κοσιοι. So for example πεντακόσιοι is 500 (πέντε=5 and -κοντα= x10).
- 1,000 is its own word (χίλιοι).
    - A suffix which means "x 1,000" is -χιλιοι. So for example πεντακισχίλιοι is 5,000 (πέντε=5 and -χιλιοι= x1,000).
- There is also a word for 10,000 (μύριοι) and for an innumerable number (μυριάδες).

All of the numbers in-between these are strung together. Here is an example from the end of the Gospel of John: "Simon Peter went aboard and hauled the net ashore, full of large fish, ἑκατὸν πεντήκοντα τριῶν of them" (John 21:11). From the information above you should be able to determine that the number is 153.

6.4.2: Ordinals

Ordinal numbers are the ordering numbers (first, second, third). Only the word "first" occurs in high frequency. Ordinals both function and are declined just like adjectives.

Table 45: Ordinal number "First"

	Masculine		Feminine		Neuter	
	sg.	pl.	sg.	pl.	sg.	pl.
nominative	πρῶτος	πρῶτοι	πρώτη	πρῶται	πρῶτον	πρῶτα
genitive	πρώτου	πρώτων	πρώτης	πρώτων	πρώτου	πρώτων
dative	πρώτῳ	πρώτοις	πρώτῃ	πρώταις	πρώτῳ	πρώτοις
accusative	πρῶτον	πρώτους	πρώτην	πρώτας	πρῶτον	πρῶτα

In translation, "first" may not always be the best choice. An ordinal may also be used to mean "prominent," "former," "earlier," or even "above all else."

6.5: The Least You Need to Know

You should be able to clearly and accurately answer these questions. Use these online flashcards (http://quizlet.com/_7tfxi) to memorize the answers:

- What endings does the Article take?
- What two things can the Article do when it is all by itself?
- What does it mean for an adjective to be in concord with a noun?
- What is an attributive adjective?
- What is a substantival adjective?
- What is a predicate adjective?
- What is the **AAA rule**?
- What is the **A(A)noN rule**?
- What is the **noA noV rule**?
- What are the special functions of the 3rd person personal pronouns? How do you know when the special functions have kicked in?
- What are demonstrative pronouns? How do they function?

- What do relative pronouns do?
- What do interrogative pronouns do?
- What do interrogative pronouns look just like? How do you tell them apart?
- What are cardinal numbers?
- Which cardinal numbers are declined?
- How are teen numbers formed?
- How are multiples of 10 formed?
- How are multiples of 100 formed?
- How are multiples of 1,000 formed?
- What are ordinals? How do they work?

6.6: Greek@Logos

Utilizing the ***Mastering Logos Bible Software*** course or the Logos help files, Logos forums, Logos wiki, and videos provided, users should take the time to learn:

- Basic Search
    - See Lecture 31 of ***Mastering Logos Bible Software***
    - Alternative: http://youtu.be/LAxK0ECzo4g
- Bible Search
    - See Lecture 30 of ***Mastering Logos Bible Software***
    - Alternative: http://youtu.be/uKs5cZDum0Q
- Clause Search
    - See Lecture 33 of ***Mastering Logos Bible Software***
    - Alternative: http://youtu.be/W4Cg8VM_MPY

6.7: Vocabulary

Word	Meaning	Type	Freq.	Derivatives
ἅγιος, -α, -ον	holy; pl. saints	adj.	233	*hagio*graphy
εἷς, μία, ἕν	one	adj.	345	
μέγας, -η, -α	large, great	adj.	243	*mega*phone

οὐδείς, οὐδεμία, οὐδέν	no one; nothing	adj.	234	
πᾶς, πᾶσα, πᾶν	every, each; [pl.] all	adj.	1243	*pan*oramic
πολύς, πολλή, πολύ	much, [pl.] many; (adv.) often	adj.	416	*poly*theism
αὐτός, αὐτή, τουτό	he, she, it (-self, same); pl. they	pron.	5597	*auto*matic
ἑαυτοῦ, -ῆς, -οῦ	himself/herself/itself; our-your-themselves	pron.	319	
ἐγώ (pl. ἡμεῖς)	I; we	pron.	2666	*ego*
ἐκεῖνος, -η, -ο	that, [pl.] those	pron.	265	
ὅς, ἥ, ὅ	who, which, what	pron.	1398	
οὗτος, αὕτη, τοῦτο	this (one); pl. these	pron.	1387	*taut*ology
σύ (pl. ὑμεῖς)	you (sg.); y'all (pl.)	pron.	2907	
τίς, τί	who? which? what? why?	pron.	556	
τις, τι	someone, anyone; something, certain one	pron.	525	

6.8: The Second Time Around

As you recognize, adjectives and pronouns use case endings, so if you have those down you do not need to focus heavily on memorization in this chapter. Instead, focus heavily on what adjectives can do (§6.2.2) and the special functions of the 3rd person personal pronoun (§6.3.3.1).

Greek has numerous types of pronouns, and not all of them are particularly frequent. Through the chapter, several pronoun types were mentioned but not shown. The following tables cover the pronouns that were not shown through the chapter.

The Article, Adjectives, Pronouns, and Numbers

Table 46: Correlative Pronouns

	"such"	"so much /great"	Masculine		Feminine		Neuter	
			sg.	*pl.*	*sg.*	*pl.*	*sg.*	*pl.*
nom.	τοι-	τοσ-	-οὗτος	-οὗτοι	-αὐτη	-αὗται	-τοῦτο	-ταῦτα
gen.	τοι-	τοσ-	-τούτου	-τούτων	-ταύτης	-τούτων	-τούτου	-τούτων
dat.	τοι-	τοσ-	-τούτῳ	-τούτοις	-ταύτῃ	-ταύταις	-τούτῳ	-τούτοις
acc.	τοι-	τοσ-	-τοῦτον	-τούτους	-ταύτην	-ταύτας	-τοῦτο	-ταῦτα

"such as"	Masculine		Feminine		Neuter	
	sg.	*pl.*	*sg.*	*pl.*	*sg.*	*pl.*
nominative	οἷος	οἷοι	οἵα	οἷαι	οἷον	οἷα
genitive	οἵου	οἵων	οἵας	οἵων	οἵου	οἵων
dative	οἵῳ	οἵοις	οἵᾳ	οἵαις	οἵῳ	οἵοις
accusative	οἷον	οἵους	οἵαν	οἵας	οἷον	οἷα

"as many as"	Masculine		Feminine		Neuter	
	sg.	*pl.*	*sg.*	*pl.*	*sg.*	*pl.*
nominative	ὅσος	ὅσοι	ὅση	ὅσαι	ὅσον	ὅσα
genitive	ὅσου	ὅσων	ὅσης	ὅσων	ὅσου	ὅσων
dative	ὅσῳ	ὅσοις	ὅσῃ	ὅσαις	ὅσῳ	ὅσοις
accusative	ὅσον	ὅσους	ὅσην	ὅσας	ὅσον	ὅσα

Table 47: Possessive Pronouns

		Masculine		Feminine		Neuter	
		Singular	*Plural*	*Singular*	*Plural*	*Singular*	*Plural*
1 sg "my"	nom.	ἐμός	ἐμοί	ἐμή	ἐμαί	ἐμόν	ἐμά
	gen.	ἐμοῦ	ἐμῶν	ἐμῆς	ἐμῶν	ἐμοῦ	ἐμῶν
	dat.	ἐμῷ	ἐμοῖς	ἐμῇ	ἐμαῖς	ἐμῷ	ἐμοῖς
	acc.	ἐμόν	ἐμούς	ἐμήν	ἐμάς	ἐμόν	ἐμά
1 pl "our"	nom.	ἡμέτερος	ἡμέτεροι	ἡμέτερα	ἡμέτεραι	ἡμέτερον	ἡμέτερα
	gen.	ἡμετέρου	ἡμετέρων	ἡμέτερας	ἡμέτερων	ἡμέτερου	ἡμέτερων
	dat.	ἡμετέρῳ	ἡμέτεροις	ἡμέτερα	ἡμέτεραις	ἡμέτερῳ	ἡμέτεροις
	acc.	ἡμέτερον	ἡμέτερους	ἡμέτεραν	ἡμέτερας	ἡμέτερον	ἡμέτερα
2 sg "your"	nom.	σός	σοί	σή	σαί	σόν	σά
	gen.	σοῦ	σῶν	σῆς	σῶν	σοῦ	σῶν
	dat.	σῷ	σοῖς	σῇ	σαῖς	σῷ	σοῖς
	acc.	σόν	σούς	σήν	σάς	σόν	σά
2 pl "your"	nom.	ὑμέτερος	ὑμέτεροι	ὑμέτερα	ὑμέτεραι	ὑμέτερον	ὑμέτερα
	gen.	ὑμετέρου	ὑμέτερων	ὑμέτερας	ὑμέτερων	ὑμέτερου	ὑμέτερων
	dat.	ὑμετέρῳ	ὑμέτεροις	ὑμέτερα	ὑμέτεραις	ὑμέτερῳ	ὑμέτεροις
	acc.	ὑμέτερον	ὑμέτερους	ὑμέτεραν	ὑμέτερας	ὑμέτερον	ὑμέτερα
3 "his/her/its their"	nom.	ἴδιος	ἴδιοι	ἴδια	ἴδιαι	ἴδιον	ἴδια
	gen.	ἰδίου	ἴδιων	ἴδιας	ἴδιων	ἴδιου	ἴδιων
	dat.	ἴδιῳ	ἴδιοις	ἴδια	ἴδιαις	ἴδιῳ	ἴδιοις
	acc.	ἴδιον	ἴδιους	ἴδιαν	ἴδιας	ἴδιον	ἴδια

Table 48: Indefinite Relative Pronouns

The Indefinite Relative is exactly as it sounds—the indefinite pronoun and the relative pronoun are put together. So a dative singular feminine form would take the dative singular feminine form of the indefinite and the relative and puts them together. The following table shows just the nominatives.

MASCULINE		NEUTER		FEMININE	
singular	*plural*	*singular*	*plural*	*singular*	*plural*
ὅστις	οἵτινες	ὅτι	ἅτινα	ἥτις	αἵτινες

Table 49: Qualitative and Quantitative Pronouns

QUALITATIVE	**Masculine**		**Feminine**		**Neuter**	
"what type?"	sg.	pl.	sg.	pl.	sg.	pl.
nominative	ποῖος	ποῖοι	ποῖα	ποῖαι	ποῖον	ποῖα
genitive	ποίου	ποίων	ποίας	ποίων	ποίου	ποίων
dative	ποίῳ	ποίοις	ποίᾳ	ποίαις	ποίῳ	ποίοις
accusative	ποῖον	ποίους	ποῖαν	ποίας	ποῖον	ποῖα

QUANTITATIVE	**Masculine**		**Feminine**		**Neuter**	
"how much?"	sg.	pl.	sg.	pl.	sg.	pl.
nominative	πόσος	πόσοι	πόση	πόσαι	πόσον	πόσα
genitive	πόσου	πόσων	πόσης	πόσων	πόσου	πόσων
dative	πόσῳ	πόσοις	πόσῃ	πόσαις	πόσῳ	πόσοις
accusative	πόσον	πόσους	πόσην	πόσας	πόσον	πόσα

Table 50: Reflexive Pronouns

	Singular			**Plural**		
MASCULINE	*1* "myself"	*2* "yourself"	*3* "himself"	*1* "ourselves"	*2* "yourselves"	*3* "themselves"
genitive	ἐμαυτοῦ	σεαυτοῦ	ἑαυτοῦ	ἑαυτῶν	ἑαυτῶν	ἑαυτῶν
dative	ἐμαυτῷ	σεαυτῷ	ἑαυτῷ	ἑαυτοῖς	ἑαυτοῖς	ἑαυτοῖς
accusative	ἐμαυτόν	σεαυτόν	ἑαυτόν	ἑαυτούς	ἑαυτούς	ἑαυτούς

NEUTER	Singular			Plural		
	1	*2*	*3*	*1*	*2*	*3*
genitive	--	--	ἑαυτοῦ	ἑαυτῶν	ἑαυτῶν	ἑαυτῶν
dative	--	--	ἑαυτῷ	ἑαυτοῖς	ἑαυτοῖς	ἑαυτοῖς
accusative	--	--	ἑαυτόν	ἑαυτούς	ἑαυτούς	ἑαυτούς

FEMININE	Singular			Plural		
	1	*2*	*3*	*1*	*2*	*3*
genitive	ἐμαυτῆς	σεαυτῆς	ἑαυτ-ῆς	ἑαυτῶν	ἑαυτῶν	ἑαυτῶν
dative	ἐμαυτῇ	σεαυτῇ	ἑαυτῇ	ἑαυταῖς	ἑαυταῖς	ἑαυταῖς
accusative	ἐμαυτήν	σεαυτήν	ἑαυτήν	ἑαυτάς	ἑαυτάς	ἑαυτάς

Table 51: Reciprocal Pronouns

Only three forms of the reciprocal pronoun exist in the NT.

- ἀλλήλων = of one another
- ἀλλήλοις = to one another
- ἀλλήλους = one another

Table 52: Negative Pronouns

singular	MASCULINE "no one"	FEMININE "no one"	NEUTER "nothing"
nominative	οὐδείς	οὐδεμία	οὐδέν
genitive	οὐδενός	οὐδεμιᾶς	οὐδενός
dative	οὐδενί	οὐδεμιᾷ	οὐδενί
accusative	οὐδένα	οὐδεμίαν	οὐδέν

Chapter 7:
Adverbs, Prepositions, Phrases, and Clauses

⇒**What's the Point:** Phrases and clauses are groups of words that work together to say something. Take a minute to look at your Greek New Testamnet. Every word in the Greek New Testament is in a phrase or a clause that is marked by punctuation like periods, commas, semi-colons etc. This punctuation was not original to the text but was inserted by editors. While we can trust for the most part the editors of our modern Greek New Testament who added the punctuation, it is because of their knowledge of Greek clauses that they knew where to place those marks in the first place. Understanding how these units are introduced and what they do in larger paragraphs helps you to better understand Greek structure.

7.1: Adverbs

Adverbs are the last of the primary parts of speech to cover in Greek (the others being nouns, verbs, and adjectives). Recall from grade school days that adverbs give more information about the verb and answer the questions *when?, where?, why?*, and *how?*. Adverbs are simple to master in Greek because there are only a dozen or so that occur in high frequency and adverbs are not declined (yippee!).

About the only thing that adverbs do differently in Greek is that they can on occasion take an article. When this occurs, the adverb is changed into a substantive. So for example, the adverb κακῶς means "badly." But when κακῶς has the article it comes to mean "the one(s) feeling badly," or more neatly translated as "the sick." Here is a NT example: "his fame spread throughout all Syria, and they brought to him all τοὺς κακῶς" (Matt 4:24).

7.2: Prepositions

Prepositions are little words that never work alone in English and Greek. You have already been briefly introduced to prepositions that attach themselves to verbs to create compound verbs (§5.2.3). When prepositions occur they will always work with at least one noun (or substantive), but often even more than that. For instance, the noun may have an article, or the noun may also have a genitive following it. This group of words, introduced by a preposition, is called a prepositional phrase.[111] Remember too that the prepositional phrase may be introduced with an article to help the reader to know what the phrase is talking about (see §6.1.2.3 to remind yourself about this). Although prepositions are small words, they can be slippery like eels. A preposition can be translated with numerous different English words depending on their context. In this *Stripped Down* approach you do not need to worry about deciding how best to translate a preposition, but know that there are numerous options based on context that you will come across as you work with the Greek New Testament and your preferred English translation.[112]

The most immediate factor for determining a preposition's function and translation is the case of the noun it is attached to (remember that a preposition is always followed by a noun/substantive). Some prepositions are snobs. which means they will only work with one case. Others are a little more friendly, they will work with two cases. Finally, there are three prepositions that are extroverts, because they work with genitive, dative, or accusative (prepositions never work with nominatives). See the following examples, which have the same preposition but the nouns following it are different cases, resulting in different translations of the preposition:

- ἐξεπλήσσοντο ἐπὶ τῇ διδαχῇ αὐτοῦ
  They were astounded by his teaching (Mark 1:22)
- ὁ Παῦλος ἑστὼς ἐπὶ τῶν ἀναβαθμῶν ...
  Paul stood on the steps ... (Acts 21:40)
- Ἰδοὺ ἕστηκα ἐπὶ τὴν θύραν
  Behold I stand at the door (Rev 3:20)

As you can see, ἐπί is followed by a dative in the first instance, a genitive in the second, and an accusative in the third. The translation of the preposition may often employ a standard Englsh translation for each case, but may vary and really depends on the relationship between the phrase and the word it is modifying.

---

[111] You will learn more about what a phrase is in §7.4.1.
[112] The spatial translations of the prepositions are often the easiest to learn. See table 55 for the translation.

7.2.1: Preposition Forms

Prepositions are not declined so they are easy to spot. However, prepositions may change slightly depending on whether the following word starts with a vowel or if the next word begins with a rough breathing. A coronis replaces the vowel on the end of the preposition, and before a rough breathing prepositions that have a stop consonant will change to a rough stop (§1.3.2).

Table 53: Preposition Forms

	when followed by a word beginning with a vowel	*when followed by a word beginning with rough breathing*
ἀνά	ἀν'	ἀν'
ἀντί	ἀντ'	ἀνθ'
ἀπό	ἀπ'	ἀφ'
διά	δι'	δι'
ἐκ	ἐξ	ἐξ
ἐπί	ἐπ'	ἐφ'
κατά	κατ'	καθ'
μετά	μετ'	μεθ'
παρά	παρ'	παρ'
ὑπό	ὑπ'	ὑφ'

7.2.2: Preposition Functions

As you work with NT Greek and use grammars, lexicons, and commentaries, you often come across descriptions of how prepositions work (terms like ablative, locative, instrumental, means, agency, etc. often come up). Look at the following English examples of the preposition "by:"

- I stayed in a cabin by the lake.
- I made the dog happy by feeding it.
- The door was opened by my daughter.

The preposition is the same, yet it is giving you different types of information in every sentence. The first example of "by" is giving you location information (called *loca-*

tive function), the second is telling you the means by which something happened (called *instrumental* function), and the third one is giving information on who did the action (called *agency* function). It is not important to memorize these functions right now, but do not discount or dismiss these little words as you interpret the NT, because they can have such a range of function and ranslation. See for example the basic uses of ἐπί from Wallace's *Greek Grammar Beyond the Basics*:

1. With Genitive
    a. Spatial: *on, upon, at, near*
    b. Temporal: *in the time of, during*
    c. Cause: *on the basis of*
2. With Dative
    a. Spatial: *on, upon, against, at, near*
    b. Temporal: *at, at the time of, during*
    c. Cause: *on the basis of*
3. With Accusative
    a. Spatial: *on, upon, to, up to, against*
    b. Temporal: *for, over a period of*

As you can see from this list, a preposition has numerous translation options, and can function in numerous ways. As you come across prepositions in your work with the NT, you may need to dig deeper into them and use a lexicon and a grammar to better understand the function of a preposition. (Lest you want to curse the person who created Greek prepositions, English prepositions are just as complex!)

In previous chapters you have learned some of the different functions of the noun case endings. It is important to know that when a noun is in a prepositional phrase, you no longer ask the question "what is the case of the noun doing?" The question instead becomes, "what is the prepositional phrase doing?" Reading about the preposition in a lexicon or grammar will help you answer this and other questions.

7.3: More Little Words

This last set of word types almost completes your introduction to the types of words in Greek (participles and infinitives each receive their own chapter). These little words are simple in that they are not inflected, and they do not pair themselves with other words as do adjectives or prepositions.

7.3.1: Conjunctions

Conjunctions connect things together in both Greek and English. The highest frequency conjunctions are included in the vocabulary sections. The following is a list of some of the main functions of conjunctions:

1. INTRODUCERS: Some conjunctions may introduce a sentence (they will come after a period or colon in your Greek NT). Conjunctions like οὖν (therefore) and γάρ (for) frequently—but not always—introduce a new sentence. These two conjunctions, as well as δέ, always occur as the second (or later) word in their clause.[113]

2. INTRODUCE A DEPENDENT CLAUSE: Many conjunctions introduce a dependent clause (which you are about to learn about in §7.4.2.2): ἵνα, ἐάν, ὅταν, ὅτε, and a few others fall into this function. These conjunctions are good to know as you come to work with and recognize Greek clauses.

3. CONNECT INDEPENDENT CLAUSES TOGETHER: Several high frequency conjunctions can at times connect two independent clauses (which you are about to learn about in §7.4.2.1). καί, δέ, and ἀλλά are the ones that can function this way.

4. CONNECT EQUALS: καί is one of the most frequent words in Greek and can do several things. καί is often a "teeter-totter" conjunction, in that it connects things of equal grammatical weight. It may connect verbs together,[114] nouns together, or clauses together. If you recall from when you first learned καί as vocabulary, it can mean "also" as well. When translated as "also," καί is an adverb, not a conjunction.

---

[113]These are called post-positive conjunctions and frequently come between an article and its noun.

[114]As you will learn in §7.4.2, a clause has only one verb. An exception is when a καί directly connects two verbs together. In these cases, the two verbs are acting as one in the clause.

7.3.2: Interjections

Interjections inject emotion into a sentence. They are small words that are not paired with any other words in the sentence. English, too, has interjections like "wow" or "hey." The most frequent interjection in Greek is ἰδού, which means "look!" or "pay attention!" Oftentimes interjections are left untranslated in English, but they add an element of emotion into the Greek NT.

7.3.3: Particles

Particle is a tricky word that is used in different ways, but for the sake of being thorough, it is introduced here. Oftentimes particle simply means "little word," and so conjunctions and interjections are often considered particles. In other cases, particles are simply words that do not fall into any other category. Some Greek particles function as word–group markers, and are often left untranslated as well.

7.4: Word Groups

You have now been introduced to all but two types of words in Greek (participles and infinitives; both will receive their own chapter). Now that we've talked about individual words, let's discuss how groups of words work together. The following discussion applies to both English and Greek.

In English and Greek, the primary parts of speech are 1) nouns, 2) verbs, 3) adjectives, and 4) adverbs. The primary parts (excluding verbs) are generally thought of as one word, but a group of words can also function like a noun, adjective, or adverb and other types of words can also function in these positions. For instance, recall from Chapter 6 that an article, an adjective, and a pronoun can all act like a noun (substantive).

The prepositions section introduced the concept of a "prepositional phrase." Notice how the following examples of prepositional phrases (word groups) function in the sentence:

1. AS A NOUN: "In the house was very hot." The phrase is acting as the subject in the sentence.
2. AS AN ADJECTIVE: "I saw the child with his mother." The phrase is acting like an adjective, telling us more about the child.

3. AS AN ADVERB: "I hit the ball with a wooden bat." The phrase is acting like an adverb, telling us the "how" of the verb

The following table breaks down how word groups work. The remainder of this chapter will be a commentary on this table.

Table 54: Greek Word Groups

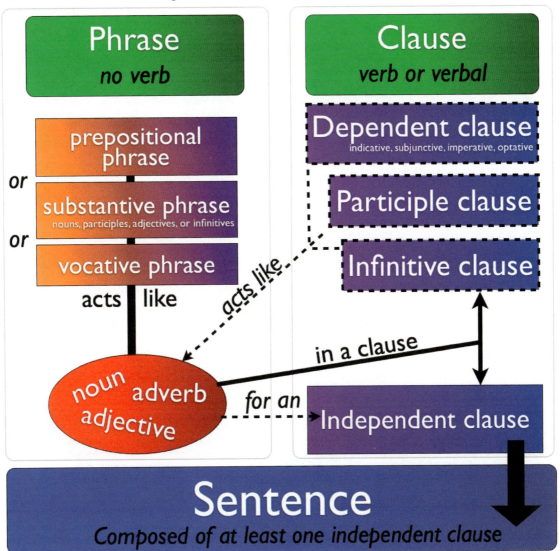

7.4.1: Phrases

Phrases, then, may be a single word or group of words that act like a noun, an adjective, or an adverb in a sentence. A phrase does not contain a regular verb,[115] so a phrase cannot be a clause all on its own. You have been shown above how a phrase can function as a noun, an adjective, or an adverb, which means that this word or group of words works together to function as a unit that have a function *within a clause (follow the solid arrow in the table above)*.

7.4.2: Clauses

A clause is a group of grammatically related words that has both a subject and verb. A clause can be as simple as just a subject and verb ("I yelled"), which can be only one word in Greek, or a more complex group of words with subject, verb, object, and indirect object ("Joe yelled commands to the soldiers"). The rest of the parts of the clause are expansions of the verb or the subject. *A clause has ONE verb*,[116] the main verb, around which the entire clause is centered.

7.4.2.1: Independent Clauses

There are two types of clauses. The first is an independent clause. An independent clause stands independently, so it needs no help from anyone. A sentence has at least one independent clause; if you do not have an independent clause, you don't have a sentence either. A sentence can have more than one independent clause, but, if too many independent clauses are connected together, run-on sentences begin to appear!

7.4.2.2: Dependent, Participle, and Infinitive Clauses

A dependent clause is a bit harder to understand as it possesses the qualities of a clause, but functions like a phrase. As a clause it has its own subject and verb, but it *is not* the main thought of a sentence. It is **dependent** on an independent clause for its existence; therefore, it can never exist on its own. Often times a complex sentence will have one independent clause and several dependent clauses that are all tied to the central independent clause.

---

[115] Participles and infinitives, as you will learn, are verbal forms, but not true verbs.
[116] See footnote 114 for the exception to this rule.

Dependent clauses are like phrases, though, in that they are a word group that together functions like a noun, adjective, or adverb to the independent clause (follow the dotted arrows in the table above). Like a phrase, they cannot live on their own, but depend on an independent clause for their existence. In the following examples, **the main verbs are bold blue**, the independent clauses are highlighted yellow, the dependent clauses are highlighted green, and *phrases are in italics*.

- We **declare** to you what **was** *from the beginning*, what we have **heard**, what we have **seen** *with our eyes*, what we have **looked** at and **touched** *with our hands* (1 John 1:1).
    - Notice how each clause has one verb
    - Notice how each dependent clause is telling you what is being "declared" in the independent clause. Each dependent clause is functioning as a noun; therefore, they are the objects of the main verb.
    - Each of the phrases in their respective clause are functioning like an adverb—the object of the verb they are with.
    - Although the independent clause comes first in the sentence *this is not always the case*.
- If we **say** that we **have** fellowship with him while we are **walking** *in darkness*, we **lie** and do not **do** what **is** true (1 John 1:6).
    - Notice how each clause has one verb.
    - Remember, a sentence (like this) can have more than one independent clause.
    - The first dependent clause and the last dependent clause are functioning as nouns—specifically the object for their respective independent clause.
    - The second dependent clause is answering the question of why?, so it is acting like an adverb of "say."

7.4.2.3: Dependent Clause Introducers

You have already been introduced to relative pronouns (§6.3.4.1), which are one of the main independent clause introducers. When you see a relative pronoun it is *always the first word in a dependent clause*. There are various other Greek words that often (not always) introduce dependent clauses—the equivalent English words do the same thing as well.

- ὅς, ἥ, ὅ: who, which, that
- ἵνα: that, in order that
- ὅπως: how, that
- ὅταν: when(ever)
- ἕως: until, while
- ἄχρι: until, as far as
- ἐάν: if

7.5: Syntax and Bible Software

By now you know how to search for specific forms of words and that Bible software can quickly provide you with the parsing information of Greek words.

Some Bible software programs go a step further by also providing syntactical information. So, for instance, you can search for a noun acting like an object (rather than just an accusative noun). The syntax information helps you to see the flow of the scriptural text. For Accordance users, the *Grammatical Syntax add-on to GNT* is the module with this information. With this module, you can view the syntactical diagrams, as well as search for syntactical information. BibleWorks does not allow for syntactical searching, but does provide diagrams for the Greek New Testament. Logos Bible Software also provides a number of syntax resources. One in particular is called the OpenText syntax resource (opentext.org), which is available for free online. The other main Logos resource is called the *Lexham Syntactic Greek New Testament*. When and if the time comes that you want to work more with the syntax of the NT, be sure to read about the resource of your choosing, as they often use their own nomenclature.

7.6: The Least You Need to Know

You should be able to clearly and accurately answer these questions. Use these online flashcards (http://quizlet.com/_7tfxu) to memorize the answers:

- What is an adverb?
- How are Greek adverbs declined?

- What is a preposition?
- What changes may occur to a preposition and why?
- How do Greek prepositions work?
- What noun cases are prepositions coupled with?
- What is a conjunction?
- What type of conjunctions are there?
- What are interjections?
- What is a phrase and what does a phrase do?
- What types of phrases are there?
- What is an independent clause?
- What is a dependent clause and what does it do?
- What composes a sentence?
- What words can introduce dependent clauses?

7.7: Greek@Logos

Utilizing the *Mastering Logos Bible Software* course or the Logos help files, Logos forums, Logos wiki, and videos provided, users should take the time to learn:
- Lexham clausal outlines and Lexham Syntactic Greek New Testament
    - See Lecture 13 of *Mastering Logos Bible Software*

These resources are included in your *Original Languages* pack. Open it alongside your Greek New Testament in a link group and explore how it displays verses.

7.8: Vocabulary

Word	Meaning	Type	Freq.	Derivatives
Ἰουδαῖος, -α, -ον	Jewish, Judean	adj.	195	
νῦν	now (adv.); the present (noun)	adv.	147	
τότε	then	adv.	160	

ἕως	(conj.) until [+gen] as far as	conj. prep.	146	
καθώς	as, even as, just as	conj.	182	
οὐδέ	and not, not even, neither, nor	conj.	143	
ἰδού	look!, Behold!	interj.	200	
ἁμαρτία, -ας, ἡ	sin	noun	173	
βασιλεία, -ας, ἡ	kingdom	noun	162	*basili*ca
δόξα, -ης, ἡ	glory	noun	166	*dox*ology
ἔθνος, -ους, τό	(sg.) nation; (pl.) Gentiles	noun	162	*eth*nic
ἔργον, -ου, τό	work, deed, action	noun	169	*ergo*nomic
ὄχλος, -ου, ὁ	crowd, multitude	noun	175	
ἄν	-ever; if, would, might (conditional, untranslatable particle)	partic.	166	
ὑπέρ	(+gen.) in behalf of (+acc.) above	prep.	150	*hyper*bole

Table 55: Prepositions Spatial Translation Chart

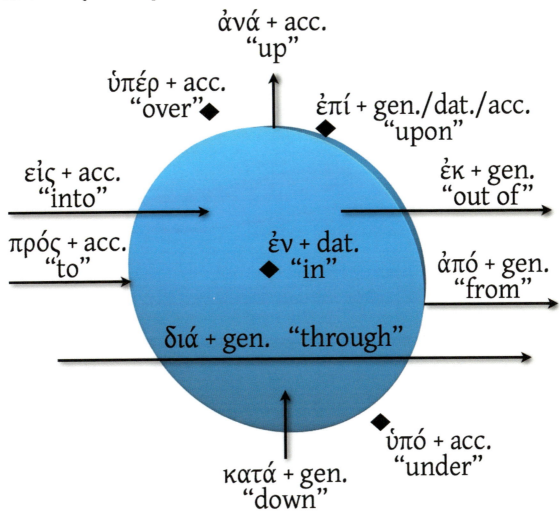

7.9: The Second Time Around

Second time around users should focus on preposition functions, as well as the phrases and clauses section. In particular, take time to memorize the particular dependent clause introducers.

Chapter 8:
Participles Stripped Down

⇒**What's the Point:** Many a grammarian has echoed the sentiments that the mastery of the Greek participle is mastery of Greek itself. Participles are robust in their meaning and usage, and it often takes several words in English to translate what a participle is doing. One out of every four verb forms is a participle, so they are everywhere! Due to their frequency and complexity of usage, it would be better to start working with participles earlier, except a student needs many other pieces in place first. Now we are ready, so let the fun begin!

8.1: Participle Description

A participle is a hybrid word because it is part adjective and part verb. Its lexical form is based on its verb stem, but its adjective nature is shown because it taking declension endings.
A participle is a hybrid word because it is part adjective and part verb. Its lexical form is based on its verb stem, but its adjective nature is shown because it taking declension endings.

Once we stray outside of the Indicative mood, the number of Greek tenses which occur reduce significantly. In the NT, participles only occur in the Present (3,687), Aorist (2,289), Perfect (673), and Future (13) tenses. Due to the scarcity of future participles, we focus on the other three tenses. The action described by an Aorist participle usually occurs prior to the main verb's action. The action described by a Present participle usually occurs at the same time as the main verb's action. The action described by a Perfect participle usually occurs prior to the main verb's action. The action of a Future participle usually occurs after the main verb's action.

Are these funky hybrid words in English, too? Of course they are. Participles describe action happening in and around the main verb. Examine the following examples:
- The dog barked at the car.
    - "bark" is the verb of the clause.
- The barking dog ran after the car.
    - "ran" is the main verb of the clause.

— Notice how the verb "bark" is no longer the main verb. "-ing" has been added to the verb and paired with "dog" to act like an adjective.

In the scene which has been portrayed, there are two actions happening in the scene, but only one is the main action (main verb). Other actions happening in and around the main verb will often use a participle to describe these peripheral actions in the clause.

8.2: How Participles Are Formed

The following table breaks down how participles are formed. There is commentary and more tables below.

Table 56: Participle Formation

Verb Parts					Adjective Parts (case, gender, number)		
tense		voice			masc.	fem.	neut.
					declension use		
Present	1st principal part	active	οντ	ουσ (fem. and dat.pl)	3rd	1st	3rd
		mid/pass		ομεν	2nd	1st	2nd
Aorist (NO augment)	3rd principal part (1Aor. ends with σα, 2Aor. does not)	active	ντ	σ (fem. and dat.pl)	3rd	1st	3rd
		middle		μεν	2nd	1st	2nd
	6th principal part (ends with θε)[117]	passive	ντ	ισ (fem. and dat.pl)	3rd	1st	3rd
Perfect	4th/5th principal part (WITH reduplication)	active	κοτ	κυι (fem.)	3rd	1st	3rd
		mid/pass		μεν	2nd	1st	2nd

---

[117] Remember from the indicative mood that some verbs drop the theta (θ).

While this table may not look too complicated, it amounts to A LOT of participle forms because of the declension endings a participle can take. The following tables show all possible participle forms of λύω (see the discussion below the tables).

As you observe the participle paradigm of λύω below, bear in mind the following points:

1. A participle's parsing information is: tense, voice, mood (participle), case, gender, number, lexical form. For example, the first participle in the table below is parsed as present, active, participle, nominative, masculine, singular, λύω.

2. The most difficult participle form to recognize is the nominative, masculine, singular form, because the case ending is ς, which is a bully and changes things.

    a. For Present active, the ς case ending kicks out the τ from the voice suffix, slips on the ν, and as it leaves it lengthens the ο to an ω. i.e. οντς becomes ων.

    b. A similar thing happens to the Perfect active; the τ drops out and lengthens the ο to an ω. I.e. κοτς becomes κως.

    c. For Aorist active and passive the ς case ending kicks out the ντ voice suffix all together (see §2.7.3, particularly note 18). so that ντς becomes ς. For the Aorist passive, the ε at the end of the tense will lengthen to ει. i.e. θεντς becomes θεις.

3. Present participle voice suffixes begin with an omicron (ο), which is actually a connecting vowel. The important thing to know is that this can cause contraction with contract verbs (remind yourself about contract verbs §5.2.2).

4. Remember the phrase "μεν are in the middle." Notice how μεν is always the middle voice suffix for every tense.

5. Present and Aorist active as well as Aorist passive have different voice suffixes for feminine participles. For Present and Aorist active, the suffix also applies to masculine and neuter dative plural forms.

6. Aorist participles:

    a. The epsilon augment is one of the markers of the Aorist tense indicative, but the augment *does not* occur with Aorist participles.

    b. The σα suffix for the Aorist active and middle indicative tense is retained for the participle (and the sigma may slip away).

c. The suffix for the Aorist passive indicative is θη and for the participle it is only slightly different: θε.

7. Perfect participles:

   a. Reduplication was the marker of the Perfect tense in the indicative mood. It still indicates Perfect for participles.

   b. Perfect active and middle indicative verbs had a κ in its suffix. A κ occurs in the Perfect participle suffix as well.

   c. The Perfect active dative plural participle loses the τ from the suffix and replaces it with a σ. (I've told you before the sigma is sinister!)

Remember, in the *Stripped Down* approach you don't need to memorize all of this material. It is more important to understand what you see as you come across participles in the NT, and recognize the patterns where you can. As you look at the following tables, compare them with the formations table and points above to understand the participle forms.

Table 57: Present Tense λύω Participles

1st Princ. Part: λύω		active			middle / passive		
		masc.	*fem.*	*neut.*	*masc.*	*fem.*	*neut.*
sg.	nom.	λύων	λύουσα	λῦον	λυόμενος	λυομένη	λυόμενον
	gen.	λύοντος	λυούσης	λύοντος	λυομένου	λυομένης	λυομένου
	dat.	λύοντι	λυούσῃ	λύοντι	λυομένῳ	λυομένῃ	λυομένῳ
	acc.	λύοντα	λύουσαν	λῦον	λυόμενον	λυομένην	λυόμενον
pl.	nom.	λύοντες	λύουσαι	λύοντα	λυόμενοι	λυόμεναι	λυόμενα
	gen.	λυόντων	λυουσῶν	λυόντων	λυομένων	λυομένων	λυομένων
	dat.	λύουσιν	λυούσαις	λύουσιν	λυομένοις	λυομέναις	λυομένοις
	acc.	λύοντας	λυούσας	λύοντα	λυομένους	λυομένας	λυόμενα

Table 58: Aorist Tense λύω Participles

3rd Princ. part: ἐλύσα		active			middle		
		masc.	*fem.*	*neut.*	*masc.*	*fem.*	*neut.*
sg.	nom.	λύσας	λύσασα	λῦσαν	λυσάμενος	λυσαμένη	λυσάμενον
	gen.	λύσαντος	λυσάσης	λύσαντος	λυσαμένου	λυσαμένης	λυσαμένου
	dat.	λύσαντι	λυσάσῃ	λύσαντι	λυσαμένῳ	λυσαμένῃ	λυσαμένῳ
	acc.	λύσαντα	λύσασαν	λῦσαν	λυσάμενον	λυσαμένην	λυσάμενον
pl.	nom.	λύσαντες	λύσασαι	λύσαντα	λυσάμενοι	λυσάμεναι	λυσάμενα
	gen.	λυσάντων	λυσασῶν	λυσάντων	λυσαμένων	λυσαμένων	λυσαμένων
	dat.	λύσασιν	λυσάσαις	λύσασιν	λυσαμένοις	λυσαμέναις	λυσαμένοις
	acc.	λύσαντας	λυσάσας	λύσαντα	λυσαμένους	λυσαμένας	λυσάμενα

6th Princ. Part: ἐλύθην		passive		
		masc.	*fem.*	*neut.*
sg.	nom.	λυθείς	λυθεῖσα	λυθέν
	gen.	λυθέντος	λυθείσης	λυθέντος
	dat.	λυθέντι	λυθείσῃ	λυθέντι
	acc.	λυθέντα	λυθεῖσαν	λυθέν
pl.	nom.	λυθέντες	λυθεῖσαι	λυθέντα
	gen.	λυθέντων	λυθεισῶν	λυθέντων
	dat.	λυθεῖσιν	λυθείσαις	λυθεῖσι(ν)
	acc.	λυθέντας	λυθείσας	λυθέντα

Table 59: Perfect Tense λύω Participles

		4th Principal Part λελύκα			5th Principal Part λελύμαι		
		active			middle / passive		
		masc.	*fem.*	*neut.*	*masc.*	*fem.*	*neut.*
sg.	n.	λελυκώς	λελυκυῖα	λελυκός	λελυμένος	λελυμένη	λελυμένον
	g.	λελυκότος	λελυκυίας	λελυκοτος	λελυμένου	λελυμένης	λελυμένου
	d.	λελυκότι	λελυκυίᾳ	λελυκότι	λελυμένῳ	λελυμένῃ	λελυμένῳ
	a.	λελυκότα	λελυκυῖαν	λελυκός	λελυμένον	λελυμένην	λελυμένον
pl.	n.	λελυκότες	λελυκυῖαι	λελυκότα	λελυμένοι	λελυμέναι	λελυμένα
	g.	λελυκότων	λελυκυιῶν	λελυκότων	λελυμένων	λελυμένων	λελυμένων
	d.	λελυκόσιν	λελυκυίαις	λελυκόσι(ν)	λελυμένοις	λελυμέναις	λελυμένοις
	a.	λελυκότας	λελυκυίας	λελυκότα	λελυμένους	λελυμένας	λελυμένα

8.3: What a Participle Can Do, pt.1

The next chapter deals in depth with what a participle can do and how they are translated. This chapter will only highlight how the participle functions adjectivally.

8.3.1: Participle Acting Like An Adjective

Since a participle is a verbal adjective, it can do the things an adjective can do:

1. A participle can be in full concord with a nearby noun that it is paired with and attribute value to the noun. If the noun has an article, so will the participle. If the noun doesn't have an article, the participle may or may not have the article. Eg: τίς ὑπέδειξεν ὑμῖν φυγεῖν ἀπὸ τῆς μελλούσης ὀργῆς; (Matt 3:7) is *who told you to flee from the coming wrath.* (This is like "the barking dog" example above.)

2. All by itself and *with an article*, a participle functions as a substantive. Eg: ὁ λύων is *the one who is loosing* or *the man who is loosing.* Remember that the gender and number of a substantive adjective affects the translation, and the same goes for participles. Eg: ἐξῆλθεν ὁ σπείρων τοῦ σπείρειν (Matt 13:3) is *a sower went out to sow.*

3. As a substantive, a nominative participle can be the object[118] of an equative verb. This includes being the object in a verbless clause (remember that a verbless clause assumes the copulative εἰμί). Eg.: ποῦ ἐστιν ὁ τεχθεὶς βασιλεὺς τῶν Ἰουδαίων; (Matt 2:2) is translated *who is <u>the one born</u> king of the Jews*? The verb here is ἐστιν (a form of εἰμί), and the participle is a predicate nominative.

8.3.2: Participle Acting Like a Verb

Although very rare in the New Testament, there are times when a participle can act as the main verb of a sentence. In these instances where the participle is acting as a finite verb, they will be translated as an indicative or imperative.

8.4: The Least You Need to Know

You should be able to clearly and accurately answer these questions. Use these online flashcards (http://quizlet.com/_7tfy6) to memorize the answers:

- What is a participle?
- What 3 tenses most frequently occur as participles?
- What are all of the components in participle parsing?
- What is the indicator for an aorist active or middle participle?
- What is the indicator for an aorist passive participle?
- What is the indicator for a perfect active or middle/passive participle?
- What is the present active voice suffix for participles?
- What is the aorist active voice suffix for participles?
- What is the aorist passive voice suffix for participles?
- What is the perfect active voice suffix for participles?
- What does it mean when a participle has an article?
- What is the most difficult participle form to recognize? Why?
- What is the suffix for all middle(/passive) participles?
- When a participle is acting like an adjective, what things can it do?
- A nominative participle with an equative verb may be doing what?

---

[118] The proper term is predicate nominative.

8.5: Greek@Logos

Utilizing the *Mastering Logos Bible Software* course or the Logos help files, Logos forums, Logos wiki, and videos provided, users should take the time to learn:

- Use the Passage Guide
  - See Lecture 15 of *Mastering Logos Bible Software*
  - Alternative: www.logos.com/support/logos5/passage-guide
- Topical Guide
  - See Lecture 18 of *Mastering Logos Bible Software*
  - Alternative: http://youtu.be/M7QcDlo_cYY
  - Alternative: http://youtu.be/Q5U-9JD3zO0
- Bible Facts
  - See Lecture 21 of *Mastering Logos Bible Software*
  - Alternative: http://youtu.be/xEJ9XModEnE

8.6: Vocabulary

Word	Meaning	Type	Freq.	Derivatives
ἄλλος, -η, -ον	other, another	adj.	155	*alle*gory
πρῶτος, -η, -ον	first, earlier; foremost	adj. adv.	155	
πάλιν	again	adv.	141	*palin*drome
καρδία, -ας, ἡ	heart	noun	156	*cardi*ac
λαός, -ου, ὁ	people; crowd	noun	142	*lai*ty
πόλις, -εως, ἡ	city	noun	162	metro*polis*
προφήτης, -ου, ὁ	prophet	noun	144	
σάρξ, σαρκός, ἡ	flesh, body	noun	147	*sarc*ophogus
σῶμα, -ματος, τό	body	noun	142	psycho*soma*tic
χάρις, -ιτος, ἡ	grace, favor	noun	155	Eu*char*ist

ὅστις, ἥτις, ὅτι	whoever/whichever/whatever; everyone, which	pron.	153
ἀγαπάω	I love, cherish	verb	143
ἀγαπάω, ἀγαπήσω, ἠγάπησα, ἠγάπηκα, ἠγάπημαι, ἠγαπήθην			
ἀφίημι	I let go, leave, permit, divorce, forgive	verb	143
ἀφίημι (ἀφίω, ἀφέω), ἀφήσω, ἀφῆκα, ——, ἀφέωμαι, ἀφέθην			
ἐγείρω	I raise up, wake	verb	144
ἐγείρω, ἐγερῶ, ἤγειρα, ——, ἐγήγερμαι, ἠγέρθην			
ζάω	I live	verb	140
ζάω, ζήσω, ἔζησα, ——, ——, ——			

8.7: The Second Time Around

In the second time around focus heavily on the formation of participles. Memorize not only the participle formation tables, but how to reproduce the λύω participle paradigm in full.

Chapter 9:
Participle Functions

⇒**What's the Point:** The challenge with participles is not only how they are formed, but how they can function. They are so numerous it is important to understand their use. Remember that the mastery of the Greek participle is mastery of Greek itself!

9.1: What a Participle Can Do

The following information covers the most common uses of the participle. In the future as you work with Greek and your preferred English translation, consult Wallace's *Greek Grammar Beyond the Basics* when you are struggling over what a participle is doing, or questioning the decision of an English translation.

9.1.1: Periphrastic Participle

Periphrastic means to combine words to form a single idea. In Greek, εἰμί is sometimes combined with a participle to convey one verb idea. It is no different in English. Sometimes "I am" can be the verb in a clause all by itself, and other times it works with a participle to convey one verbal idea. For example, "I am hungry" or "I am a teacher" has "I am" as the verb working on its own. "I am kicking the ball" has "am" working with the participle "kicking" to form one verbal idea. You may be wondering why Greek didn't just use a regular indicative verb to indicate the same thing as a periphrastic construction, like "I kick the ball." Good question! Periphrastic constructions are somewhat redundant but do add emphasis for effect. One thing to note is that because εἰμί and works with the participle as a package, it is no longer considered an equative verb.

Periphrastic participles are almost always nominative, and regularly follow the εἰμί form. They combine with εἰμί to work in Present, Imperfect, Future, and Perfect tenses:

- Present periphrastic construction: Present εἰμί + Present participle
    - ὅ ἐστιν μεθερμηνευόμενον Κρανίου Τόπος (Mark 15:22)
      which is *translated* place of the skull.

- Imperfect periphrastic construction: Imperfect εἰμί + Present participle[119]
    - ἦν προσδεχόμενος τὴν βασιλείαν τοῦ θεοῦ (Mark 15:43)
      he was waiting for the kingdom of God.
- Future periphrastic construction: Future εἰμί + Present participle
    - ἔσεσθε μισούμενοι ὑπὸ πάντων διὰ τὸ ὄνομά μου (Matt 10:22)
      you will be hated by all because of my name.
- Perfect periphrastic construction: Present εἰμί[120] + Perfect participle
    - χάριτί ἐστε σεσῳσμένοι διὰ πίστεως (Eph 2:8)
      by grace you have been saved through faith.

9.1.2: Genitive Absolute

A genitive absolute participle phrase stands 'absolutely alone' within the sentence. This type of phrase is very similar to using parentheses in English sentences. The participle is always in the genitive case, and has a noun or pronoun in concord. The genitive (pro)noun it is with is not in concord with any other noun in the sentence. *When you see a genitive absolute, say "when."* E.g.: ἐξελθόντων αὐτῶν ἀπὸ Βηθανίας ἐπείνασεν (Mark 11:12) is translated as *when they came* from Bethany, he was hungry.

9.1.3: Adverbial Participle

Most participles act adverbially, and when a participle does act adverbially *it will always be anarthrous*.[121] Remember that participles give you information about other actions happening in and around the main verb's action. It is here that the verbal idea of a participle is emphasized because grammatically it functions as a dependent clause that can have its own object or other phrases. In fact, even though it is one word in Greek, an adverbial participle is often translated as a whole dependent clause in English! It is also not always easy to translate the tense of a participle (present participles will sometimes be translated as a past tense rather than a durative), but *context determines the function*.

The following is a list of the types of adverbial information a participle can convey. The listing of functions is in order of regularity (i.e. temporal is the dominant function).

---

[119] Remember that there are no Imperfect participles.
[120] Remember that there are no Perfect forms of εἰμί.
[121] This means it has no article.

In the sentence examples, the participle clauses are underlined, the participle is red, and the participle's translation is italicized.

1. SIMULTANEOUS TEMPORAL ACTION—A participle can indicate an action happening at the same time as the main verb's action. The participle will always be in the Present tense.
   - Περιπατῶν δὲ παρὰ τὴν θάλασσαν τῆς Γαλιλαίας εἶδεν δύο ἀδελφούς (Matt 4:18)
     While he walked by the sea of Galilee he saw two brothers.

2. PRECEDING TEMPORAL ACTION—A participle can indicate an action that happened prior to the main verb's action. The participle will always be in the Aorist tense.
   - Τότε Ἡρῴδης λάθρᾳ καλέσας τοὺς μάγους ἠκρίβωσεν παρ᾽ αὐτῶν τὸν χρόνον... (Matt 2:7)
     Then *after he* secretly *called* the magi, Herod learned from them the time...

3. PURPOSE or RESULT—A participle can indicate the purpose or result of the main verb's action.
   - τοῦτο δὲ ἔλεγεν πειράζων αὐτόν (John 6:6)
     But he was saying this *in order to test* him.
   - πατέρα ἴδιον ἔλεγεν τὸν θεὸν ἴσον ἑαυτὸν ποιῶν τῷ θεῷ (John 5:18)
     he was also calling God his own Father, *thereby making* himself equal to God.

4. CAUSE—A participle can indicate the action which caused the main verb's action.
   - οἱ πατριάρχαι ζηλώσαντες τὸν Ἰωσὴφ ἀπέδοντο εἰς Αἴγυπτον (Acts 7:9)
     Because the patriarchs *were jealous* of Joseph, they sold him into Egypt.

5. CONDITION—A participle can indicate a conditional action that needs to happen before the main verb's action occurs.
   - θερίσομεν μὴ ἐκλυόμενοι (Gal 6:9)
     We will reap *if we* do not *give up*.

6. CONCESSION—A concessive participle introduces an (inconvenient) action that is occurring, but the main verb's action is still happening in spite of the participle's action.

- γνόντες τὸν θεὸν οὐχ ὡς θεὸν ἐδόξασαν (Rom 1:21)
  Although they knew God, they did not honor him as God.

7. MEANS—A participle can indicate the action that provides the means for the main verb's action.

    - οἵτινες ὅλους οἴκους ἀνατρέπουσιν διδάσκοντες ... αἰσχροῦ (Titus 1:11)
      they are upsetting whole families *by teaching* shameful things

8. MANNER—A participle can indicate the manner in which the main verb's action is occurring.

    - ἐπορεύοντο χαίροντες (Acts 5:41)
      They went *with rejoicing*.

9. REDUNDANT—A participle can indicate action related to the main verb's action, but it is not essential to the main verb's action. Because the participle is redundant, either it OR the main verb is left untranslated. In the example below, the participle is translated, the main verb is not.

    - ἀποκριθεὶς δὲ ὁ Ἰησοῦς εἶπεν πρὸς αὐτόν (Matt 3:15)
      But Jesus *answered* him.

9.2: Understanding Participle Function and Translation

In the *Stripped Down* approach, you do not need to determine participle function and translation on your own. What you do need to do is understand how and why modern translators come to the decisions they have (and decide if you agree!). Translation is interpretation, and in the case of adverbial participles you will find that you may disagree at times with English translations. The following flowchart is a "determination device" for participles. As you come across Greek participles in the NT and study them in conjunction with English translation(s), take the time to see how the participle has flowed through the flowchart. The following points are items to note as you use and study the flowchart:

- A participle with an article instantly means its 'adjectival quality' has kicked in.
- A nominative participle (with or without an article) that is in a clause with an equative verb or in a verbless clause is a predicate nominative OR a periphrastic construction with a form of εἰμί.

- A genitive participle that has a (pro)noun in concord nearby (and that genitive is not connected to any other noun), is likely a genitive absolute.
- An anarthrous[122] participle is most often an adverbial participle. But, an anarthrous participle in concord with a nearby noun can be acting like an indefinite attributive adjective.
- The adverbial functions in the flowchart are listed in order of frequency. i.e. temporal functions are the most common.
- Remember, the flowchart does not cover everything a participle can do. Consult Wallace's *Greek Grammar Beyond the Basics* to understand the other minor functions.

---

[122] Anarthrous means no article.

Table 60: Participle Flowchart

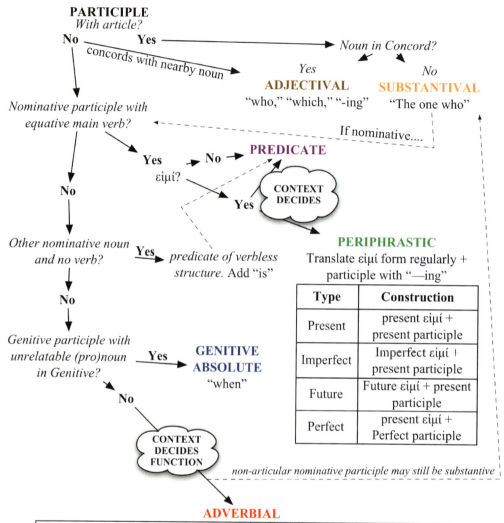

9.2.1: The Subject of an Adverbial Participle

An adverbial participle functions as a dependent clause that is describing an action happening in and around the main verb, so it only makes sense that there is someone or something doing the action. The way a participle indicates who did the action is by placing the participle in concord with a noun in the clause, or in concord with the 'built-in' pronoun of the main verb. A pronoun, not present in the Greek, is often added to the English translation of these types of participles to indicate the doer of the participle action. The following examples (taken from §9.1), highlight how the participle is in concord with a substantive in the clause. The participle is in red, the participle translation is in red, and the pronoun provided in English (but not present in Greek) is bold.

- Περιπατῶν δὲ παρὰ τὴν θάλασσαν τῆς Γαλιλαίας εἶδεν δύο ἀδελφούς (Matt 4:18)

  *While **he** walked* by the sea of Galilee he saw two brothers.
    - Participle Parsing: pres., act., ptc., nom., masc., sg., περιπατέω.
    - There are three 'actors' in this section: the sea (acc., fem., sg.), brothers (acc., masc., pl.), and the built in subject of the verb εἶδεν (3rd person singular). This built-in pronoun is the subject of the clause.
    - This means the participle's parsing matches the built-in he/she/it of the main verb. That is why "he" is supplied in the translation of the participle.

- Τότε Ἡρῴδης λάθρᾳ καλέσας τοὺς μάγους ἠκρίβωσεν παρ' αὐτῶν τὸν χρόνον... (Matt 2:7)

  Then *after **he** secretly called* the magi, Herod learned from them the time...
    - Participle Parsing: aor., act., ptc., nom., masc., sg., καλέω.
    - There are two 'actors' in this section: Herod (nom., masc., sg.) and the Magi (acc., masc., pl.). In this case the built-in pronoun is not necessary because the Greek has provided the subject (Herod).
    - Since the participle's parsing matches Herod, "he" is supplied in the translation of the participle.

- θερίσομεν μὴ ἐκλυόμενοι (Gal 6:9)

  We will reap *if **we*** do not *give up*.
    - Participle Parsing: pres., m/p., ptc., nom., masc., pl., ἐκλύω.

- There is only one 'actor' in this section, the "we" built into the main verb θερίσομεν (which is 1ˢᵗ person plural).
- The participle's parsing matches the built-in pronoun so "we" is supplied in the translation of the participle.

- γνόντες τὸν θεὸν οὐχ ὡς θεὸν ἐδόξασαν (Rom 1:21)
  Although they knew God, they did not honor him as God.
  - Participle Parsing: aor., act., ptc., nom., masc., pl., γινώσκω.
  - There are two 'actors' in this section: God (acc., masc., sg.) and the built-in subject of the verb (3ʳᵈ person pl.).
  - The participle's parsing matches the built-in subject of the verb. That is why "they" is supplied in the translation of the participle.

9.2.2: The Tense Of A Participle

As mentioned before, a Present tense participle *usually* indicates an action concurrent with the main verb, while Aorist and Perfect tense participles usually indicates action prior to the action of the main verb.

The tense of participles is yet another example of how it is often difficult to translate Greek into good English. Often times Present participles end up being translated as past tense. Notice this example:

- Περιπατῶν δὲ παρὰ τὴν θάλασσαν τῆς Γαλιλαίας εἶδεν δύο ἀδελφούς (Matt 4:18)
  While he walked by the sea of Galilee he saw two brothers.
  - Participle Parsing: pres., act., ptc., nom., masc., sg., περιπατέω.
  - The participle is present and would more accurately be translated as *while walking* by the sea...

9.3: The Least You Need to Know

You should be able to clearly and accurately answer these questions. Use these online flashcards (http://quizlet.com/_7tfyd) to memorize the answers:

- What is a periphrastic participle?
- How is a present periphrastic construction made?

Participle Functions

- How is an imperfect periphrastic construction made?
- How is a future periphrastic construction made?
- How is a perfect periphrastic construction made?
- What is a genitive absolute? How do you translate it?
- What is an adverbial participle?
- What function is an anarthrous participle usually performing?
- How is the subject of an adverbial participle determined?
- What does a present tense participle usually indicate?
- What does an aorist tense participle usually indicate?
- What does a perfect tense participle usually indicate?

9.4: Greek@Logos

Utilizing the *Mastering Logos Bible Software* course or the Logos help files, Logos forums, Logos wiki, and videos provided, users should take the time to learn:

- How to use the Exegetical Guide
    - See Lecture 16 of *Mastering Logos Bible Software*
    - Alternative: http://youtu.be/tof8W4NFZg0
- How to use the Sermon Starter
    - See Lecture 18 of *Mastering Logos Bible Software*
    - Alternative: http://youtu.be/JvGFbHstPtk
- How to save and access your layouts
    - See Lecture 6 of *Mastering Logos Bible Software*
    - Alternative: See the "Layouts & History" articles at www.logos.com/videos

9.5: Vocabulary

Word	Meaning	Type	Freq.	Derivatives
δύο	two	adj.	135	duo
νεκρός, -ά, -όν	dead	adj.	128	*necro*sis

ὅταν	whenever	conj.	123	
αἰών, -ῶνος, ὁ	age, eternity	noun	122	eon
ἀρχιερεύς, -έως, ὁ	chief priest, high priest	noun	122	
δοῦλος, -ου, ὁ	slave, servant	noun	124	
δύναμις, -εως, ἡ	power, ability	noun	119	*dyna*mite
ζωή, -ῆς, ἡ	life	noun	135	*zoo*logy
θάνατος, -ου, ὁ	death	noun	120	eu*thana*sia
φωνή, -ῆς, ἡ	sound	noun	139	*phon*e
σύν	(+dat) with	prep.	128	sy*n*thesis
ἀποστέλλω	I send (away)	verb	132	*apost*le
ἀποστέλλω, ἀποστελῶ, ἀπέστειλα, ἀπέσταλκα, ἀπέσταλμαι, ἀπεστάλην				
βάλλω	I throw	verb	122	*ball*istic
βάλλω, βαλῶ, ἔβαλον, βέβληκα, βέβλημαι, ἐβλήθην				
βλέπω	I see	verb	133	
βλέπω, βλέψω, ἔβλεψα, ——, ——, ——				
παραδίδωμι	I entrust, hand over, betray	verb	119	
παραδίδωμι, παραδώσω, παρέδωκα, παραδέδωκα, παραδέδομαι, παρεδόθην				

9.6: The Second Time Around

The second time around is all about practice in working with participles. Through the exercises for this section continually focus on how the participle flows through the participle flow chart. You would also do well to try your best to memorize the flowchart and try and recreate it from memory.

Chapter 10:
Non-Indicative Verbs

⇒**What's the Point:** Wandering outside of the Indicative mood takes us into the realm of possibility. When a command is given, request is made, or a possibility is discussed, verbs in the Subjunctive, Imperative, and Optative are used. 3,556 of these non-indicative verbs occur, which is almost 1 in 4 verbs in the New Testament.

10.1: Introduction

Indicative verbs are finite verbs that have a proper subject. Finite verbs are the main verb in their clause. This is in contrast to participles and infinitives, which are not true verbs. Whereas the indicative mood *indicates* reality, non-indicative moods do not indicate reality. Non-indicative moods suggest possibility in varying degrees.

Compare the following sentences:
- I am going to have pizza for supper. (indicative)
- You should have pizza for supper. (subjunctive)
- I may have pizza for supper. (subjunctive)
- Do not go to have pizza for supper! (imperative)
- Mom, please make pizza for supper. (imperative)
- If I just so happen to have pizza for supper, I'll let you know. (optative)

Only the first sentence expresses certainty of action, while all of the remaining sentences have varying degrees of probability regarding the action of having pizza for supper. If these sentences were in Greek, the first sentence would use the indicative mood, because it is the only sentence that represents certainty in contrast to the non-indicative moods that express probability. The *subjunctive* mood expresses something that is probable. The *imperative* mood is used to express commands or requests. The *optative* mood expresses an action that is only remotely possible.

10.2: Subjunctive Mood

The subjunctive mood expresses probability. In other words, Greek uses the subjunctive mood to indicate an action that will probably happen. In English we also have this mood, and most often express it with words like "may," "might," "should," "could," "when," "whenever," or "if." These are the words that are used when translating the subjunctive mood as well. Sometimes an English translator will have to supply one of these words to the translation, but quite often the Greek will have one of these words in the sentence already. Subjunctive verb parsing is the same as indicative verbs—tense, voice, mood, person, number, lexical form.

10.2.1: How the Subjunctive is Formed

The subjunctive occurs primarily in the present and aorist tenses. Of the 1,868 subjunctive verbs, only 10 of them are perfect tense, and 7 are future tense.

The primary marker of the subjunctive mood is a lengthened connecting vowel. Whereas in the indicative mood the connecting vowel is epsilon (ε) or omicron (o), in the subjunctive the connecting vowel is eta (η) or omega (ω).

Table 61: Subjunctive Formation

	tense		connecting vowel		inflected endings
Present	1st principal part	active	ω / η		primary active
		mid/pass	ω / η		primary middle/passive
Aorist (NO augment)	3rd principal part (1Aor. ends with σ,[123] 2Aor. does not)	active	ω / η		primary active
		middle	ω / η		primary middle/passive
	6th principal part (ends with θ)[124]	passive	ω / η		primary active

---

[123]Remember that σα has been the regular indicator of the aorist in the other verb forms.
[124]Remember from the indicative mood that some verbs drop the theta (θ).

As you may notice from the formation table, the subjunctive can be tricky to spot in Greek because it is often similar to the indicative. Like the infinitive and participle, 2Aorist forms end up looking just like the present tense, but with a different stem.

An additional difficulty with the subjunctive is the lengthened connecting vowel. If you remember from our discussion of contract verbs (§5.2.2), stems that end with a vowel lengthen. This means that indicative contract verbs and subjunctive verbs are sometimes identical. In the *Stripped Down* approach, you do not need to worry about identifying these troublesome forms, just know that they exist and let your bible software do the work for you.

As with all other verb forms, the usual quirks of Greek appear in the subjunctive: contract verbs contract (and thus look identical), liquid verbs cause sigmas to disappear, the aorist sigma will interact with stop consonants, and the θ of the aorist passive can also interact with a stop consonant.

Table 62: λύω Subjunctive Paradigm

Parts		1st λύω		3rd ἔλυσα				6th ἐλύθην
tense & voice		present active	present m/p	aorist active	2aorist active	aorist middle	2aorist middle	aorist passive
sg	1	λύω	λύωμαι	λύσω	λάβω	λύσωμαι	λάβωμαι	λυθῶ
sg	2	λύῃς	λύῃ	λύσῃς	λάβῃς	λύσῃ	λάβῃ	λυθῇς
sg	3	λύῃ	λύηται	λύσῃ	λάβῃ	λύσηται	λάβηται	λυθῇ
pl	1	λύωμεν	λυώμεθα	λύσωμεν	λάβωμεν	λυσώμεθα	λαβώμεθα	λυθῶμεν
pl	2	λύητε	λύησθε	λύσητε	λάβητε	λύσησθε	λάβησθε	λυθῆτε
pl	3	λύωσι	λύωνται	λύσωσι	λάβωσι	λύσωνται	λάβωνται	λυθῶσι

Table 63: εἰμί Subjunctive Paradigm[125]

person and number		present	translation
sg	1ˢᵗ	ὦ	*I might be*
sg	2ⁿᵈ	ᾖς	*you might be*
sg	3ʳᵈ	ᾖ	*he/she/it might be*
pl	1ˢᵗ	ὦμεν	*we might be*
pl	2ⁿᵈ	ἦτε	*y'all might be*
pl	3ʳᵈ	ὦσι (ν)	*they might be*

10.2.2: Understanding Subjunctive Translation and Function

The tense of a subjunctive retains its essential difference (internal aspect vs. external aspect), but, when it comes to translating, the present and aorist subjunctive often end up being translated the same.

As mentioned previously, sometimes the Greek sentence has a word that provides the necessary context for it to be possible reality (like "if," "whenever," etc.). Other times the translator needs to provide one of the many words that make the reality possible (e.g. "could," "might," etc.) For the most part, when a subjunctive is the main verb of an independent clause the translator needs to add a helper word. However, *most subjunctives live in dependent clauses*. Remember that dependent clauses function like an adjective, adverb, or noun for the independent clause. Dependent clauses, particularly those with a subjunctive verb, frequently are introduced by particular words.

The following table summarizes most of the subjunctive functions and their translation.

---

[125]Notice how the subjunctive forms of εἰμί are identical to the present active forms of λύω, without the λυ.

Table 64: Subjunctive Function Table

	Function	Cue	Translation
Independent Clause	hortatory *to exhort or command*	1st person plural	"let us"
	deliberative *asks a question*	interrogative pronoun, ποῦ, and/or question mark (;)	"shall we....?"
	emphatic negation *a decisive negation*	aorist with οὐ μή	"never"
	prohibitive *a negative command*	aorist with μή	"do not"
Dependent Clause	purpose or result *purpose/result of the independent clause*	ἵνα or ὅπως	"(in order) to" "as a result"
	indefinite relative *acts as a noun or as an adjective*	indefinite relative pronoun or relative pronoun (ὅς, ἥ, ὅν) sometimes followed by ἄν or [independent clause lacks substantive]	"who(ever)", etc *[acts as subject or object]* "may, "might," etc.
	temporal *tells when the main verb action will occur*	ὅταν, ἕως, ἄχρι, μέχρι	*translate cue word*
	conditional	ἐάν	*translate cue word*

10.2.2.1: Subjunctive in Independent Clauses

1. HORTATORY: A hortatory subjunctive offers an exhortation or command. The subjunctive verb will usually be a 1st person plural verb, and is usually translated with "let us."

    • διέλθωμεν εἰς τὸ πέραν (Mark 4:35)
    Let us go to the other side.

2. DELIBERATIVE: A deliberative subjunctive asks a question, real or rhetorical. The subjunctive will frequently be introduced with an interrogative pronoun, and

the NT editors will add the question mark (;). Translation is usually "shall we...?"

- μὴ μεριμνήσητε λέγοντες· τί φάγωμεν; (Matt 6:31)
  Do not be anxious, saying, '*What* should we eat?'

3. EMPHATIC NEGATION: An aorist subjunctive with οὐ μή is a decisive negation, usually translated as "never....!"

- οἱ λόγοι μου οὐ μὴ παρέλθωσιν (Matt 24:35)
  My words will *never* pass away.

4. PROHIBITIVE: An aorist subjunctive with μή is a negative command, usually translated as "do not."

- μὴ φοβηθῇς παραλαβεῖν Μαρίαν τὴν γυναῖκά σου (Matt 1:20)
  Do not be afraid to take Mary as your wife.

10.2.2.2: Subjunctive in Dependent Clauses

1. PURPOSE or RESULT: As with infinitives and participles, purpose or result is sometimes hard to differentiate. The subjunctive dependent clause will be introduced by ἵνα or ὅπως. ἵνα is usually translated as "so that" or "(in order) to."

- προσηνέχθησαν αὐτῷ παιδία ἵνα τὰς χεῖρας ἐπιθῇ αὐτοῖς (Matt 19:13)
  Children were brought to him *in order that* he might lay his hands on them

2. INDEFINITE RELATIVE: An indefinite relative dependent clause functions as the subject or object of the independent clause.

- [ὃς δ' ἂν πίῃ ἐκ τοῦ ὕδατος] οὗ ἐγὼ δώσω αὐτῷ, οὐ μὴ διψήσει εἰς τὸν αἰῶνα (John 4:14)
  [But *whoever* drinks of the water] that I will give him will never thirst again.

3. TEMPORAL: A subjunctive in a temporal dependent clause tells when the main verb object will occur.

- τὸν θάνατον τοῦ κυρίου καταγγέλλετε ἄχρι οὗ ἔλθῃ (1 Cor 11:26)
  you do proclaim the Lord's death *until* he comes.

10.2.3: Conditional Sentences

Whenever you see the word "if" in an English or Greek sentence, you are encountering a conditional sentence, and can expect a "then" independent clause to follow. "If" indicates possibility, thus subjunctive verbs are often found in conditional sentences.

There is a further element of logic in Greek conditional sentences that is not present in English conditional sentences, and this logic is difficult to add to an English translation (yet another great reason to know how to work with Greek!). Greek conditional sentences are complex beasts, but basically the grammar of a conditional sentence determines whether or not the conditional sentence is already determined to be true or false. In English we assume "if" sentences are up in the air, but not so in Greek.

1. When the "if" verb is indicative in Greek, the sentence is *not* up in the air—the writer/speaker assumes the sentence to be true or false already.
    a. It is assumed false if the tense is imperfect, aorist, or pluperfect.
    b. It is assumed true if the tense is any of the remaining indicative tenses.
2. When the "if" verb is subjunctive, the assumption is then undetermined but possible (like an English conditional sentence).
3. When the "if" verb is optative, the assumption is undetermined but only remotely possible (like an English conditional sentence).

Observe the following sentences:
- εἰ (if) γὰρ ἐπιστεύετε Μωϋσεῖ, ἐπιστεύετε ἂν ἐμοί (John 5:46)
  If you believed Moses, [then] you would believe me.
    – The verb in the "if" dependent clause is imperfect indicative. Indicative = determined. Imperfect = false.
    – IN OTHER WORDS, the assumption is that they DO NOT BELIEVE Moses. The translation could be " If you believed Moses, then you would believe me —but you didn't, so you don't."
- εἰ (if) δὲ ἐν πνεύματι θεοῦ ἐγὼ ἐκβάλλω τὰ δαιμόνια, ἄρα ἔφθασεν ἐφ᾽ ὑμᾶς ἡ βασιλεία τοῦ θεοῦ. (Matt 12:28)
  But if it is by the Spirit of God that I cast out demons, then the kingdom of God has come to you.

- Whereas in the English translation you may be wondering if Jesus is casting out demons by the Spirit of God, the Greek is crystal clear. The "if" verb in the dependent clause is present indicative. Indicative = determined. Present = true.
- IN OTHER WORDS, the assumption is that IT IS by the Spirit of God that Jesus casts out demons.

• καὶ εἶπεν αὐτῷ· ταῦτά σοι πάντα δώσω, ἐὰν(if) πεσὼν προσκυνήσῃς μοι. (Matt 4:9)

And he said to him, "All these I will give you, if you will fall down and worship me."

- The verb in the "if" dependent clause is subjunctive. Subjunctive = possible.
- *In other words*, there is no assumption on the devil's part here. The conditional sentence indicates only the possibility that Jesus might fall down and worship him.

10.3: Imperative

The imperative mood expresses probability, but in a different way than subjunctive. The imperative is used primarily to express commands or requests. This means that the imperative only expresses the will or desire of the speaker—the ball is in the court of the person receiving the command or request. For the most part, an imperative going from a superior to an inferior is a command, and an imperative going from an inferior to a superior is a request. Imperative verb parsing include the same as indicative verbs: tense, voice, mood, person, number, and lexical form.

10.3.1: How the Imperative is Formed

The imperative occurs primarily in the present and aorist tenses. Of the 1,636 imperative verbs, only 4 of them are perfect tense. Since the imperative is aways directed towards other people or objects, it has no 1st person forms.

Whereas the indicative and subjunctive used primary and secondary endings, the imperative mood has its own set of endings.

Table 65: Imperative Endings

person		Active set	Middle/Passive set
singular	2nd	--(ε), ς, θι/τι, ον	σο, (ου), αι
singular	3rd	τω	σθω
plural	2nd	τε	σθε
plural	3rd	τωσαν	σθωσαν

Like participles and the subjunctive, 2Aorist forms end up looking just like the present tense, but with a different stem. If you recall the primary active endings, you may notice that the second person plural (active) ending is identical in form. The identical forms for these verbs means that context is the only indicator of whether or not a verb is an indicative or an imperative. The other difficult factor with imperatives is the second person singular forms of verbs, which vary in their endings.

Table 66: Imperative Formation

tense			connecting vowel	inflected endings
Present	1st principal part	active	ε	active set
Present	1st principal part	mid/pass	ε	middle/passive set
Aorist (NO augment)	3rd principal part (1Aor. ends with σα, 2Aor. does not)	active	2Aor: ε	active set
Aorist (NO augment)	3rd principal part (1Aor. ends with σα, 2Aor. does not)	middle	2Aor: ε	middle/passive set
Aorist (NO augment)	6th principal part (ends with θη)	passive	--	active set

As with all other verb forms, the usual quirks of Greek appear in the imperative: contract verbs contract, liquid verbs cause sigmas to disappear, the aorist sigma will interact with stop consonants, and the θ of the aorist passive may drop out. Remember, in the *Stripped Down* approach, you don't need to worry about memorizing these endings. Just be familiar with the endings and understand how imperatives are formed.

Table 67: λύω Imperative Paradigm

Parts		1st λύω		3rd ἔλυσα				6th ἐλύθην
tense & voice		present active	present m/p	aorist active	2aorist active	aorist middle	2aorist middle	aorist passive
sg	2	λῦε	λύου	λῦσον	λάβε	λῦσαι	λαβοῦ	λύθητι
	3	λυέτω	λυέσθω	λυσάτω	λαβέτω	λυσάσθω	λαβέσθω	λυθήτω
pl	2	λύετε	λύεσθε	λύσατε	λάβετε	λύσασθε	λάβεσθε	λύθητε
	3	λυέτωσαν	λυέσθωσαν	λυσάτωσαν	λαβέτωσαν	λυσάσθωσαν	λαβέσθωσαν	λυθήτωσαν

Table 68: εἰμί Imperative Paradigm

		present	translation
sg	2nd	ἴσθι	you be!
	3rd	ἔστω (ἤτω)	let him/her/it be!
pl	2nd	ἔστε	y'all be!
	3rd	ἔστωσαν	let them be!

10.3.2: Understanding Imperative Translation and Function

As with the subjunctive, the nuance of the aorist or present tense imperative is often difficult to translate into English. Remember that aorist represents external aspect, present internal aspect. This means that an aorist imperative is generally commanding the action as a whole, while the present commands an action in progress.

1. COMMAND: The most common function of the imperative is to issue a command, usually from a superior to an inferior.

    • ἀκολούθει μοι (Mark 2:14)
      Follow me!

    • εἰ τις ὑμῶν λείπεται σοφίας, αἰτείτω παρὰ τοῦ . . . θεοῦ (Jas 1:5)
      If anyone of you lacks wisdom, let him ask of God.

– Notice that the English translation of this 3rd person imperative sounds more like a suggestion in English, but it is a command in Greek.

2. PROHIBITION: A prohibition is also a command, but it is a command NOT to do something. The negative μή will occur with the imperative.

- μὴ μεθύσκεσθε οἴνῳ (Eph 5:18)
  Do not get drunk with wine.

3. REQUEST: An imperative becomes a request when spoken from an inferior to a superior. Whereas God frequently speaks with imperatives to command, imperatives occur in prayers (and elsewhere) to make requests.

- ἐλθέτω ἡ βασιλεία σου· γενηθήτω τὸ θέλημά σου (Matt 6:10-11)
  Let your kingdom come, let your will be done.

10.4: Optative

The optative mood is one step further away from possibility than the subjunctive, so it is the subjunctive's weaker brother. There are only 68 optative verbs in the NT, which is less than 1% of the verbs in the NT. They are translated in a similar way to the subjunctive. Since the optative occurs so infrequently, it is best to simply consult Wallace's *Greek Grammar Beyond the Basics* when you run into an optative.

The optative occurs only in the present and aorist tenses. The active endings are a bit like μι verb endings, and a bit like secondary endings, so we'll call them μι-ish endings. The marker of the optative is an iota (ι) after the stem or connecting vowel.

Table 69: Optative Formation

tense		connecting vowel		optative marker	optative endings
Present	1st principal part	active	o	ι	μι-ish endings
		mid/pass	o	ι	secondary mid/pass
Aorist (NO augment)	3rd principal part (1Aor. ends with σα,[126] 2Aor. does not)	active	2Aor: o	ι	μι-ish endings
		middle	2Aor: o	ι	secondary mid/pass
	6th principal part (ends with θε)[127]	passive	--	ιη	secondary active

Table 70: λύω Optative Paradigm

Parts		1st λύω		3rd ἔλυσα				6th ἐλύθην
tense & voice		present active	present m/p	aorist active	2aorist active	aorist middle	2aorist middle	aorist passive
sg	1st	λύοιμι	λυοίμην	λύσαιμι	λάβοιμι	λυσαίμην	λαβοίμην	λυθείην
	2nd	λύοις	λύοιο	λύσαις	λάβοις	λύσαιο	λάβοιο	λυθείης
	3rd	λύοι	λύοιτο	λύσαι	λάβοι	λύσαιτο	λάβοιτο	λυθείη
pl	1st	λύοιμεν	λυοίμεθα	λύσαιμεν	λάβοιμεν	λυσαίμεθα	λαβοίμεθα	λυθείημεν
	2nd	λύοιτε	λύοισθε	λύσαιτε	λάβοιτε	λύσαισθε	λάβοισθε	λυθείητε
	3rd	λύοιεν	λύοιντο	λύσαιεν	λάβοιεν	λύσαιντο	λάβοιντο	λυθείησαν

---

[126] Remember that σα has been the regular indicator of the aorist in the other verb forms.
[127] Remember from the indicative mood that some verbs drop the theta (θ).

Non-Indicative Verbs

10.5: The Least You Need to Know

You should be able to clearly and accurately answer these questions. Use these online flashcards (http://quizlet.com/_7tfyk) to memorize the answers:

- What are the 3 non-indicative moods?
- What do the 3 non-indicative moods indicate?
- What tenses occur in the non-indicative moods?
- What does the subjunctive mood indicate?
- What kinds of words in English are used to translate a subjunctive?
- What is the grammatical marker of the subjunctive?
- What kind of clause are most subjunctives found in?
- What is a conditional sentence?
- What does it mean to say a Greek conditional sentence has been determined?
- How does Greek show that a conditional sentence has been undetermined?
- How does Greek show that a conditional sentence is possible?
- How does Greek show that a conditional sentence is only remotely possible?
- What is the most common function of the imperative mood?
- What is the grammatical marker of the imperative?
- What does the optative mood indicate?
- What is the grammatical marker of the optative?

10.6: Greek@Logos

Utilizing the *Mastering Logos Bible Software* course or the Logos help files, Logos forums, Logos wiki, and videos provided, users should take the time to learn:

- How to use the Timeline
  - See Lecture 23 of *Mastering Logos Bible Software*
  - Alternative: http://youtu.be/0VT5IzkJcrY
- How to use the Bible Sense Lexicon
  - See Lecture 22 of *Mastering Logos Bible Software*
  - Alternative: Search "bible sense lexicon" in Logos's interior help files to learn. (*note:* The Bible Sense lexicon decides the semantic domain of

each word for you. While this is an incredibly useful tool, it is still important for you to be able to do this for yourself, which is why this resource is only being introduced now, and it is still incomplete.)

10.7: Vocabulary

Word	Meaning	Type	Freq.	Derivatives
ἴδιος, -α, -ον	one's own; his/her/its	adj.	114	*idio*m
μόνος, -η, -ον	alone, only	adj.	114	*mono*logue
ὅλος, -η, -ον	(adj.) whole, complete; (adv.) entirely	adj.	109	*who*l*e*
βασιλεύς, -έως, ὁ	king	noun	115	*basil*ica
ἐκκλησία, -ας, ἡ	assembly, church, congregation	noun	114	*ecclesi*ology
οἶκος, -ου, ὁ	house, home	noun	114	*eco*logy
ὅσος, -α, -ον	as great as, as many as, as much, how much	pron.	110	
ἀπέρχομαι	I depart, go away	verb	117	
ἀπέρχομαι, ἀπελεύσομαι, ἀπῆλθον, ἀπελήλυθα, ——, ——				
ἀποθνήσκω	I die, am about to die, am freed from	verb	111	
ἀποθνήσκω, ἀποθανοῦμαι, ἀπέθανον, ——, ——, ——				
ζητέω	I seek, desire	verb	117	
ζητέω, ζητήσω, ἐζήτησα, ἐζήτηκα, ——, ἐζητήθην				
κρίνω	I judge, decide, prefer	verb	114	*cri*tic
κρίνω, κρινῶ, ἔκρινα, κέκρικα, κέκριμαι, ἐκρίθην				
μέλλω	I am about to, intend	verb	109	
μέλλω, μελλήσω, ἔμελλον, ——, ——, ——				
μένω	I remain, live, abide, stay	verb	118	
μένω, μενῶ, ἔμεινα, μεμένηκα, ——, ——				

παρακαλέω	I call, urge, exhort, comfort, beseech	verb	109	*parac*lete
παρακαλέω, ——, παρεκάλεσα, ——, παρακέκλημαι, παρεκλήθην				

10.8: The Second Time Around

Second time around students should focus on the formation tables so that the λύω subjunctive and impera- tive paradigms can be created from memory. The optative is so infrequent that you do not need to focus on it, even in the second time around.

Chapter 11:
Infinitives Stripped Down

⇒**What's the Point:** While not quite as difficult or frequent as participles, infinitives are nonetheless another verbal form that is peppered throughout the NT. One out of every ten verb forms is an infinitive, so they occur quite often. Infinitives are another hybrid form (part verb and part noun), so they can function in numerous ways.

11.1: Infinitive Description

An infinitive is another hybrid word that is part noun and part verb. Its meaning is derived from its verb stem, so its lexical form is a verb. Infinitives have their own unique set of endings (a small set), and are limited primarily to Present tense (994) and Aorist tense (1, 242; 393 of them are 2Aorist forms). There are 49 Perfect tense infinitives, and 5 Future infinitives.[128]

Are these funky hybrid words in English too? Of course they are. *Like participles, infinitives describe action happening in and around the main verb*. Like a participle, the verbal part of an infinitive will often act adverbially or work with the main verb. Other times, an infinitive's noun characteristics make the infinitive function as a substantive that is usually the subject or object of the main verb. Like nouns, an infinitive can have an article, but they only ever take neuter singular articles. An infinitive in English usually has "to" in front of it, e.g. "to go." This is often, but not always, a good way to translate a Greek infinitive.

11.2: How Infinitives Are Formed

Infinitives are indeclinable verbal forms, so they do not take primary or secondary endings like Indicative verbs. They also do not take case endings like participles. The

---

[128] 4 of the 5 future infinitives are ἔσεσθαι, the future infinitive form of εἰμί.

simplicity of infinitives makes them easy to spot, although like participles they can do many things.

The following table breaks down how infinitives are formed, and there is commentary on the table below.

Table 71: Infinitive Formation

tense		voice					paradigm
			connecting vowel+ending			*= **final ending***	
Present	1st principal part	active	ε	+	εν	= ειν	λύειν
		mid/pass	ε	+	σθαι	= εσθαι	λύεσθαι
Aorist (NO augment)	3rd principal part *(1Aor. ends with σα, 2Aor. does not)*	active	--	+	ι	= σαι	λῦσαι
		active (2Aor.)	ε	+	εν	= ειν	βαλεῖν
		middle	--	+	σθαι	= σασθαι	λύσασθαι
		middle (2Aor.)	ε	+	σθαι	= εσθαι	βαλέσθαι
	6th principal part *(ends with θη)*	passive	--	+	ναι	= θηναι	λυθῆναι
Perfect	4th/5th principal part *(WITH reduplication)*	active	--	+	κεναι[129]	= κεναι	λελυκέναι
		mid/pass	--	+	σθαι	= σθαι	λελύσθαι

Infinitive formation is relatively straightforward because infinitives do not have case like participles, or person and number like indicative verbs. Keep in mind the following points as you study the table above:

1. The parsing of infinitives is the simplest of all inflected forms; tense, voice, mood (infinitive), lexical form.
2. Notice that σα is still the Aorist active and middle indicator, and θη is the Aorist passive indicator.

---

[129]Remember that a kappa suffix is characteristic of the Perfect tense.

3. 2Aorist forms are recognized by the altered stem. The endings of a 2Aorist form are just like the Present tense.
4. For the Aorist active and middle, remember that the sigma is slippery and may disappear in liquid verbs (see §1.3.1 and §1.3.2).
5. For the Aorist passive, remember that the θ sometimes disappears (§4.3.1.4).
6. Notice that Reduplication is still the indicator of the Perfect tense, and active forms still have a κ(ε) in the ending.
7. Like any contract verb form, a vowel at the end of a stem can collide with the connecting vowel and cause changes.
8. εἰμί occurs in a single infinitive form, εἶναι. Like εἰμί anywhere else, it does not have voice. So εἶναι is parsed as present infinitive.

11.3: What An Infinitive Can Do

An infinitive has a wide range of uses, so like participles it is wise to consult Wallace's *Greek Grammar Beyond the Basics* when you are struggling over what an infinitive is doing, or questioning the decision of an English translation. The following information covers the most common usages. The infinitive (and its article) will be red, with the infinitive phrase underlined. The infinitive's translation will be italicized.

11.3.1: Infinitive as Subject (nominative)

When there is no subject in the clause, an infinitive (or the infinitive phrase) may be acting as the subject. The infinitive as subject will frequently have a nominative neuter singular article, but not always.

- Ἐμοὶ γὰρ τὸ ζῆν Χριστὸς καὶ τὸ ἀποθανεῖν κέρδος. (Phil 1:21)
  For me, *to live* is Christ and *to die* is gain.
    – This verse is 2 verbless clauses (the assumed verb is ἔστιν, "is")
    – In both clauses, the infinitive has the nominative neuter singular article.

11.3.2: Infinitive as Object (accusative)

When there is no object in the clause, an infinitive (or the infinitive phrase) may be acting as the object. The infinitive as object will frequently have an accusative neuter singular article, but not always. When the infinitive is the object the usually-simple infinitive translation (adding "to" before it) does not always work.

- ἤδη ποτὲ ἀνεθάλετε τὸ ὑπὲρ ἐμοῦ φρονεῖν (Phil 4:10)
  now at last you have revived *concern* for me.

11.3.3: Appositional Infinitive or Epexegetical Infinitive (accusative)

When a clause already has an object (an accusative noun) and you *also* have an infinitive (or infinitive phrase) with an accusative neuter article, it is acting alongside the actual direct object. Occasionally, a genitive infinitive may also function in this manner. Apposition and Epexegetical are two roles a second accusative in the sentence can perform. In general, they are giving you more information about the object, but the difference is subtle and not always easy to distinguish. Apposition renames the object, while epexegetical further defines it (it exegetes the object a little bit for you). Another thing to note is that an epexegetical infinitive is essential to the sentence, it can't be removed without losing something. An appositional infinitive, though, can usually be removed without loss of meaning. However, even these distinctions do not always work well. Just remember, it is a second accusative in the clause tied to the actual object.

- Τοῦτο γάρ ἐστιν θέλημα τοῦ θεοῦ, ὁ ἁγιασμὸς ὑμῶν, ἀπέχεσθαι ὑμᾶς ἀπὸ τῆς πορνείας (1 Thess 4:3)
  For this is the will of God, your holiness: that *you abstain* from fornication.
    - "the will of God" is the object of the clause, while "your holiness" is an epexegetical noun.
    - "that you abstain from fornication" is the infinitive phrase, functioning in apposition.
- δέδωκα ὑμῖν τὴν ἐξουσίαν τοῦ πατεῖν ἐπάνω ὄφεων καὶ σκορπίων (Luke 10:19)
  I have given you authority *to tread* on snakes and scorpions.
    - "authority" is the object of the clause
    - The infinitive phrase is epexegetical, describing the object more.

11.3.4: Infinitive in Indirect Discourse

Often an infinitive can follow a verb (including a participle) of perception (e.g. "I know") or communication (e.g. "they said"). This type of infinitive will be anarthrous (i.e. no article). When an infinitive is functioning in this way, it is usually translated the same as the main verb in the sentence, and this verb is usually an indicative or an imperative. It may be translated with the typical infinitive "to" in front, it may use "that," or quotation marks may indicate the indirect discourse.

- ὁ λέγων ἐν αὐτῷ μένειν ... (1Jn 2:6)
  The one who says '*I remain* in him'...
    – In this example the communication verb is a participle
    – Notice how an acceptable translation would also be "The one who says *that he remains* in him..."
- τίνα με λέγετε εἶναι; (Mark 8:29)
  who do you say *that I am*.
    – In this example the main verb is a communication word
    – The infinitive εἶναι ("to be") is translated as a first person indicative.

11.3.5: Complementary Infinitive

If someone said to you "I want," you would be thinking, "you want what?!" The verb "I want" demands some help: "I want *to eat* supper." Notice how "I want" needs an infinitive to complete its thought. This is what is called a complementary infinitive. Numerous Greek (and English) verbs demand some help from a complementary infinitive.

- καὶ ἤρξαντο τίλλειν στάχυας καὶ ἐσθίειν (Matt 12:1)
  and they began *to pluck* heads of grain and *to eat*.

11.3.6: Adverbial Infinitive

Like participles, the predominant function of an infinitive is adverbial. Unlike a participle, though, the construction of an adverbial infinitive makes the type of adverbial function clear. Most adverbial infinitives are preceded by the accusative neuter singular article (τό) *and* a preposition. An adverbial infinitive can also be preceded by a conjunction. Occasionally, the infinitive by itself or the infinitive with a genitive article can also act adverbially.

1. PURPOSE or RESULT—An infinitive or infinitive phrase can indicate the purpose or result of the main verb's action. These two functions are very closely linked and sometimes hard to tell apart. Words like *to, so that, in order to,* or *as a result* are often used to translate. The constructions can be: 1) just the infinitive, 2) τοῦ + infinitive, 3) εἰς τό + infinitive, or 4) ὥστε + infinitive.

- Μὴ νομίσητε ὅτι ἦλθον <u>καταλῦσαι</u> τὸν νόμον (Matt 5:17)
  Do not think that I have come *(in order) to destroy* the law
- καὶ ἀπήγαγον αὐτὸν <u>εἰς τὸ σταυρῶσαι</u> (Matt 27:31)
  and they led him away *to crucify* him.

2. PURPOSE—While the previous constructions can all indicate the purpose or result of the main verb, there are two particular constructions that indicate purpose. Words like *to, so that,* and *in order to* are often used to translate. The constructions can be: 1) πρὸς τό + infinitive or 2) ὡς + infinitive.[130]

   - ἐγὼ δὲ λέγω ὑμῖν ὅτι πᾶς ὁ βλέπων γυναῖκα <u>πρὸς τὸ ἐπιθυμῆσαι</u>... (Matt 5:28)
     But I say to you that anyone who looks at a woman *in order to lust*...

3. CAUSE—The infinitive phrase διὰ τό + infinitive will indicate <u>the cause of the main verb</u>. The translation is relatively straightforward, just translate διά as it should be, *because*.

   - καὶ εὐθέως ἐξανέτειλεν <u>διὰ τὸ μὴ ἔχειν</u> βάθος γῆς (Matt 13:5)
     and they sprang up quickly, *because they had* no depth of soil.

4. TIME: ANTECEDENT—The infinitive phrase μετὰ τό + infinitive can indicate an action that occurred <u>prior to</u> the action of the main verb. The translation is straightforward, simply translate μετὰ as it should be, *after*.

   - <u>μετὰ τὸ ἐγερθῆναί</u> με προάξω ὑμᾶς εἰς τὴν Γαλιλαίαν. (Matt 26:32)
     after I have been raised I will go before you into Galilee.

5. TIME: SIMULTANEOUS—The infinitive phrase ἐν τῷ + infinitive can indicate an action that occurs <u>at the same time as</u> the action of the main verb. The translation of this type uses *while* or *as*.

   - καὶ <u>ἐν τῷ σπείρειν αὐτὸν</u> ἃ μὲν ἔπεσεν παρὰ τὴν ὁδόν (Matt 13:4)
     and *while* he *sowed*, some seeds fell on the road.

6. TIME: SUBSEQUENT—The infinitive phrase can indicate an action that occurred <u>after</u> the action of the main verb. The construction will be 1) πρὸ τοῦ + infinitive, 2) πρὶν + infinitive, or 3) πρὶν ἤ + infinitive. The translation is straightforward, simply translate πρὸ or πρὶν as they should be, *before*.

---

[130] ὡς + infinitive can also indicate result, but this is rare.

- ὁ πατὴρ ὑμῶν ὧν χρείαν ἔχετε <u>πρὸ τοῦ ὑμᾶς αἰτῆσαι</u> αὐτόν (Matt 6:8)
  your Father knows what you need *before* you *ask* him.

11.4: Understanding Infinitive Function and Translation

In the *Stripped Down* approach, you do not need to determine infinitive function and translation on your own. What you do need to do is understand how and why modern translators have come to the decisions they have. Infinitive translation is more straightforward than participles, particularly adverbial participles. The following flowchart is a "determination device" for infinitives. As you come across Greek infinitives in the NT and study them in conjunction with English translation(s), take the time to see how the infinitive has flowed through the flowchart. The following points are items to note as you use and study the flowchart:

- A lone infinitive is the most flexible construction, as it can perform any function.
- Preposition + article + infinitive is the most common construction, and is *always* adverbial.
- conjunction + infinitive is *always* adverbial.
- If your infinitive has the article τό, your bible software will parse it for you as nominative or accusative. This helps to determine if the infinitive is the subject (nominative), object (accusative), appositional (accusative), or epexegetical (accusative).
- While the standard "to _____" translation is adequate in some situations, it does not always work when bringing the infinitive into English. Sometimes the infinitive is translated more like an indicative, an imperative, or a participle.
- The adverbial functions in the flowchart are listed in order of frequency. i.e. purpose and result functions are the most common.
- Remember, the flowchart does not cover everything an infinitive can do. Consult Wallace's *Greek Grammar Beyond the Basics* to understand the other minor functions.

Table 72: Infinitive Flowchart

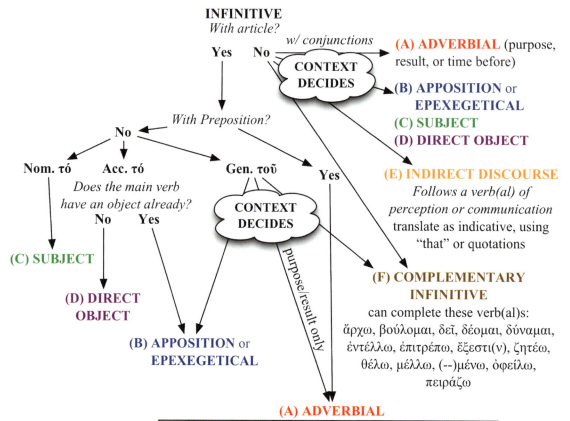

Adverbial Use	Constructions	Translation
purpose or result	just infinitive ------- εἰς τό + infinitive τοῦ + infinitive ------- ὥστε + infinitive	"to" "so that" "in order to" "as a result"
purpose	πρὸς τό + infinitive ------- ὡς + infinitive	"to" "so that" "in order to"
cause	διὰ τό + infinitive	"because"
time: antecedent	πρὸ τοῦ + infinitive ------- πρίν (ἤ) + infinitive	"before"
time: simultaneous	ἐν τῷ + infinitive	"while" or "as"
time: subsequent	μετὰ τό + infinitive	"after"

11.4.1: The Sort-of-Subject of an Infinitive

Because an adverbial infinitive is describing an action happening in and around the main verb, it only makes sense that there is someone or something doing the action at times. Like a participle, an infinitive is not a true verb, so it does not have a proper subject, but there is someone or something in the clause that is doing the action of the infinitive. This sort-of-subject will be an accusative noun or pronoun.[131] Sometimes it is the subject of the verbs, sometimes it is the object of the verb: eg: "I asked him *to go* wash his hands." Other times, though, the infinitive phrase will have an accusative acting as the sort-of-subject. Sometimes, an infinitive phrase will even have 2 accusatives, one acting as the sort-of-subject, and the other acting as the object of the infinitive. This accusative sort-of-subject is a time when an accusative (normally object) is translated as a nominative (normally subject). (taken from §11.3), highlight how the infinitive is connected to its sort-of-subject in the clause. The infinitive is in red, the phrase is underlined, its sort-of-subject will be blue, and the infinitive translation is *italicized*.

- καὶ ἐν τῷ σπείρειν αὐτὸν ἃ μὲν ἔπεσεν παρὰ τὴν ὁδόν (Matt 13:4)
  and *while he sowed*, some seeds fell on the road.
    - The pronoun that is part of the infinitive phrase is in the accusative. The regular translation of αὐτὸν would be "him," but because it is the sort-of-subject of the infinitive, it is translated as "he."

- ὁ πατὴρ ὑμῶν ὧν χρείαν ἔχετε πρὸ τοῦ ὑμᾶς αἰτῆσαι αὐτόν (Matt 6:8)
  your Father knows what you need *before you ask* him.
    - In this example there are 2 accusatives in the infinitive phrase. The first is the sort-of-subject, and the second is the object of the infinitive.

- μετὰ τὸ ἐγερθῆναί με προάξω ὑμᾶς εἰς τὴν Γαλιλαίαν. (Matt 26:32)
  after I have been raised I will go before you into Galilee.
    - Like the first example, the pronoun με is an accusative and would regularly be translated as "me." Since it is the sort-of-subject of the infinitive, it is translated as "I."

- καὶ ἀπήγαγον αὐτὸν εἰς τὸ σταυρῶσαι (Matt 27:31)
  and they led him away *to crucify* him.

---

[131]It may also be a predicate nominative.

– Notice how in the Greek there is no extra pronoun in the infinitive phrase. The object of the sentence is the sort-of-subject. To clarify this, most translations repeat the pronoun again at the end.

11.4.2: The Tense Of An Infinitive

As with participles, the tense of an infinitive is often hard to translate. Technically speaking, a present tense infinitive displays internal aspect, an aorist tense infinitive displays external aspect, and a perfect tense infinitive is stative.[132] However, when it comes to translating these aspectual differences of an infinitive into readable English, the tense does not usually come through. Present and aorist infinitives are usually translated the same, while perfect infinitives often have the word "have" or "had" in its translation. Remember, in the *Stripped Down* approach, you don't need to make these translation decisions! You just need to understand the choices modern English translations make and understand what they have left out!

11.5: The Least You Need to Know

You should be able to clearly and accurately answer these questions. Use these online flashcards (http://quizlet.com/_7tfyr) to memorize the answers:

- What is an infinitive?
- What type of articles do infinitives take?
- What 3 tenses occur as infinitives?
- What are all of the components in infinitive parsing?
- What is the indicator for an aorist active or middle infinitive?
- What is the indicator for an aorist passive infinitive?
- What is the indicator for a perfect active or middle/passive infinitive?
- What is the present active suffix for infinitives?
- What is the suffix for all middle(/passive) infinitives (except Aorist passive)?
- What is a complementary infinitive?
- How are infinitives translated in indirect discourse?

---

[132] The aspect of the Greek tenses were discussed in §4.1.3.

- Why is an infinitive all by itself the most difficult to translate?
- An infinitive with an article and preposition is always performing what function?
- What is an infinitive phrase and what can it do?
- What is the "sort-of-subject" of an infinitive?

11.6: Greek@Logos

Utilizing the *Mastering Logos Bible Software* course or the Logos help files, Logos forums, Logos wiki, and videos provided, users should take the time to learn:

- How to utilize Logos notes, highlighting, and clippings
    - See Lectures 40–42 of *Mastering Logos Bible Software*
    - See the "Notes, Highlights & Clipping" articles on www.logos.com/videos

11.7: Vocabulary

Word	Meaning	Type	Freq.	Derivatives
ἀγαθός, -ή, -όν	good, useful	adj.	102	
καλός, -ή, -όν	good, beautiful	adj.	100	*call*igraphy
ἐκεῖ	there, in that place	adv.	105	
ὅτε	when	conj.	103	
ἐξουσία, -ας, ἡ	authority, power	noun	102	
ὁδός, -οῦ, ἡ	way, road, journey; conduct	noun	100	odometer
ὀφθαλμός, -οῦ, ὁ	eye, sight	noun	100	*ophthamo*logy
ψυχή, -ῆς, ἡ	soul, life, self	noun	103	*psych*ology
ὥρα, -ας, ἡ	hour; occasion, moment	noun	106	

πῶς	how?	partic.	103	
ἀλλήλων (-οις, -ους)	one other (of one another, to one another)	pron.	100	par*allel*
αἴρω	I raise, take up, take away	verb	101	*aor*ta
αἴρω, ἀρῶ, ἦρα, ἦρκα, ἦρμαι, ἤρθην				
ἀνίστημι	I rise, get up; I raise	verb	108	
ἀνίστημι, ἀναστήσω, ἀνέστησα, ἀνέστηκα, ἀνέστημαι, ἀνεστάθην				
δεῖ	it is necessary	verb	101	
δεῖ [Imperfect, ἔδει]				
σῴζω (σώζω)	I save, heal, deliver, rescue	verb	106	
σῴζω (σώζω), σώσω, ἔσωσα, σέσωκα, σέσωμαι, ἐσώθην				
τίθημι	I put, place	verb	100	
τίθημι, θήσω, ἔθηκα, τέθεικα, τέθειμαι, ἐτέθην				

11.8: The Second Time Around

There are not many infinitive endings, so be sure the second time around that you have them memorized and can create a λύω table from memory. In addition, focus on the infinitive flowchart and analyze every infinitive you come across in exercises. Do your best to memorize the infinitive flowchart and practice creating it from memory.

Where Do I Go From Here?

If you've made it this far, your brain probably hurts but it was worth it! The goal of this *Stripped Down* approach is to make the original language of the NT accessible to you without compromising a proper un- derstanding of the grammar, and to understand how to utilize the latest tools. You may have heard your professor say, "a little bit of Greek is a dangerous thing." Just go on YouTube and you'll swiftly find that many preachers and teachers who do not really know Greek (or Hebrew) frequently use it and make mistakes. It was necessary to cover all of the basics in order to help you realize the complex machine that is Koine Greek. You hopefully realize now that working with the Greek NT alongside your preferred English translation is and will be incredibly rewarding for your study of the NT for life. No English translation is perfect, and even the best translations out there lose something in their interpretive choices.

Going Beyond

For those of you who have completed this book, you understand Greek and can work with it using your bible software. Picking up and reading a Greek NT on its own is a different beast altogether and you are not yet equipped for that. With another few months of hard work, though, you can get to the point where you can start reading sections of the Greek NT with a nice Greek NT like *The UBS Greek New Testament: A Reader's Edition*. Here are some suggestions if you want to go beyond:

1. Each chapter has a *Second Time Around* section at the end of the chapter. Go through each chapter again, and the *Second Time Around* section will give you some tips on what to focus on. In a few cases it also offers some advanced information.
2. Do the additional exercises for another 11 weeks that are included in the workbook.
3. Practice parsing. I recommend ParseGreek for iOS and Android. If you do not have an iOS or Android device, then use the Mac/PC program called *Paradigms Master Pro*. The additional workbook exercises will ask you to work with these programs.

4. Increase your vocabulary. Many of the popular full-year introductory grammars aim to teach you all words that occur 50x or more. The first pass through this text has taught you all words that occur 100x or more plus all proper nouns that occur 50x, a total of 161 words. To get to 50x or more, you need to learn 149 more words. I would actually recommend going a little bit further, to all words that occur 30x or more, which would be 300 words more—461 words all together. I recommend this because the *Reader's Greek New Testament* (recommended below) works on the assumption that you know up to 30x. To aid in your vocabulary acquisition, I have assembled 12 lists of words in Appendix A, placed into groups of about 25. A 13th list provides some of the highest frequency irregular verb forms. I recommend FlashGreek Pro for iOS and Android, as it is designed to be compatible with this grammar.

5. STOP using your Bible software, and start practicing reading. If you want to get to the point of reading Greek on your own, it is time to flex your brain muscle more. In addition to this grammar I also recommend the *Reader's Greek New Testament* mentioned above.

Appendix A: Additional Vocabulary Lists

List 1
frequency: 99-90

Word	Meaning	Type	Freq.
αἷμα, -ματος, τό	blood	noun	97
ἀκολουθέω	I follow, accompany	verb	90
ἀπόλλυμι	I destroy, kill; I perish, die	verb	90
ἄρτος, -ου, ὁ	bread, loaf, food; burden	noun	97
γεννάω	I bear, beget, produce	verb	97
διδάσκω	I teach	verb	97
δικαιοσύνη, -ης, ἡ	righteousness, justice	noun	92
εἰρήνη, -ης, ἡ	peace, health	noun	92
ἐνώπιον	(+gen) before, in front of	preposition	94
ἕτερος, -α, -ον	other, another, different	adjective	98
ἔτι	yet, still	adverb	93
θάλασσα, -ης, ἡ	sea, lake	noun	91
κάθημαι	I sit (down), live	verb	91
μηδείς, μηδεμία, μηδέν	no one, nothing	adjective	90
οἰκία, -ας, ἡ	house, home	noun	93
περιπατέω	I walk (around), live	verb	95
πίπτω	I fall	verb	90
πούς, ποδός, ὁ	foot	noun	93
τέκνον, -ου, τό	child, descendent	noun	99
τόπος, -ου, ὁ	place, position; opportunity	noun	94
φοβέω (mid. φοβεόμαι)	I fear	verb	95

List 2
frequency: 89-79

Word	Meaning	Type	Freq.
ἀναβαίνω	I go up, come up, rise up, advance	verb	82
ἀπόστολος, -ου, ὁ	apostle	noun	80
ἄρχομαι (ἄρχω)	I begin; I rule over	verb	86
δίκαιος, -α, -ον	right, righteous, just	adjective	79
ἕκαστος, -η, -ον	each, every	adjective	82
ἐκβάλλω	I cast out, send out, drive out	verb	81
ἑπτά (indecl.)	seven	adjective	88
καιρός, -οῦ, ὁ	(appointed) time, season	noun	85
καταβαίνω	I come down, go down	verb	81
μᾶλλον	more, rather	adverb	81
μήτηρ, μητρός, ἡ	mother	noun	83
Μωϋσῆς, -έως, ὁ	Moses	proper noun	80
ὅπου (ποῦ)	where, whereas	conjunction	82
οὔτε	neither	conjunction	87
πέμπω	I send	verb	79
πληρόω	I fill, fulfill, complete	verb	86
προσέρχομαι	I come to	verb	86
προσεύχομαι	I pray	verb	85
ὑπάγω	I depart, go away; I draw off	verb	79
ὥστε	therefore, so that, in order that	conjunction	83

List 3
frequency: 78-70

Word	Meaning	Type	Freq.
αἰτέω	I ask, demand	verb	70
αἰώνιος, -ος, -ον	eternal	adjective	71
ἀνοίγω	I open, unlock, disclose	verb	77
ἀποκτείνω (ἀποκτέννω)	to kill	verb	74
βαπτίζω	I baptize, wash, dip, immerse	verb	77
δώδεκα (indecl.)	twelve	adjective	75
ἐμός, -ή, -όν	my, mine	adjective	76
ἔσομαι	I shall be (future of εἰμί)	verb	
εὐαγγέλιον, -ου, τό	good news, gospel	noun	76
ἱερόν, -οῦ, τό	temple	noun	72
κεφαλή, -ῆς, ἡ	head	noun	75
μαρτυρέω	I bear witness, testify	verb	76
πίνω	I drink	verb	73
πονηρός, -ά, -όν	evil, bad, wicked	adjective	78
πρόσωπον, -ου, τό	face, appearance, presence	noun	76
πῦρ, πυρός, τό	fire	noun	71
σημεῖον, -ου, τό	sign, miracle	noun	77
στόμα, -ματος, τό	mouth	noun	78
τηρέω	I keep, guard, observe	verb	70
ὕδωρ, ὕδατος, τό	water	noun	76
φῶς, φωτός, τό	light	noun	73
χαίρω	I rejoice	verb	74

List 4
frequency: 69-62

Word	Meaning	Type	Freq.
ἄγω	I bring, lead, arrest	verb	67
ἀπολύω	I release, divorce	verb	66
γραμματεύς, -έως, ὁ	scribe, secretary	noun	63
δαιμόνιον, -ου, τό	demon	noun	63
δοκέω	I think, suppose, seem	verb	62
εἴτε	(even) if; whether...or, or, either/or	conjunction	65
ἐντολή, -ῆς, ἡ	commandment, law	noun	67
ἔξω	[adv.] without; (+gen) out, outside	adverb; preposition	63
ἐρωτάω	I ask, request, entreat	verb	63
θέλημα, -ματος, τό	will, desire, wish	noun	62
θρόνος, -ου, ὁ	throne, seat	noun	62
Ἰσραήλ, ὁ	Israel	noun	68
καρπός, -οῦ, ὁ	fruit, crop, result	noun	66
ὄρος, -ους, τό	mountain, high hill	noun	63
πιστός, -ή, -όν	faithful, believing; reliable	adjective	67
πλοῖον, -ου, τό	boat, ship	noun	67
πρεσβύτερος, -α, -ον	older; elder	adjective	66
ῥῆμα, -ματος, τό	word, thing	noun	68
σάββατον, -ου, τό	sabbath, week	noun	68
τρεῖς, τρεῖς, τρία	three	adjective	69
φέρω	I bear, carry, produce, bring	verb	66
φημί	I say, affirm	verb	66

List 5
frequency: 61-56

Word	Meaning	Type	Freq.
ἀγαπητός, -ή, -όν	beloved	adjective	61
ἀσπάζομαι	I greet, salute, welcome	verb	59
δέχομαι	I take, receive	verb	56
διδάσκαλος, -ου, ὁ	teacher	noun	59
δοξάζω	I praise, honor, glorify	verb	61
ἐπερωτάω	I ask (for), question, demand	verb	56
εὐθύς (εὐθέως)	immediately (adv.); straight (adj.)	adverb	59
ἤδη	now, already	adverb	61
θεωρέω	I look at, behold, see, observe	verb	58
ἱμάτιον, -ου, τό	garment, cloak, clothing	noun	60
κηρύσσω	I proclaim, preach	verb	61
λίθος, -ου, ὁ	stone	noun	59
μέσος, -η, -ον	middle; (prep +gen) in the middle; (adv.) among	adjective	58
μηδέ	nor, and not, but not	conjunction	56
νύξ, νυκτός, ἡ	night	noun	61
προσκυνέω	I worship; I do obeisance	verb	60
συνάγω	I gather together, invite	verb	59
συναγωγή, -ῆς, ἡ	synagogue, meeting, gathering	noun	56
τοιοῦτος, -αύτη, -οῦτο(ν)	such, of such kind	pronoun	57
τρίτος, -η, -ον	third	adjective	56
ὑπάρχω	I am, exist; I possess	verb	60
χαρά, -ᾶς, ἡ	joy, delight, gladness	noun	59
ὧδε	here; in this way, so, thus	adverb	61

List 6
frequency: 55-50

Word	Meaning	Type	Freq.
ἄρα	then, therefore	particle	52
ἀρχή, -ῆς, ἡ	beginning, first; ruler	noun	55
γλῶσσα, -ης, ἡ	tongue, language	noun	50
γραφή, -ῆς, ἡ	written document, scripture	noun	50
δεξιός, -ά, -όν	right, right hand, right side	adjective	54
διό	therefore, for this reason	conjunction	53
ἐλπίς, -ίδος, ἡ	hope	noun	53
ἐπαγγελία, -ας, ἡ	promise	noun	52
ἔσχατος, -η, -ον	last, least, end	adjective	52
εὐαγγελίζω (mid. εὐαγγελίζομαι)	I bring good news, preach, announce	verb	54
κακός, -ή, -όν	evil, bad, wrong, harm	adjective	50
κράζω	I call out, cry out	verb	55
λοιπός, -ή, -όν	remaining; (adv.) henceforth, finally	adjective	55
μακάριος, -α, -ον	blessed, happy	adjective	50
ὅπως	how, (so) that, in order that	conjunction	53
οὐχί	not, no	particle	54
παιδίον, -ου, τό	child, infant	noun	52
παραβολή, -ῆς, ἡ	parable	noun	50
πείθω	I persuade, believe, trust	verb	52
πλείων, -ων, -ον	larger, more, greater (comparative of πόλυς)	adjective	55
σοφία, -ας, ἡ	wisdom	noun	51
σπείρω	I sow	verb	52
τυφλός, -ή, -όν	blind	adjective	50
χρόνος, -ου, ὁ	time	noun	54

List 7
frequency: 49-46

Word	Meaning	Type	Freq.
ἁμαρτωλός, -ός, -όν	sinner, sinful	adjective	47
ἀποδίδωμι	I give back, pay	verb	48
ἄχρι (ἄχρις)	(+gen) until	conjunction, preposition	49
ἔμπροσθεν	(+gen) before, in front of	adverb, preposition	48
ἔρημος, -ος, -ον	desolate, wilderness, desert	adjective	48
ἔτος, -ους, τό	year	noun	49
θηρίον, -ου, τό	wild animal	noun	46
καθίζω	I sit, set, place	verb	46
κρατέω	I grasp, am strong, take possession	verb	47
κρίσις -εως, ἡ	judgment, decision	noun	47
μείζων (μείζον)	greater, larger (comparative of μέγας)	adjective	48
μικρός, -ά, -όν	small, little; a little, a short time	adjective	46
οὐαί	woe! how terrible?	interjection	46
οὐκέτι	no longer	adverb	47
παραλαμβάνω	I take along, accept, receive	verb	49
ποῦ	where?	particle	48
πρό	(+gen) before, above	preposition	47
προσφέρω	I bring, I offer	verb	47
σταυρόω	I crucify	verb	46
σωτηρία, -ας, ἡ	salvation, deliverance	noun	46
φανερόω	I reveal, make known	verb	49
φόβος, -ου, ὁ	fear, terror; reverence	noun	47
φυλακή, -ῆς, ἡ	guard, watch, prison	noun	47
χρεία, -ας, ἡ	need	noun	49

List 8
frequency: 45-43

Word	Meaning	Type	Freq.
ἁμαρτάνω	I sin	verb	43
ἀπαγγέλλω	I report, tell, bring news	verb	45
γενεά, -ᾶς, ἡ	generation	noun	43
δεύτερος, -α, -ον	second	adjective	43
δέω	I bind, stop	verb	43
διέρχομαι	I go/pass through	verb	43
διώκω	I pursue, persecute	verb	45
ἐπιγινώσκω	I know	verb	44
Ἡρῴδης, ου, ὁ	Herod	proper noun	43
θαυμάζω	I marvel, wonder	verb	43
θεραπεύω	I serve, heal	verb	43
θλῖψις, -ψεως, ἡ	affliction, trouble, tribulation, oppression	noun	45
Ἰουδαία, -ας, ἡ	Judea	proper noun	44
Ἰούδας, α, ὁ	Judas/Judah	proper noun	44
ἴσθι	you be! (Imperative of εἰμί)	verb	
κατοικέω	I settle, dwell, inhabit	verb	44
ναός, -ου, ὁ	temple; palace	noun	45
ὅμοιος, -α, -ον	like, similar	adjective	45
σεαυτοῦ -ῆς	of yourself (sing.)	pronoun	43
σπέρμα, -ματος, τό	seed, offspring	noun	43
φωνέω	I call, to shout	verb	43

List 9
frequency: 42-40

Word	Meaning	Type	Freq.
ἀνάστασις, -εως, ἡ	standing up, resurrection	noun	42
ἄξιος, -α, -ον	worthy	adjective	41
ἐγγίζω	I bring near, come near	verb	42
ἐργάζομαι	I work	verb	41
ἑτοιμάζω	I prepare	verb	40
εὐλογέω	I bless	verb	41
Ἰάκωβος, -οῦ, ὁ	Jacob; James	proper noun	42
καινός, -ή, -όν	new	adjective	42
κλαίω	I weep, cry	verb	40
λογίζομαι	I count, think, calculate	verb	40
μέρος, -ους, τό	part	noun	42
μισέω	I hate	verb	40
μνημεῖον, -ου, τό	tomb, monument	noun	40
οἰκοδομέω	I build	verb	40
ὀλίγος, -η, -ον	little, few	adjective	40
πάντοτε	always	adverb	41
παρίστημι (παριστάνω)	I present, offer; (intrans.:) I stand by	verb	41
πάσχω	I suffer	verb	42
σήμερον	today	adverb	41
τέλος, -ους, τό	end, goal; tribute	noun	40
τέσσαρες	four	adjective	41
τιμή, -ῆς, ἡ	honor	noun	41
χωρίς	separately (adv.) (+gen) without	adverb; preposition	41

List 10
frequency: 39-37

Word	Meaning	Type	Freq.
ἀκάθαρτος, ἀκάθαρτος, ἀκάθαρτον	unclean	adjective	32
ἀναγινώσκω	I read	verb	32
ἅπας, ἅπασα, ἅπαν	all, every	adjective	34
ἀρνέομαι	I deny	verb	33
ἀσθενέω	I be weak	verb	33
βιβλίον, -ου, τό	scroll, papyrus strip	noun	34
βλασφημέω	I slander, blaspheme	verb	34
διαθήκη, -ης, ἡ	covenant	noun	33
διακονία, -ας, ἡ	service, ministry	noun	34
δυνατός, δυνατή, δυνατόν	possible, strong, able	adjective	32
ἐκπορεύομαι	I go, come out	verb	33
ἐχθρός, ἐχθρά, ἐχθρόν	hostile, enemy	adjective	32
ἥλιος, -ου, ὁ	sun	noun	32
Ἰωσήφ, ὁ	Joseph	proper noun	35
μάρτυς, μάρτυρος, ὁ	witness	noun	35
μέλος, μέλους, τό	body part; musical part, melody	noun	34
μετανοέω	I repent	verb	34
μήτε	and not; neither . . . nor	conjunction	34
ναί	yes	particle	33
οἶνος, -ου, ὁ	wine	noun	34
ὀπίσω	(+gen) after (prep.); back (adv.)	adverb, improper prep.	35
ὀφείλω	I am obligated, I owe	verb	35
παραγγέλλω	I command	verb	32
ποῖος, ποῖα, ποῖον	what kind of, which	pronoun	33
πτωχός, πτωχή, πτωχόν	poor	adjective	34
ὑπομονή, -ης, ἡ	endurance; staying	noun	32
ὑποστρέφω	I return	verb	35

List 11
frequency: 36-33

Word	Meaning	Type	Freq.
ἀγρός, -οῦ, ὁ	field	noun	36
ἅπας, ἅπασα, ἅπαν	all, every	adjective	34
ἀρνέομαι	I deny	verb	33
ἄρτι	now	adverb	36
ἀσθενέω	I be weak	verb	33
βιβλίον, -ου, τό	scroll, papyrus strip	noun	34
βλασφημέω	I slander, blaspheme	verb	34
διαθήκη, -ης, ἡ	covenant	noun	33
διακονία, -ας, ἡ	service, ministry	noun	34
ἐκπορεύομαι	I go, come out	verb	33
ἐπιστρέφω	I turn back, return, turn	verb	36
εὐθέως	immediately, at once, suddenly	adverb	36
Ἰωσήφ, ὁ	Joseph	proper noun	35
μάρτυς, -υρος, ὁ	witness	noun	35
μέλος, -ους, τό	body part; musical part, melody	noun	34
μετανοέω	I repent	verb	34
μήτε	and not; neither . . . nor	conjunction	34
ναί	yes	particle	33
οἶνος, -ου, ὁ	wine	noun	34
ὀπίσω	back (adv.); (+gen) after (prep.)	adverb; preposition	35
ὀργή, -ῆς, ἡ	wrath; anger	noun	36
οὖς, ὠτός, τό	ear	noun	36
ὀφείλω	I am obligated, I owe	verb	35
περιτομή, -ῆς, ἡ	circumcision	noun	36
ποῖος, -α, -ον	what kind of, which	pronoun	33
προσευχή, -ῆς, ἡ	prayer	noun	36
πτωχός, -ή, -όν	poor	adjective	34

Σατανᾶς, -ᾶ, ὁ	Satan	noun	36
ὑποστρέφω	I return	verb	35
Φίλιππος, -ου, ὁ	Philip	proper noun	36
ὥσπερ	as, just as	conjunction	36

List 12
frequency: 32-30

Word	Meaning	Type	Freq.
ἀγοράζω	I buy	verb	30
ἀκάθαρτος, -ος, -ον	unclean	adjective	32
ἀναγινώσκω	I read	verb	32
ἄνεμος, -ου, ὁ	wind	noun	31
ἀρνίον, -ου, τό	lamb, small lamb	noun	30
δείκνυμι (δείκνυω)	I show, explain	verb	30
διδαχή, -ῆς, ἡ	teaching	noun	30
δυνατός, -ή, -όν	possible, strong, able	adjective	32
ἐγγύς	(+gen) near	adverb; preposition	31
ἐλπίζω	I hope	verb	31
ἔξεστι(ν)	it is right, possible	verb	31
ἐπικαλέω (ἐπικαλέομαι)	I call on	verb	30
ἐχθρός, -ά, -όν	hostile, enemy	adjective	32
ἥλιος, -ου, ὁ	sun	noun	32
ἱερεύς, -έως, ὁ	priest	noun	31
καθαρίζω	I cleanse	verb	31
ὁμοίως	likewise	adverb	30
παραγγέλλω	I command	verb	32
παρρησία, -ας, ἡ	boldness	noun	31
πλῆθος, -ους, τό	multitude	noun	31
πλήν	but, nevertheless (conj.) (+gen) only, except	conjunction; preposition	31
ποτήριον, -ου, τό	cup	noun	31
σκότος, -ους, τό	darkness	noun	31
συνείδησις, -εως, ἡ	conscience	noun	30
συνέρχομαι	I come together; I go together	verb	30

ὑπομονή, -ῆς, ἡ	endurance; staying	noun	32
φαίνω	I appear, shine	verb	31
φυλάσσω	I guard, keep	verb	31
φυλή, -ῆς, ἡ	tribe	noun	31

List 13
Frequent Principal Parts of Irregular Verbs

Word	Meaning	Type
ἀκήκοα	I have heard (perfect of ἀκούω)	verb
ἀπέθανον	I died (Aorist of ἀποθνήσκω)	verb
γέγονα	I have become (perfect of γίνομαι)	verb
ἔβαλον	I threw (Aorist of βάλλω)	verb
ἐγενόμην	I had been (Aorist middle of γίνομαι)	verb
ἔγνων	I knew (Aorist of γινώσκω)	verb
εἶδον	I saw (2nd Aorist of ὁράω)	verb
εἶπον	I said (2nd Aorist of λέγω)	verb
ἔλαβον	I took, received (Aorist of λαμβάνω)	verb
ἐλήλυθα	I have come, gone (perfect of ἔρχομαι)	verb
ἐληλύθειν	I was coming (pluperfect of ἔρχομαι)	verb
ἔπεσον	I fall, fell (2Aorist of πίπτω)	verb
ἔπιον	I drank (Aorist of πίνω)	verb
ἔσχον	I had (Aorist of ἔχω)	verb
εὕρηκα	I have found (Aorist of εὑρίσκω)	verb
εὗρον	I found (Aorist of εὑρίσκω)	verb
ἔφαγον	I ate (Aorist of ἐσθίω)	verb
ἤγαγον	I brought, lead (Aorist of ἄγω)	verb
ἦλθον	I came, went (2nd Aorist of ἔρχομαι)	verb
ἤνεγκα	I brought, bore, carried (Aorist of φέρω)	verb

Appendix B: Principal Parts

All asterisked items indicate 2Aorist forms.

First	Second	Third	Fourth	Fifth	Sixth
ἀγαπάω	ἀγαπήσω	ἠγάπησα	ἠγάπηκα	ἠγάπημαι	ἠγαπήθην
ἄγω	ἄξω	ἤγαγον*	ἀγείοχα	ἦγμαι	ἤχθην
αἴρω	ἀρῶ	ἦρα	ἦρκα	ἦρμαι	ἤρθην
αἰτέω	αἰτήσω	ᾔτησα	ᾔτηκα	ᾔτημαι	ᾐτήθην
ἀκολουθέω	ἀκολουθήσω	ἠκολούθησα	ἠκολούθηκα	ἠκολούθημαι	ἠκολουθήθην
ἀκούω	ἀκούσω	ἤκουσα	ἀκήκοα	ἤκουσμαι	ἠκούσθην
ἀναβαίνω	ἀναβήσομαι	ἀνέβην*	ἀναβέβημα	----------	----------
ἀνίστημι	ἀναστήσω	ἀνέστησα	ἀνέστηκα	ἀνέστημαι	ἀνεστάθην
ἀνοίγω	ἀνοίξω	ἀνέῳξα	ἀνέῳγα	ἀνέῳγμαι	ἀνεῴχθην
ἀπαγγέλλω	ἀπαγγελῶ	ἀπήγγειλα	----------	ἀπήγγελμαι	ἀπηγγέλην
ἀπέρχομαι	ἀπελεύσομαι	ἀπῆλθον*	ἀπελήλυθα	----------	----------
ἀποθνῄσκω	ἀποθανοῦμαι	ἀπέθανον*	----------	----------	----------
ἀποκρίνομαι	----------	ἀπεκρινάμην	----------	----------	ἀπεκρίθην
ἀποκτείνω	ἀποκτενῶ	ἀπέκτεινα	----------	----------	ἀπεκτάνθην
ἀπόλλυμι	ἀπολέσω	ἀπώλεσα	ἀπώλεκα	ἀπολώλεσμαι	ἀπωλέσθην
ἀπολύω	ἀπολύσω	ἀπέλυσα	----------	ἀπολέλυμαι	ἀπελύθην
ἀποστέλλω	ἀποστελῶ	ἀπέστειλα	ἀπέσταλκα	ἀπέσταλμαι	ἀπεστάλην
ἄρχω	ἄρξω	ἦρξα	----------	----------	----------
ἀσπάζομαι	----------	ἠσπασάμην	----------	----------	----------
ἀφίημι	ἀφήσω	ἀφῆκα	----------	ἀφέωμαι	ἀφέθην
βάλλω	βαλῶ	ἔβαλον*	βέβληκα	βέβλημαι	ἐβλήθην
βαπτίζω	βαπτίσω	----------	ἐβάπτισα	βεβάπτισμαι	ἐβαπτίσθην
βλέπω	βλέψω	ἔβλεψα	----------	----------	----------
γεννάω	γεννήσω	ἐγέννησα	γεγέννηκα	γεγέννημαι	ἐγεννήθην
γίνομαι	γενήσομαι	ἐγενόμην*	γέγονα	γεγένημαι	ἐγενήθην
γινώσκω	γνώσομαι	ἔγνων*	ἔγνωκα	ἔγνωσμαι	ἐγνώσθην
γράφω	γράψω	ἔγραψα	γέγραφα	γέγραμμαι	ἐγράφην

First	Second	Third	Fourth	Fifth	Sixth
δέχομαι	δέξομαι	ἐδεξάμην	----------	δέδεγμαι	ἐδέχθην
διδάσκω	διδάξω	ἐδίδαξα	----------	----------	ἐδιδάχθην
δίδωμι	δώσω	ἔδωκα	δέδωκα	δέδομαι	ἐδόθην
δοκέω	----------	ἔδοξα	----------	----------	----------
δοξάζω	δοξάσω	ἐδόξασα	----------	δεδόξασμαι	ἐδοξάσθην
δύναμαι	δυνήσομαι	----------	----------	----------	ἠδυνήθην
ἐγείρω	ἐγερῶ	ἤγειρα	----------	ἐγήγερμαι	ἠγέρθην
εἰσέρχομαι	εἰσελεύσομαι	εἰσῆλθον*	εἰσελήλυθα	----------	----------
ἐκβάλλω	ἐκβαλῶ	ἐξέβαλον*	----------	----------	ἐξεβλήθην
ἐξέρχομαι	ἐξελεύσομαι	ἐξῆλθον*	ἐξελήλυθα	----------	----------
ἐπερωτάω	ἐπερωτήσω	ἐπηρώτησα	----------	----------	----------
ἔρχομαι	ἐλεύσομαι	ἦλθον*	ἐλήλυθα	----------	----------
ἐρωτάω	ἐρωτήσω	ἠρώτησα	----------	----------	----------
ἐσθίω	φάγομαι	ἔφαγον*	----------	----------	----------
εὐαγγελίζω	----------	εὐηγγέλισα	----------	εὐηγγέλισμαι	εὐηγγελίσθην
εὑρίσκω	εὑρήσω	εὕρησα (εὗρον)*	εὕρηκα	----------	εὑρέθην
ἔχω	ἕξω	ἔσχον*	ἔσχηκα	----------	----------
ζάω	ζήσω	ἔζησα	----------	----------	----------
ζητέω	ζητήσω	ἐζήτησα	----------	----------	ἐζητήθην
θέλω	----------	ἠθέλησα	----------	----------	----------
θεωρέω	θεωρήσω	ἐθεώρησα	----------	----------	----------
ἵστημι	στήσω	ἔστησα (ἔστην)	ἕστηκα	----------	ἐστάθην
κάθημαι	καθήσομαι	----------	----------	----------	----------
καλέω	καλέσω	ἐκάλεσα	κέκληκα	κέκλημαι	ἐκλήθην
καταβαίνω	καταβήσομαι	κατέβην*	καταβέβηκα	----------	----------
κηρύσσω	----------	ἐκήρυξα	----------	----------	ἐκηρύχθην
κράζω	κράξω	ἔκραξα	κέκραγα	----------	----------
κρατέω	κρατήσω	ἐκράτησα	κεκράτηκα	κεκράτημαι	----------

Appendix B

First	Second	Third	Fourth	Fifth	Sixth
κρίνω	κρινῶ	ἔκρινα	κέκρικα	κέκριμαι	ἐκρίθην
λαλέω	λαλήσω	ἐλάλησα	λελάληκα	λελάλημαι	ἐλαλήθην
λαμβάνω	λήμψομαι	ἔλαβον*	εἴληφα	----------	----------
λέγω	ἐρῶ	εἶπον*	εἴρηκα	εἴρημαι	ἐρρέθην
μαρτυρέω	μαρτυρήσω	ἐμαρτύρησα	μεμαρτύρηκα	μεμαρτύρημαι	ἐμαρτυρήθην
μέλλω	μελλήσω	----------	----------	----------	----------
μένω	μενῶ	ἔμεινα	μεμένηκα	----------	----------
οἶδα	εἰδήσω	----------	οἶδα (εἰδῆτε=subj.)		
ὁράω	ὄψομαι	εἶδον*	ἑώρακα (ἑόρακα)	----------	ὤφθην
ὀφείλω	----------	----------	----------	----------	----------
παραδίδωμι	παραδώσω	παρέδωκα	παραδέδωκα	παραδέδομαι	παρεδόθην
παρακαλέω	----------	παρεκάλεσα	----------	παρακέκλημαι	παρεκλήθην
πείθω	πείσω	ἔπεισα	πέποιθα	πέπεισμαι	ἐπείσθην
περιπατέω	περιπατήσω	περιεπάτησα	----------	----------	----------
πίνω	πίομαι	ἔπιον*	πέπωκα	----------	----------
πίπτω	πεσοῦμαι	ἔπεσον* (ἔπεσα)	πέπτωκα	----------	----------
πιστεύω	πιστεύσω	ἐπίστευσα	πεπίστευκα	πεπίστευμαι	ἐπιστεύθην
πληρόω	πληρώσω	ἐπλήρωσα	----------	πεπλήρωμαι	ἐπληρώθην
ποιέω	ποιήσω	ἐποίησα	πεποίηκα	πεποίημαι	----------
πορεύομαι	πορεύσομαι	----------	----------	πεπόρευμαι	ἐπορεύθην
προσέρχομαι	----------	προσῆλθον*	προσελήλυθα	----------	----------
προσεύχομαι	προσεύξομαι	προσηυξάμην	----------	----------	----------
προσκυνέω	προσκυνήσω	προσεκύνησα	----------	----------	----------
σπείρω	----------	ἔσπειρα	----------	ἔσπαρμαι	ἐσπάρην
συνάγω	συνάξω	συνήγαγον*	----------	συνῆγμαι	συνήχθην
σῴζω (σώζω)	σώσω	ἔσωσα	σέσωκα	σέσωμαι	ἐσώθην

First	Second	Third	Fourth	Fifth	Sixth
τηρέω	τηρήσω	ἐτήρησα	τετήρηκα	τετήρημαι	ἐτηρήθην
τίθημι	θήσω	ἔθηκα	τέθεικα	τέθειμαι	ἐτέθην
ὑπάγω	----------	----------	----------	----------	----------
ὑπάρχω	----------	----------	----------	----------	----------
φέρω	οἴσω	ἤνεγκα*	ἐνήνοχα	----------	ἠνέχθην
φοβέω	----------	----------	----------	----------	ἐφοβήθην
χαίρω	χαρήσομαι	ἐχάρην (ἐχαίρησα)	----------	----------	ἐχάρην

Appendix C: Using the BDAG Lexicon

Bauer, Walter, Frederick W. Danker, William Arndt, and Walter Bauer, eds. *A Greek-English Lexicon of the New Testament and Other Early Christian Literature*. 3d ed. Chicago Press, 2000.

The BDAG lexicon is a highly respected Greek lexicon for the New Testament and other Christian literature. Some professors may want to utilize BDAG rather than the Louw & Nida lexicon used through the textbook, or some students may want to learn how to access another lexicon. This section covers BDAG in the same detail Louw & Nida was covered through the textbook.

11.9: Nouns in the BDAG Lexicon[133]

The goal of the Stripped Down approach is to help you access the language using the best tools. One of the most important items in your toolkit when working with Greek is a lexicon. As mentioned previously, this grammar will utilize the BDAG lexicon.

You will come to see that all translation is interpretation.[134] Simply take a look at the entry of a few different words in your lexicon and you will see that there can sometimes be numerous translation options for a single word.[135] This is why it is important to not only learn the main gloss while learning vocabulary, but also to be able to access a lexicon when looking closer at New Testament passages. A proper translation of a word is only yielded when the meaning of the word in **that specific** context in understood.

11.9.1: A Noun's Stem

Beyond giving you the various glosses for a noun, some of the first information a lexicon relates to a reader is the stem of a word and its gender. Remember, a noun's stem determines what declension endings a word uses. The biggest reason readers need a lexicon to help them with identifying a stem is because of 3rd declension nouns (those that

---

[133] To read more about the BDAG lexicon, I encourage you to read this online essay by Rodney Decker: www.ntresources.com/documents/UsingBDAG.pdf

[134] That's why not every English translation is the same and why it is important for you to be able to work with the primary language of the New Testament.

[135] These options for translating a word are often called glosses.

end in a consonant) because the lexical form (nominative singular) of a 3rd declension noun does not show the stem the way 1st and 2nd declension nominative singular nouns do (those pesky consonant interactions). A lexicon will help you identify the stem by showing you the genitive singular ending directly after the word is introduced (see examples below).

11.9.2: A Noun's Gender

Chapter 6 introduced the Greek article (the word "the") which was in chapter one's vocabulary. But three forms are important to understand now as you begin your work in the BDAG lexicon. The masculine singular form of "the" is ὁ. The feminine singular form of "the" is ἡ. The neuter singular form of "the" is τό. In a lexicon, after a noun and its genitive ending, an article will occur[136] to indicate the gender of the noun (see examples below).

11.9.3: BDAG Lexicon Noun Examples

| Lexical form (nominative singular) | Genitive ending to reveal stem | Article to indicate gender | Earliest known uses of the word | A basic gloss if applicable |

ἄνθρωπος, ου, ὁ (Hom.+; loanw. in rabb.; ἡ ἄνθρωπος [Hdt. 1, 60, 5] does not appear in our lit.) 'human being, man, person'.

ἡμέρα, ας, ἡ (Hom.+; loanw. in rabb.)

πνεῦμα, ατος, τό (πνέω; Aeschyl., Pre-Socr., Hdt.+. On the history of the word s. Rtzst., Mysterienrel.3 308ff).

11.9.4: Lexicon Definitions

As mentioned before, most Greek nouns do not have just one English word to translate it. A lexicon will categorize the various different translation options and provide you

---

[136] In some lexicons (like Louw, Johannes P. and Eugene A. Nida. *Greek-English Lexicon Of The New Testament: Based On Semantic Domains*. 2 vols. New York: United Bible Societies, 1989) the lexicon will indicate gender with *m*, *f*, or *n*.

with information on what texts translate the word in that manner, will provide examples, and will cite significant secondary sources for the word. The sub-categories may be up to four categories deep (1. a. α.[137] א.[138]).

Do not make the mistake of reading the entire entry of a word when you are doing a word study. The first thing you do is look at the entry in its entirety, in particular noting the major categories and sub-categories. The following is a condensation of the categories of πνεῦμα, *without the additional information* of each category (this example categorizes three levels deep):

1. **air in movement, *blowing, breathing***
    a. *wind*
    b. *the breathing out of air, blowing, breath*
2. **that which animates or gives life to the body, *breath, (life-)spirit***
3. **a part of human personality, *spirit***
    a. when used with σάρξ, the flesh, it denotes the immaterial part 2 Cor 7:1; Col 2:5. *Flesh and spirit*=the whole personality....
    b. as the source and seat of insight, feeling, and will, gener.[139] as the representative part of human inner life....
    c. spiritual state, state of mind, disposition ἐν ἀγάπῃ πνεύματί τε πραΰτητος *with love and a gentle spirit*....
4. **an independent noncorporeal being, in contrast to a being that can be perceived by the physical senses, *spirit***
    a. God personally
    b. good, or at least not expressly evil *spirits* or *spirit-beings*
    c. *evil spirits*
5. **God's being as controlling influence, with focus on association with humans, *Spirit, spirit***

---

[137]This level uses Greek letters.
[138]This level uses Hebrew letters.
[139]The BDAG lexicon uses abbreviations extensively: gener. means generally, w. means with, art. means article, gen. means genitive, and abs. means absolute. One of the great advantages of having BDAG as an Accordance module is that every abbreviation is hyperlinked to be able to access quickly. In other forms of the lexicon, you will need to access the list of abbreviations in the box.

- a. the Spirit of God
- b. the Spirit of Christ
- c. Because of its heavenly origin and nature this Spirit is called *(the) Holy Spirit*
    - α. w. the art. τὸ πνεῦμα τὸ ἅγιον
    - β. without the art.
- d. abs.
    - α. w. the art. τὸ πνεῦμα.
    - β. without the art. πνεῦμα
- e. The Spirit is more closely defined by a gen. of thing....
- f. Of Christ 'it is written' in Scripture....
- g. The (divine) Pneuma stands in contrast to everything that characterizes this age or the finite world....
    - α. in contrast to σάρξ....
    - β. in contrast to σῶμα....
    - γ. in contrast to γράμμα....
    - δ. in contrast to the wisdom of humans 1 Cor 2:13.

6. **the Spirit of God as exhibited in the character or activity of God's people or selected agents**, *Spirit, spirit*
    - a. πνεῦμα is accompanied by another noun....
    - b. Unless frustrated by humans in their natural condition, the Spirit of God produces a spiritual type of conduct....
    - c. The Spirit inspires certain people of God....
    - d. The Spirit of God, being one, shows the variety and richness of its life....
    - e. One special type of spiritual gift....
    - f. The Spirit leads and directs Christian missionaries in their journeys....

7. **an activating spirit that is not fr. God,** *spirit*
8. **an independent transcendent personality,** *the Spirit*

Every division in the example above has a lot of information in it, including bibliographic information for those who want to do even deeper word studies. <u>Most of the time you will not have to read this information, so learn how to spot the important stuff</u>. Notice too how our word example πνεῦμα in many different divisions are translated as "spirit." But each time the word is translated as "spirit" under the different divisions there are different nuances to the meaning of the word. This is why the information provided in a lexicon is so important: it helps you understand the nuances of meaning in translation.

Finally, after you have taken an overview, take the time to find out where BDAG placed your word for the verse you are studying. Please take note, the authors of BDAG were brilliant *but they were not infallible*. You may disagree with the decision BDAG made over the word in question.

11.10: *BDAG Lexicon Adjective Examples*

Adjective information is similar in the lexicon to nouns. One of the main differences in the first information is that adjectives do not have gender, so feminine and neuter endings will be shown instead.

Lexical form (nominative singular) — Feminine and neuter ending — When the word first appears, etc. — information on the comparative and superlative forms

ἀγαθός, ή, όν, (Hom.+) Comp. ἀμείνων (not in NT, but e.g. PGM 5, 50; 6, 2; Jos., Bell. 5, 19, Ant. 11, 296) 1 Cl 57:2; IEph 13:2; 15:1; βελτίων, also κρείσσων........

11.10.1: Lexicon Definitions

Definitions for adjectives will follow the same basic structure as nouns, but be careful to note how the lexicon highlights the two main uses of an adjective (attributive and substantive). The following is a condensation of the categories of ἀγαθός, without the additional information of each category:

1. **pert. to meeting a relatively high standard of quality**, of things.
    a. adj. *useful, beneficial* καρποί

    b. used as a pure subst.: sg. (Hom. et al.; ins, pap, LXX), **ἀγαθόν, οῦ, τό** *the good*
- α. quite gener. τὰ ἀγαθά σου
- β. *possessions, treasures*
- γ. possessions of a higher order

2. **pert. to meeting a high standard of worth and merit**, *good*
    a. as adj.
- α. of humans and deities
- β. of things characterized esp. in terms of social significance and worth

    b. as subst., sg. (s. 1b). Opp. (τὸ) κακόν
- α. that which is beneficial or helpful
- β. τὰ ἀ. (ἀληθινὰ ἀ. Orig., C. Cels 7, 21, 10) good deeds

Looking at the above example, notice that when the adjective is attributive, it is noted as "adj." (i.e. adjective). When the word is acting as a substantive it is noted as "subst." (i.e. substantive).

Appendix D: Glossary

The following glossary lists all Greek words introduced in the textbook along with their meaning, part of speech, frequency, and section introduced.

Ἀβραάμ, ὁ Abraham (pr. noun), ch 1
ἀγαθός, -ή, -όν good, useful (adj.), ch 11
ἀγαπάω I love, cherish (verb), ch 8
ἀγάπη, -ης, ἡ love (noun), ch 10
ἀγαπητός, -ή, -όν beloved (adj.), list 5
ἄγγελος, -ου, ὁ messenger, angel (noun), ch 4
ἅγιος, -α, -ον holy; pl. saints (adj.), ch 6
ἀγοράζω I buy (verb), list 12
ἀγρός, -οῦ, ὁ field (noun), list 11
ἄγω I bring, lead, arrest (verb), list 4
ἀδελφός, -οῦ, ὁ brother (noun), ch 2
αἷμα, -ματος, τό blood (noun), list 1
αἴρω I raise, take up, take away (verb), ch 11
αἰτέω I ask, demand (verb), list 3
αἰών, -ῶνος, ὁ age, eternity (noun), ch 9
αἰώνιος, -ος, -ον eternal (adj.), list 3
ἀκάθαρτος, -ος, -ον unclean (adj.), list 12
ἀκολουθέω I follow, accompany (verb), list 1
ἀκούω I hear (verb), ch 4
ἀλήθεια, -ας, ἡ truth, reality, faithfulness (noun), ch 10
ἀλλά (ἀλλ') but, yet, except (conj.), ch 2
ἀλλήλων (-οις, -ους) one other (of one another, to one another) (pron.), ch 11
ἄλλος, -η, -ον other, another (adj.), ch 8
ἁμαρτάνω I sin (verb), list 8
ἁμαρτία, -ας, ἡ sin (noun), ch 7
ἁμαρτωλός, -ός, -όν sinner, sinful (adj.), list 7
ἀμήν amen, truly (particle), ch 9
ἄν (conditional, untranslatable particle) -ever; if, would, might (particle), ch 7
ἀναβαίνω I go up, come up, rise up, advance (verb), list 2
ἀναγινώσκω I read (verb), list 12
ἀνάστασις, -εως, ἡ standing up, resurrection (noun), list 9
ἄνεμος, -ου, ὁ wind (noun), list 12
ἀνήρ, ἀνδρός, ὁ man, husband (noun), ch 3
ἄνθρωπος, -ου, ὁ man, person (noun), ch 2
ἀνίστημι I rise, get up; I raise (verb), ch 11
ἀνοίγω I open, unlock, disclose (verb), list 3
ἄξιος, -α, -ον worthy (adj.), list 9
ἀπαγγέλλω I report, tell, bring news (verb), list 8
ἅπας, ἅπασα, ἅπαν all, every (adj.), list 11
ἀπέρχομαι I depart, go away (verb), ch 10
ἀπό (ἀπ', ἀφ') [+gen] (away) from (prep.), ch 2
ἀποδίδωμι I give back, pay (verb), list 7
ἀποθνήσκω I die, am about to die, am freed from (verb), ch 10
ἀποκρίνομαι I answer (verb), ch 4
ἀποκτείνω (ἀποκτέννω) I kill (verb), list 3
ἀπόλλυμι I destroy, kill; I perish, die (verb), list 1
ἀπολύω I release, divorce (verb), list 4
ἀποστέλλω I send (away) (verb), ch 9
ἀπόστολος, -ου, ὁ apostle (noun), list 2
ἅπτω (ἅπτομαί) I touch, hold, grasp; I light, ignite (verb), list 10
ἄρα then, therefore (particle), list 6
ἀρνέομαι I deny (verb), list 11
ἀρνίον, -ου, τό lamb, small lamb (noun), list 12
ἄρτι now (adv.), list 11
ἄρτος, -ου, ὁ bread, loaf, food; burden (noun), list 1
ἀρχή, -ῆς, ἡ beginning, first; ruler (noun), list 6
ἀρχιερεύς, -έως, ὁ chief priest, high priest (noun), ch 9

ἄρχομαι (ἄρχω) I begin; I rule over (verb), list 2
ἄρχων, -χοντος, ὁ ruler (noun), list 10
ἀσθενέω I be weak (verb), list 11
ἀσπάζομαι I greet, salute, welcome (verb), list 5
αὐτός, αὐτή, τουτό he, she, it (-self, same); pl. they (pron.), ch 6
ἀφίημι I let go, leave, permit, divorce, forgive (verb), ch 8
ἄχρι (ἄχρις) (+gen) until (prep.), list 7
βάλλω I throw (verb), ch 9
βαπτίζω I baptize, wash, dip, immerse (verb), list 3
βασιλεία, -ας, ἡ kingdom (noun), ch 7
βασιλεύς, -έως, ὁ king (noun), ch 10
βιβλίον, -ου, τό scroll, papyrus strip (noun), list 11
βλασφημέω I slander, blaspheme (verb), list 11
βλέπω I see (verb), ch 9
βούλομαι I will, want (verb), list 10
Γαλιλαία, ας, ἡ Galilee (pr. noun), ch 1
γάρ for, so, then (conj.), ch 1
γενεά, -ᾶς, ἡ generation (noun), list 8
γεννάω I bear, beget, produce (verb), list 1
γῆ, -ῆς, ἡ land, earth (noun), ch 3
γίνομαι I become, am, exist, happen, take place, am born, am created (verb), ch 5
γινώσκω I know, come to know, realize, learn (verb), ch 5
γλῶσσα, -ης, ἡ tongue, language (noun), list 6
γραμματεύς, -έως, ὁ scribe, secretary (noun), list 4
γραφή, -ῆς, ἡ written document, scripture (noun), list 6
γράφω I write (verb), ch 4
γυνή, -αικός, ἡ woman, wife (noun), ch 3
δαιμόνιον, -ου, τό demon (noun), list 4
Δαυίδ, ὁ David (pr. noun), ch 1
δέ but, and (conj.), ch 1
δεῖ it is necessary (verb), ch 11
δείκνυμι (δείκνυω) I show, explain (verb), list 12
δεξιός, -ά, -όν right, right hand, right side (adj.), list 6
δεύτερος, -α, -ον second (adj.), list 8
δέχομαι I take, receive (verb), list 5

δέω I bind, stop (verb), list 8
διά (δι') (+gen) through; (+acc) because of (prep.), ch 2
διάβολος, -ος, -ον enemy, adversary; devil (adj.), list 10
διαθήκη, -ης, ἡ covenant (noun), list 11
διακονέω I serve, wait on (verb), list 10
διακονία, -ας, ἡ service, ministry (noun), list 11
διδάσκαλος, -ου, ὁ teacher (noun), list 5
διδάσκω I teach (verb), list 1
διδαχή, -ῆς, ἡ teaching (noun), list 12
δίδωμι I give (out), entrust, give back, put, grant, allow (verb), ch 5
διέρχομαι I go/pass through (verb), list 8
δίκαιος, -α, -ον right, righteous, just (adj.), list 2
δικαιοσύνη, -ης, ἡ righteousness, justice (noun), list 1
δικαιόω I justify, vindicate, pron.ce righteous (verb), list 10
διό therefore, for this reason (conj.), list 6
διώκω I pursue, persecute (verb), list 8
δοκέω I think, suppose, seem (verb), list 4
δόξα, -ης, ἡ glory (noun), ch 7
δοξάζω I praise, honor, glorify (verb), list 5
δοῦλος, -ου, ὁ slave, servant (noun), ch 9
δύναμαι I am able, I am powerful, I can (verb), ch 4
δύναμις, -εως, ἡ power, ability (noun), ch 9
δυνατός, -ή, -όν possible, strong, able (adj.), list 12
δύο two (adj.), ch 9
δώδεκα (indecl.) twelve (adj.), list 3
ἐάν if (ever), when (ever), although (+subj.) (conj.), ch 3
ἑαυτοῦ, -ῆς, -οῦ himself/herself/itself; our-your-themselves (pron.), ch 6
ἐγγίζω I bring near, come near (verb), list 9
ἐγγύς (+gen) near (prep.), list 12
ἐγείρω I raise up, wake (verb), ch 8
ἐγώ (pl. ἡμεῖς) I; we (pron.), ch 6
ἔθνος, -ους, τό (sg.) nation; (pl.) Gentiles (noun), ch 7
εἰ if (particle), ch 2

εἰμί I am (verb), ch 5
εἰρήνη, -ης, ἡ peace, health (noun), list 1
εἰς (+acc) into, in; to, toward; among (prep.), ch 1
εἷς, μία, ἕν one (adj.), ch 6
εἰσέρχομαι I enter, come in(to), go in(to) (verb), ch 5
εἴτε (even) if; whether...or, or, either/or (conj.), list 4
ἐκ (ἐξ) (+gen) from, out of, of, by (prep.), ch 1
ἕκαστος, -η, -ον each, every (adj.), list 2
ἐκβάλλω I cast out, send out, drive out (verb), list 2
ἐκεῖ there, in that place (adv.), ch 11
ἐκεῖθεν from there (adv.), list 10
ἐκεῖνος, -η, -ο that, [pl.] those (pron.), ch 6
ἐκκλησία, -ας, ἡ assembly, church, congregation (noun), ch 10
ἐκπορεύομαι I go, come out (verb), list 11
ἐλπίζω I hope (verb), list 12
ἐλπίς, -ίδος, ἡ hope (noun), list 6
ἐμαυτοῦ -ῆς of myself, my own (pron.), list 10
ἐμός, -ή, -όν my, mine (adj.), list 3
ἔμπροσθεν (+gen) before, in front of (prep.), list 7
ἐν (+dat) in, on, by (prep.), ch 1
ἐντολή, -ῆς, ἡ commandment, law (noun), list 4
ἐνώπιον (+gen) before, in front of (prep.), list 1
ἐξέρχομαι I go out (verb), ch 5
ἔξεστι(ν) it is right, possible (verb), list 12
ἐξουσία, -ας, ἡ authority, power (noun), ch 11
ἔξω (+gen) out, outside; [adv.] without (adv., improper prep.), list 4
ἐπαγγελία, -ας, ἡ promise (noun), list 6
ἐπερωτάω I ask (for), question, demand (verb), list 5
ἐπί (ἐπ', ἐφ') (+gen) on, over, when; (+dat) on the basis of, at; (+acc) on, to, against, for (prep.), ch 1
ἐπιγινώσκω I know (verb), list 8
ἐπιθυμία, ἡ desire, lust (noun), list 10
ἐπικαλέω (ἐπικαλέομαι) I call on (verb), list 12
ἐπιστρέφω I turn back, return (verb), list 11
ἐπιτίθημι I lay on, place, put, add (verb), list 10

ἑπτά (indecl.) seven (adj.), list 2
ἐργάζομαι I work (verb), list 9
ἔργον, -ου, τό work, deed, action (noun), ch 7
ἔρημος, -ος, -ον desolate, wilderness, desert (adj.), list 7
ἔρχομαι I come, go (verb), ch 5
ἐρωτάω I ask, request, entreat (verb), list 4
ἐσθίω I eat (verb), ch 5
ἔσομαι I shall be (future of εἰμί) (verb), list 3
ἔσχατος, -η, -ον last, least, end (adj.), list 6
ἕτερος, -α, -ον other, another, different (adj.), list 1
ἔτι yet, still (adv.), list 1
ἑτοιμάζω I prepare (verb), list 9
ἔτος, -ους, τό year (noun), list 7
εὐαγγελίζω (mid. εὐαγγελίζομαι) I bring good news, preach, announce (verb), list 6
εὐαγγέλιον, -ου, τό good news, gospel (noun), list 3
εὐθέως immediately, at once, suddenly (adv.), list 11
εὐθύς (εὐθέως) immediately (adv); straight (adj) (adv.), list 5
εὐλογέω I bless (verb), list 9
εὑρίσκω I find (verb), ch 5
εὐχαριστέω I give thanks (verb), list 10
ἐχθρός, -ά, -όν hostile, enemy (adj.), list 12
ἔχω I have (verb), ch 4
ἕως (conj.) until; (prep.) [+gen] as far as (conj.), ch 7
ζάω I live (verb), ch 8
ζητέω I seek, desire (verb), ch 10
ζωή, -ῆς, ἡ life (noun), ch 9
ἤ or, than; (ἤ... ἤ either...or) (particle), ch 3
ἤδη now, already (adv.), list 5
ἥλιος, -ου, ὁ sun (noun), list 12
ἡμέρα, -ας, ἡ day (noun), ch 2
Ἡρῴδης, ου, ὁ Herod (pr. noun), list 8
θάλασσα, -ης, ἡ sea, lake (noun), list 1
θάνατος, -ου, ὁ death (noun), ch 9
θαυμάζω I marvel, wonder (verb), list 8
θέλημα, -ματος, τό will, desire, wish (noun), list 4
θέλω I want, wish, will, desire (verb), ch 4

θεός, -οῦ, ὁ God, god (noun), ch 1
θεραπεύω I serve, heal (verb), list 8
θεωρέω I look at, behold, see, observe (verb), list 5
θηρίον, -ου, τό wild animal (noun), list 7
θλῖψις, -ψεως, ἡ affliction, trouble, tribulation, oppression (noun), list 8
θρόνος, -ου, ὁ throne, seat (noun), list 4
θύρα, -ας, ἡ door (noun), list 10
Ἰάκωβος, -ου, ὁ Jacob; James (pr. noun), list 9
ἴδιος, -α, -ον one's own; his/her/its (adj.), ch 10
ἰδού look!, Behold! (interj.), ch 7
ἱερεύς, -έως, ὁ priest (noun), list 12
ἱερόν, -οῦ, τό temple (noun), list 3
Ἱεροσόλυμα, τά or ἡ Jerusalem (pr. noun), ch 1
Ἱερουσαλήμ, ἡ Jerusalem (pr. noun), ch 1
Ἰησοῦς, -οῦ, ὁ Jesus, Joshua (pr. noun), ch 1
ἱκανός, -ή, -όν sufficient, able, worthy (adj.), list 10
ἱμάτιον, -ου, τό garment, cloak, clothing (noun), list 5
ἵνα in order that, that (conj.), ch 2
Ἰουδαία, -ας, ἡ Judea (pr. noun), list 8
Ἰουδαῖος, -α, -ον (adj.) Jewish; (noun) Jew, Judean (adj.), ch 7
Ἰούδας, α, ὁ Judas/Judah (pr. noun), list 8
ἴσθι you be! (Imperative of εἰμί) (verb), list 8
Ἰσραήλ, ὁ Israel (noun), list 4
ἵστημι I stand, set, place; I cause to stand (verb), ch 5
Ἰωάννης, -ου, ὁ John (pr. noun), ch 1
Ἰωσήφ, ὁ Joseph (pr. noun), list 11
καθαρίζω I cleanse (verb), list 12
κάθημαι I sit (down), live (verb), list 1
καθίζω I sit, set, place (verb), list 7
καθώς as, even as, just as (conj.), ch 7
καί and, even, also (conj.), ch 1
καινός, -ή, -όν new (adj.), list 9
καιρός, -οῦ, ὁ (appointed) time, season (noun), list 2
κακός, -ή, -όν evil, bad, wrong, harm (adj.), list 6
καλέω I call, name, invite (verb), ch 4
καλός, -ή, -όν good, beautiful (adj.), ch 11

καλῶς well, rightly (adv.), list 10
καρδία, -ας, ἡ heart (noun), ch 8
καρπός, -οῦ, ὁ fruit, crop, result (noun), list 4
κατά (κατ', καθ') (+gen) down from, against; (+acc) according to, throughout, during (prep.), ch 3
καταβαίνω I come down, go down (verb), list 2
κατοικέω I settle, dwell, inhabit (verb), list 8
καυχάομαι I boast, glory (verb), list 10
κεφαλή, -ῆς, ἡ head (noun), list 3
κηρύσσω I proclaim, preach (verb), list 5
κλαίω I weep, cry (verb), list 9
κόσμος, -ου, ὁ world, universe (noun), ch 4
κράζω I call out, cry out (verb), list 6
κρατέω I grasp, am strong, take possession (verb), list 7
κρίνω I judge, decide, prefer (verb), ch 10
κρίσις -εως, ἡ judgment, decision (noun), list 7
κύριος, -ου, ὁ lord, Lord (noun), ch 1
λαλέω to sound, talk, speak (verb), ch 4
λαμβάνω I take, receive (verb), ch 5
λαός, -οῦ, ὁ people; crowd (noun), ch 8
λέγω I say, speak (verb), ch 5
λίθος, -ου, ὁ stone (noun), list 5
λογίζομαι I count, think, calculate (verb), list 9
λόγος, -ου, ὁ word, matter (noun), ch 2
λοιπός, -ή, -όν (noun) rest; (adj.) remaining; (adv.) henceforth, finally (adj.), list 6
λύω I loosen, release (verb), ch 4
μαθητής, -οῦ, ὁ disciple, student (noun), ch 3
μακάριος, -α, -ον blessed, happy (adj.), list 6
μᾶλλον more, rather (adv.), list 2
μαρτυρέω I bear witness, testify (verb), list 3
μαρτυρία, -ας, ἡ testimony (noun), list 10
μάρτυς, -υρος, ὁ witness (noun), list 11
μέγας, -η, -α large, great (adj.), ch 6
μείζων (μείζον) greater, larger (comparative of μέγας) (adj.), list 7
μέλλω I am about to, intend (verb), ch 10
μέλος, -ους, τό body part; musical part, melody (noun), list 11

μέν on the one hand, indeed [or left untranslated] (particle), ch 5

μένω I remain, live, abide, stay (verb), ch 10

μέρος, -ους, τό part (noun), list 9

μέσος, -η, -ον middle; (prep +gen) in the middle; (adv) among (adj.), list 5

μετά (μετ', μεθ') (+gen) with; (+acc) after (prep.), ch 3

μετανοέω I repent (verb), list 11

μή not, no; lest (conj.), ch 1

μηδέ nor, and not, but not (conj.), list 5

μηδείς, μηδεμία, μηδέν no one, nothing (adj.), list 1

μήτε and not; neither . . . nor (conj.), list 11

μήτηρ, μητρός, ἡ mother (noun), list 2

μικρός, -ά, -όν small, little; a little, a short time (adj.), list 7

μισέω I hate (verb), list 9

μνημεῖον, -ου, τό tomb, monument (noun), list 9

μόνος, -η, -ον alone, only (adj.), ch 10

Μωϋσῆς, -έως, ὁ Moses (pr. noun), list 2

ναί yes (particle), list 11

ναός, -ου, ὁ temple; palace (noun), list 8

νεκρός, -ά, -όν dead (adj.), ch 9

νόμος, -ου, ὁ law (noun), ch 3

νῦν now (adv.); the present (noun) (adv.), ch 7

νύξ, νυκτός, ἡ night (noun), list 5

ὁ, ἡ, τό the (article), ch 1

ὁδός, -οῦ, ἡ way, road, journey; conduct (noun), ch 11

οἶδα I know, understand (verb), ch 5

οἰκία, -ας, ἡ house, home (noun), list 1

οἰκοδομέω I build (verb), list 9

οἶκος, -ου, ὁ house, home (noun), ch 10

οἶνος, -ου, ὁ wine (noun), list 11

ὀλίγος, -η, -ον little, few (adj.), list 9

ὅλος, -η, -ον (adj.) whole, complete; (adv.) entirely (adj.), ch 10

ὅμοιος, -α, -ον like, similar (adj.), list 8

ὁμοίως likewise (adv.), list 12

ὄνομα, -ματος, τό name, reputation (noun), ch 3

ὀπίσω (+gen) after (prep.); back (adv.) (prep.), list 11

ὅπου (ποῦ) where, whereas (conj.), list 2

ὅπως how, (so) that, in order that (conj.), list 6

ὁράω I see, notice, experience (verb), ch 5

ὀργή, -ῆς, ἡ wrath; anger (noun), list 11

ὄρος, -ους, τό mountain, high hill (noun), list 4

ὅς, ἥ, ὅ who, which, what (pron.), ch 6

ὅσος, -α, -ον as great as, as many as, as much, how much (pron.), ch 10

ὅστις, ἥτις, ὅτι whoever/whichever/whatever; everyone, which (pron.), ch 8

ὅταν whenever (conj.), ch 9

ὅτε when (conj.), ch 11

ὅτι because, that, since (conj.), ch 1

οὐ, οὐκ, οὐχ not (particle), ch 1

οὐαί woe! how terrible? (interj.), list 7

οὐδέ and not, not even, neither, nor (conj.), ch 7

οὐδείς, οὐδεμία, οὐδέν no one; nothing (adj.), ch 6

οὐκέτι no longer (adv.), list 7

οὖν therefore, then, accordingly (conj.), ch 2

οὐρανός, -οῦ, ὁ heaven, sky (noun), ch 2

οὖς, ὠτός, τό ear (noun), list 11

οὔτε neither (conj.), list 2

οὗτος, αὕτη, τοῦτο this (one); pl. these (pron.), ch 6

οὕτως thus, so, in this manner (adv.), ch 3

οὐχί not, no (particle), list 6

ὀφείλω I am obligated, I owe (verb), list 11

ὀφθαλμός, -οῦ, ὁ eye, sight (noun), ch 11

ὄχλος, -ου, ὁ crowd, multitude (noun), ch 7

παιδίον, -ου, τό child, infant (noun), list 6

πάλιν again (adv.), ch 8

πάντοτε always (adv.), list 9

παρά (παρ') (+gen) from; (+dat) beside, in the presence of, with; (+acc) alongside of, other than (prep.), ch 4

παραβολή, -ῆς, ἡ parable (noun), list 6

παραγγέλλω I command (verb), list 12

παραγίνομαι I come, I appear (verb), list 10

παραδίδωμι I entrust, hand over, betray (verb), ch 9

παρακαλέω I call, urge, exhort, comfort, beseech (verb), ch 10

παραλαμβάνω I take along, accept, receive (verb), list 7

παρίστημι (παριστάνω) I present, offer; (intrans.:) I stand by (verb), list 9

παρρησία, -ας, ἡ boldness (noun), list 12

πᾶς, πᾶσα, πᾶν every, each; [pl.] all (adj.), ch 6

πάσχω I suffer (verb), list 9

πατήρ, πατρός, ὁ father (noun), ch 2

Παῦλος, -ου, ὁ Paul (pr. noun), ch 1

πείθω I persuade, believe, trust (verb), list 6

πειράζω I tempt, test (verb), list 10

πέμπω I send (verb), list 2

πέντε (indecl.) five (adj.), list 10

περί (+gen) about, concerning; (+acc) around (prep.), ch 3

περιπατέω I walk (around), live (verb), list 1

περισσεύω I abound (verb), list 10

περιτομή, -ῆς, ἡ circumcision (noun), list 11

Πέτρος, -ου, ὁ Peter (pr. noun), ch 1

Πιλᾶτος, -ου, ὁ Pilate (pr. noun), ch 1

πίνω I drink (verb), list 3

πίπτω I fall (verb), list 1

πιστεύω I believe (in), have faith, trust (verb), ch 4

πίστις, -εως, ἡ faith, belief, trust (noun), ch 3

πιστός, -ή, -όν faithful, believing; reliable (adj.), list 4

πλανάω I deceive (verb), list 10

πλείων, -ων, -ον larger, more, greater (comparative of πόλυς) (adj.), list 6

πλῆθος, -ους, τό multitude (noun), list 12

πλήν (+gen) only, except (prep.); but, nevertheless (conj.) (prep.), list 12

πληρόω I fill, fulfill, complete (verb), list 2

πλοῖον, -ου, τό boat, ship (noun), list 4

πνεῦμα, -ματος, τό wind, spirit (noun), ch 2

ποιέω I do, make (verb), ch 4

ποῖος, -α, -ον what kind of, which (pron.), list 11

πόλις, -εως, ἡ city (noun), ch 8

πολύς, πολλή, πολύ much, [pl.] many; (adv.) often (adj.), ch 6

πονηρός, -ά, -όν evil, bad, wicked (adj.), list 3

πορεύομαι I go, proceed, live (verb), ch 4

ποτήριον, -ου, τό cup (noun), list 12

ποῦ where? (particle), list 7

πούς, ποδός, ὁ foot (noun), list 1

πράσσω I do, I accomplish (verb), list 10

πρεσβύτερος, -α, -ον older; elder (adj.), list 4

πρό (+gen) before, above (prep.), list 7

πρόβατον, -ου, τό sheep (noun), list 10

πρός (+gen) for; (+dat) at; (+acc) to, against (prep.), ch 1

προσέρχομαι I come to (verb), list 2

προσευχή, -ῆς, ἡ prayer (noun), list 11

προσεύχομαι I pray (verb), list 2

προσκυνέω I worship; I do obeisance (verb), list 5

προσφέρω I bring, I offer (verb), list 7

πρόσωπον, -ου, τό face, appearance, presence (noun), list 3

προφήτης, -ου, ὁ prophet (noun), ch 8

πρῶτος, -η, -ον first, earlier, foremost (adj.), ch 8

πτωχός, -ή, -όν poor (adj.), list 11

πῦρ, πυρός, τό fire (noun), list 3

πῶς how? (particle), ch 11

ῥῆμα, -ματος, τό word, thing (noun), list 4

σάββατον, -ου, τό sabbath, week (noun), list 4

σάρξ, σαρκός, ἡ flesh, body (noun), ch 8

Σατανᾶς, -ᾶ, ὁ Satan (noun), list 11

σεαυτοῦ -ῆς of yourself (sing.) (pron.), list 8

σημεῖον, -ου, τό sign, miracle (noun), list 3

σήμερον today (adv.), list 9

Σίμων, Σίμωνος, ὁ Simon (pr. noun), ch 1

σκότος, -ους, τό darkness (noun), list 12

σοφία, -ας, ἡ wisdom (noun), list 6

σπείρω I sow (verb), list 6

σπέρμα, -ματος, τό seed, offspring (noun), list 8

σταυρόω I crucify (verb), list 7

στόμα, -ματος, τό mouth (noun), list 3

σύ (pl. ὑμεῖς) you (sg.); y'all (pl.) (pron.), ch 6

σύν (+dat) with (prep.), ch 9
συνάγω I gather together, invite (verb), list 5
συναγωγή, -ῆς, ἡ synagogue, meeting, gathering (noun), list 5
συνείδησις, -εως, ἡ conscience (noun), list 12
συνέρχομαι I come together; I go together (verb), list 12
σῴζω (σώζω) I save, heal, deliver, rescue (verb), ch 11
σῶμα, -ματος, τό body (noun), ch 8
σωτηρία, -ας, ἡ salvation, deliverance (noun), list 7
τέ and (so), so [consec: both...and] (conj.), ch 3
τέκνον, -ου, τό child, descendent (noun), list 1
τέλος, -ους, τό end, goal; tribute (noun), list 9
τέσσαρες four (adj.), list 9
τηρέω I keep, guard, observe (verb), list 3
τίθημι I put, place (verb), ch 11
τιμή, -ῆς, ἡ honor (noun), list 9
τις, τι someone, anyone; something, certain one (pron.), ch 6
τίς, τί who? which? what? why? (pron.), ch 6
τοιοῦτος, -αύτη, -οῦτο(ν) such, of such kind (pron.), list 5
τόπος, -ου, ὁ place, position; opportunity (noun), list 1
τότε then (adv.), ch 7
τρεῖς, τρεῖς, τρία three (adj.), list 4
τρίτος, -η, -ον third (adj.), list 5
τυφλός, -ή, -όν blind (adj.), list 6
ὕδωρ, ὕδατος, τό water (noun), list 3
υἱός, -οῦ, ὁ son, descendant; child (noun), ch 2
ὑπάγω I depart, go away; I draw off (verb), list 2
ὑπάρχω I am, exist; I possess (verb), list 5
ὑπέρ (+gen.) in behalf of; (+acc.) above (prep.), ch 7
ὑπό (ὑπ', ὑφ') (+gen) by; (+acc) under (prep.), ch 3
ὑπομονή, -ῆς, ἡ endurance; staying (noun), list 12
ὑποστρέφω I return (verb), list 11
ὑποτάσσω I subject; I submit (verb), list 10
φαίνω I appear, shine (verb), list 12
φανερόω I reveal, make known (verb), list 7
Φαρισαῖος, -ου, ὁ Pharisee (pr. noun), ch 1
φέρω I bear, carry, produce, bring (verb), list 4
φημί I say, affirm (verb), list 4
Φίλιππος, -ου, ὁ Philip (pr. noun), list 11
φοβέω (mid. φοβεόμαι) I fear (verb), list 1
φόβος, -ου, ὁ fear, terror; reverence (noun), list 7
φυλακή, -ῆς, ἡ guard, watch, prison (noun), list 7
φυλάσσω I guard, keep (verb), list 12
φυλή, -ῆς, ἡ tribe (noun), list 12
φωνέω I call, to shout (verb), list 8
φωνή, -ῆς, ἡ sound (noun), ch 9
φῶς, φωτός, τό light (noun), list 3
χαίρω I rejoice (verb), list 3
χαρά, -ᾶς, ἡ joy, delight, gladness (noun), list 5
χάρις, -ιτος, ἡ grace, favor (noun), ch 8
χείρ, χειρός, ἡ hand; arm; finger (noun), ch 4
χρεία, -ας, ἡ need (noun), list 7
Χριστός, -οῦ, ὁ Christ (pr. noun), ch 1
χρόνος, -ου, ὁ time (noun), list 6
χωρίς (+gen) without (prep.); separately (adv) (prep.), list 9
ψυχή, -ῆς, ἡ soul, life, self (noun), ch 11
ὧδε here; in this way, so, thus (adv.), list 5
ὥρα, -ας, ἡ hour; occasion, moment (noun), ch 11
ὡς as, while (conj.), ch 2
ὥσπερ as, just as (particle), list 11
ὥστε therefore, so that, in order that (conj.), list 2